# Like Lions They Fought

# Like Lions They Fought

*The Zulu War and the Last Black Empire in South Africa*

Robert B. Edgerton

SOUTHERN
BOOK PUBLISHERS

*South African edition published in 1988 by*
*Southern Book Publishers (Pty) Ltd*
*P.O. Box 548*
*Bergvlei*
*2012*

*1st edition, 1st impression*



*ISBN 1 86812 151 8*

*Printed in Great Britain*

I offer you screams of a thousand mad men
Who scream to those without mercy
Who scream over the graveyards
Of skeletons, piled on piles,
Bones dislocated from their joints.
. . . I offer them to you to shout them to the world!
—from "The Screams," by Mazisi Kunene

# Contents

# Preface

The war between the British and the Zulus in 1879 is one of the most dramatic in the history of Western imperialism. In one of the war's opening battles, the British suffered their most shocking defeat in all their colonial wars. Later that same day, another British force successfully fought off a series of Zulu attacks. Eleven of the survivors received Britain's highest decoration, the Victoria Cross, more than have won it in any other battle before or since. The Zulus eventually lost the war, but their bravery and military skill astonished and fascinated not only the British but much of the Western world. Accounts of the war began to appear before 1879 had ended, and they have continued over the years with scores of new books and articles appearing since the war's centennial in 1979.

Much of this material is relatively inaccessible in the United States, although the most authoritative overview of the war—*The Washing of the Spears*—written by an American, Donald T. Morris, was published in 1965. The book was written at the suggestion of Ernest Hemingway, who thought there was a need for a readable account of this war between British Imperial forces and one of the last great African Kingdoms. Morris did his research well enough for his book to earn praise from South African scholars, but it does contain some errors, and in it the war is viewed almost entirely through the eyes of the British.

In the two decades since Morris's book appeared, there has been an outpouring of new material about the war. Many British and South African scholars have published new interpretations of the war, including a large amount of previously unavailable primary material in the form of letters, diaries, interviews, and military testimony. This material helps to answer many questions about the British role in the war, from the political considerations that led them to invade Zululand to the feelings of the soldiers who did the fighting. At the same time, more accounts by Zulu survivors of the war have been made available. This new material, complemented by older accounts published during or just after the war, makes it possible to reexamine this epic colonial war as it was experienced by men on both sides.

The modern study of men in war pioneered by Ardant du Picq, S. L. A. Marshall, Morris Janowitz, and others has recently been popularized by the British military historians John Keegan and Richard Holmes, and by psychologists such as Norman Dixon. As valuable as their work is, it is confined to European and American soldiers. Anthropologists, who specialize in the study of non-European peoples, have not filled the gap. They have provided many worthwhile descriptions and analyses of ''primitive'' war, but they have seldom turned their attention to colonial wars, particularly not in Africa. In the breech, investigation of the wars fought by non-European peoples against colonial armies has been left largely to historians or journalists, and while much of their work is of high quality, it understandably concentrates on the experiences of the European forces. This book explores the meaning of warfare for the different men who were involved. It describes how both the British and the Zulus experienced their combat, why they fought so hard, why they sometimes ran, and how they felt about fighting and about one another. This was a terribly personal war in which, unlike modern wars, much of the fighting was at very close range, black men against white, spears against bayonets.

The British were at the pinnacle of their imperial power and confidence. Their soldiers were professional, well-armed, and led by experienced officers. The Zulus were armed and powerful too, and they were confident, if not quite as confident as the British. It was a war of grandeur, with masses of elaborately uniformed men running and riding into battle, sure of their power and virtue, reinforced by their belief in their kings, officers, gods, and rituals. Unlike more recent wars in which unseen foes killed one another at a distance, in this war great numbers of black men and white fought hand to hand, and they fought with such bravery—and sometimes with such ferocity—that we of a later age, a softer one perhaps, must still marvel at them, just as we may recoil from their violence. They fought like lions, black against white, again and again, battle after battle, until the British proved themselves too strong. In the perspective of history, it was not a war that changed the world very much, but it was undeniably a war in which men fought as hard as men have ever done before or since. It is those men, Zulu and British, and their ferocious combat that the following pages will describe and try to understand.

# Acknowledgments and Sources

A word about the sources: Published material about various aspects of the war is voluminous. Books, edited collections of letters, diaries, reminiscences, newspaper and periodical articles, and testimony reproduced in the British Parliamentary Papers, in "Blue Books" that record the testimony from military courts of inquiry, and in other sources, comprise hundreds of thousands of pages. Unpublished letters and diaries also abound, as do interviews with African participants in the war. The material is mountainous, but it is also imcomplete. On the British side, the views of the surviving officers are fairly well represented (although many of them never wrote about their experiences), and many of the literate soldiers also wrote letters that have survived, but the majority of those ill-educated men left no record of their thoughts. The Zulu sources are even less adequate. Both during and shortly after the war many Zulus described aspects of the war, including the actual combat. Others spoke later, when their memories may have been less vivid. Nevertheless, these materials include the views of young warriors as well as older ones, men of high rank and commoners, men who fought loyally and others who deserted to the British. There is much more information in this Zulu material than previous writers have utilized, and despite the fact that most of this material was obtained through interpretation, it is probably a reliable record of many aspects of the Zulu War experience. To be sure, some aspects of the Zulu War experience remain almost entirely unknown, but at this date, more than a century after the battle, it is unlikely that much new material will come to light.

The spelling of Zulu words has varied over the years since the war. During the war, the Zulu King's name was usually spelled "Cetywayo." Later, "Cetshwayo" became the most common spelling. To avoid confusion I have used "Cetshwayo" throughout (other spellings will sometimes appear in quoted material) even though this is not a phonetic rendering of his name. The initial consonant which has traditionally been represented as "C" is a dental click sounding something like "Tsch," and the rest of the Zulu King's name sounds something like "etschwhyuh." The accent is on the syllable, "why," and the last syllable is almost inaudible. There is now a standard Zulu orthography that changes the spellings of rivers, place names, and sites of battles from the spellings used in the older literature, but to avoid confusion between my account and the older material I use, I have retained the older spellings.

My interest in the Anglo-Zulu War began to take shape when I first went to Africa in 1961 to do anthropological research. The influence of King Shaka's conquests in the early nineteenth century was evident in many parts of East Africa. When I consulted the books that had been written about the war of 1879, it was obvious that the story of that colonial war had been told very superficially. A short time later I ran across unpublished material about the war in London, and I visited several regimental museums, including that of the 24th Regiment, where Major G. J. B. Egerton, Regimental Secretary of the 24th, helped me to understand the war through the eyes of the officers and men of that ill-fated regiment. I also made a brief trip to Natal to visit the battlefields and consult with Dr. Killic Campbell, whose collection of materials about the war is invaluable. But before I had progressed very far with my research for a book about the Anglo-Zulu War, Morris's *The Washing of the Spears* was published. Morris had not written the book as I would have, but his book was good enough to cause me to set my plans aside. It was not until the centennial year of 1979, when so much new material began to appear, that I realized there was more than needed to be written about the war, particularly from the Zulus' point of view.

I am grateful to Grace Davis, Janell Demyan, and Esther Rose, who valiantly typed innumerable drafts of this book, to Rachel Blachly for preparing the maps, and to various anonymous librarians and archivists who helped me to locate fugitive materials in several parts of the world. That gracious scholar, Dr. Killie Campbell, helped beyond measure. I also want to thank everyone who commented on earlier drafts of this book, particularly Marcia Gaston, Jorja Prover, Hilarie Kelly, and Chad Oliver. The encouragement of the Zulu scholar Mazisi Kunene meant a great deal to me. I want to thank my editor, Grant Ujitusa, for his support and helpful suggestions, and to the copy editor at The Free Press, Norman Sloan, "bravo!" Of course, I alone am responsible for the contents of the book.

# Chapter 1

# "Never Has Such a Disaster Happened to the English Army"

The most improbable military defeat in British colonial history took place on January 22, 1879, on a rocky plain in Zululand. A few days earlier, a large force of veteran British troops accompanied by their African allies had invaded the Zulu Kingdom. In the previous year, those same British soldiers had easily defeated large African armies that had risen against British rule in South Africa. The "redcoats" were tough men, lean and hardened by African campaigning. They were well disciplined, armed with artillery and modern rifles, and supremely confident that no African army—no rabble of "niggers," as they said—could stand against them. Their only fear was that the Zulus would run away before British fire power could slaughter them. The Zulu army did not run away. At a place called Isandlwana it attacked.

As the British column slowly moved toward Isandlwana, its officers, all of whom were mounted, often rode ahead to scout or simply to enjoy the scenery. The panorama was magnificent. In the crystal clear air, men could see details of distant mountains and hills as if they were close enough to touch. Some officers tried to sketch the landscape, while others simply marveled at what they saw. Some hills were barren and rocky; others were densely forested with immense trees, rising toward the billowing clouds overhead. Recent rains had brought up fragrant green grasses that contrasted with the older brown hues and the red soil. In valleys were ferns, vines, creepers, and glorious flowers in red, purple, white, and yellow, some as big as a man's hat. In the distance, acacia trees with red, white, orange, and yellow blossoms dotted the landscape. There were brightly colored birds too, and butterflies darted everywhere.

An officer who looked down on the British army from a distant hill was thrilled by the spectacle: wagons, oxen, and redcoats marching with the sun flashing off their polished steel. Khaki uniforms were being introduced in some parts of the British Empire, but these men, two battalions of the 24th Regiment, wore blue trousers, scarlet tunics, tropical cork sun helmets covered by white canvas, and white leather belts and straps. No one knew it then, but the Zulu War was the last time British troops would wear their red coats into battle. The army was not as elegant as the Grenadier Guards on parade—the men's red coats were worn, and their white helmets were dirty—but it was a stirring sight nevertheless to see the "red soldiers," as the Zulus called them, marching in huge square formations to the beat of drums played by brightly uniformed ten- and eleven-year-old drummer boys. Many of the men were Welsh, and sometimes they sang in powerful baritone voices. One favorite was the chorus of a current music hall rage:

> We don't want to fight, but by jingo if we do,
> We've got the ships, we've got the men, and
> got the money too.

It was the origin of "jingoism."

To the men marching over the rolling green hills of Zululand, their progress seemed not quite so grand. Some of the British soldiers later commented on the incredible cacophony of sound the army made. Oxen bellowed as drivers cracked 30-foot whips so loudly that some men thought they were rifle shots. Ungreased wheels squeaked. The native African soldiers who had joined the British on the campaign laughed and talked in incomprehensible languages. Colonial horsemen recruited from South Africa to act as scouts laughed and shouted too, sometimes in Dutch, German, or French. British officers rode back and forth trying to yell loudly enough for their orders to be heard over the din. In the early morning rain, thick mud sucked at the men's boots, by now so worn that rocks sometimes cut through the flimsy soles. Before midday a hot sun was overhead, and the wet wool tunics began to steam. So did the soaked animals.

The smell was not pleasant to most of the men, but one soldier remarked it was better than the usual stink of mens' sweat. In those days before deodorants, the soldiers often wore the same sweat-soaked uniforms for weeks at a time. With the hot sun came flies, thousands of them, and the men flailed their arms trying to keep them out of their eyes and mouths. Scores of men were suffering from diarrhea and had to fall out of the column to defecate. Others were running high fevers, usually from malaria or typhoid, and they suffered from thirst and fatigue.

As sweat stains spread on the men's tunics, soldiers swore at their discomfort and complained that the African soldiers who accompanied them seemed ''too jolly by half.'' Not all the officers were off enjoying a canter over distant hills. Artillery officers (who wore blue coats, not red) cursed mightily as their horses foundered trying to pull their six heavy cannons and their rocket battery through the mud, and transport officers swore just as grandly when their heavily laden supply wagons sank to their axles.

The army camped at Isandlwana. Two days later, the Zulus attacked. When the fighting ended, fifty-two British officers, 806 British soldiers, and about five hundred of their African allies lay dead. Only a handful of white men escaped with their lives. The fighting had been brutal. British bayonets had been bent, and broken Zulu spears lay everywhere. One British soldier lay impaled by his own bayonet, which had been driven through his mouth a foot deep into the rock-hard ground. Next to him a Zulu lay with a bayonet driven completely through his skull. In some parts of the camp it was almost impossible to walk without stepping on a dead man. There were bodies everywhere—not only men, but horses, mules, oxen, even dogs impaled by spears. One officer's Irish setter was pinned to the ground by a spear, his two spare horses had been killed too, and his African groom lay speared to death between them. Two British drummer boys were hung up by their chins on butchers' hooks, their stomachs cut open like sheep. Most of the white men lay on their backs with their hands clenched, their faces contorted in agony.

Almost all of the more than 1,300 dead men had been disemboweled—turned onto their backs, then slashed open with a spear from sternum to groin. Their intestines had spilled out onto the ground where the Zulus' bare feet had smashed them, spreading a stinking ooze across the plain. A few men had been scalped, and some had been mutilated, their genitals cut off and stuffed into their mouths, or their lower jaws chopped off and taken away as bearded trophies of victory. A few bodies were headless. For some reason, a dozen or so heads of British soldiers had been arranged in a perfect circle. Some of the British died singly under wagons, in tents, and in dead embraces with Zulu warriors, the Zulus killed by bayonets, the Britons by spears. Others died in lines and clumps where they fought. Fifty British infantrymen were killed so close together that all were touching as they lay. Most of the Zulu dead had been carried away from the battlefield, but some Zulus lay where they had fallen; most of them had been covered by their shields.

Many of the British tents had been burned, but some still stood, spattered by blood and brains, ripped by spear thrusts and bullets. Almost all of the bodies had been stripped; more than a thousand rifles and 500,000 rounds of ammunition had been removed from the battleground, but the ground was still littered with blood-soaked scarlet tunics, white sun helmets, portraits, photographs, letters, books, toothbrushes, shaving kits, sausage, flour, sugar, and chocolate; tins of milk, meat, and jam; officer's portmanteaus, writing desks, and boots; tent pegs, shovels, canvas stretchers with bamboo handles, money, and officers' checkbooks. Broken glass from bottles of beer and champagne mingled with thousands of empty cartridge cases. Dozens of pet dogs lay dead among the men, as did a pet monkey on a leash.

More British officers died in this one battle than were killed in all the fighting at Waterloo. No British battalion had ever before lost so many of its officers in a single battle. Six companies of a veteran British regiment had been killed to the last man. That, too, was unheard of. As a British transport officer who escaped wrote in a letter home, "Never has such a disaster happened to the English army."[1]

It was anything but a bloodless victory for the Zulus. British fire had been murderous, and when they ran out of ammunition they had fought hand to hand. Many Zulus died on the battleground, and many others were badly wounded, most to die later. In all, more than three thousand were killed.[2]

When news of the "disaster," as it was called, reached England on February 12, the reaction was disbelief, then shock. A few commentators gave credit to the Zulus. For example, *The Times* reported that previous doubts among the British about the courage and skill of the Zulus had been resolved: "We now have ample proof not only of their valour but also of their skill in strategy."[3] Others immediately assumed that British leaders had "bungled." But for most, the reaction was simply shock. Colonel (later General Sir) Richard Harrison was one of thousands of British officers and soldiers who received orders on February 12 to stand by for shipment to South Africa. He wrote: "Many a time have the people of England been startled by the accounts received from some seat of war; but never, I think, has such a shock been felt at home as when the morning papers proclaimed that an organised British force had been almost annihilated by the badly armed though brave warriors of the Kaffir king, Cetshwayo, on the borders of Zululand."[4]

In later battles, more Zulus would die—many more—and eventually they would be defeated. But after Isandlwana, "Zulu" was a household word in Britain. Zulus were feared, admired, hated, and misunderstood, always misunderstood. Their courage was often made into fanaticism—they were "not afraid of death." Their way of life was distorted, their threat to white ''civilization'' exaggerated. Mysterious, menacing, and intriguing, the Zulus were now on center stage. The British public wanted to know what manner of men these Zulus were who could charge into British guns, die by the hundreds, yet charge again and win. The British Government and the British army were asking the same question.

The most common belief was that the British were crushed by the irresistible charge of thousands of blood-lusting, screaming black warriors. That version of what happened has been repeated many times, perhaps as dramatically in the writings of T. H. White as anywhere else. In 1933 White (later to become famous for *The Once and Future King*) wrote a novel called *Farewell Victoria*. In it he described the Zulus as an ''army of ants, automatically fearless and unforgiving. . . . It was like fighting a different and incalculable species—a species like the termites.'' The English troops, as he called them, stood in their squares, bravely firing a hail of bullets, but ''The Zulus came on, blood-lusting, incomprehensible. These death-disdaining stabbers were black, were impossible. Their bodies smelt strangely; their expressions were inhuman; their cries were in a foreign tongue, were those of beasts and cattle.''[5]

Death-disdaining, incomprehensible, inhuman, black, blood-lusting beasts! It is all there in White's hysterical prose. It need hardly be said that White misunderstood the Zulus, and so did the British who fought them in 1879. The Zulus misunderstood the British too. Their war was an epic of misunderstanding.

To understand why a British force fought and died at Isandlwana, some historical background is necessary. At the outbreak of war in 1879, there were about 23,000 whites and about 300,000 Africans in the British Colony of Natal, which bordered the Zulu Kingdom on the south. Many of those Africans were refugees from Zululand or belonged to tribes displaced by earlier Zulu wars. The threat of a large and powerful Zulu army just across the 100 mile-long Tugela and Buffalo river border separating Natal from Zululand had troubled the residents of Natal off and on for many years, but in fact no Zulu army had threatened Natal for decades. Even as war clouds gathered in 1878, Natal newspapers sometimes pointed out that the Zulus were good neighbors. One of Natal's most respected citizens wrote: ''The Zulus never went to war with us, but we with them; they have always been excellent neighbours; for thirty years they have never been accused of stealing a sheep, or an ox, or a horse from the Natal side.''[6] Although most of the British colonists of Natal had learned to live with the Zulu Kingdom as their neighbor, some British officials had not. At the time of the Zulu war, the British Empire covered one-fourth of the world's land surface—the richest and most powerful empire in history. Africa, however, had not come into the empire as a prize acquisition. It had not provided large markets for British goods, and it had few riches to exploit. But about two decades before the battle at Isandlwana, all that began to change. Africa began to look promising after all.

The European expansion that eventually led British troops into Zululand began at the end of the fifteenth century, although it is likely that Arab traders who sailed down the east coast of Africa in search of slaves and other wealth fought with Africans for centuries before the first Europeans arrived. When the Europeans did arrive, they wasted no time before they began to kill the people they met. When Bartholomeu Dias rounded the Cape of Good Hope in 1488 and put ashore for water, his men were the first Europeans to see the people they called Hottentots, small cattle-herding people who were physically similar to the even smaller people they called Bushmen. When the Hottentots seemed less than pleased to see the Portuguese sailors, Dias promptly put an arrow from his crossbow through one of them, and the rest ran away. The first European to see Natal and Zululand, farther to the north, was Vasco da Gama in 1497. Da Gama didn't go ashore, but for the next 150 years other Portuguese sailors did, and they fought the people they met—Hottentots usually, Bushmen sometimes, and now and then taller, darker people who were the ancestors of the Zulus. The Portuguese called them all "kaffirs," an Arabic word meaning infidel.

By 1650 Dutch sailors had forced the Portuguese out of southern African waters. They established a permanent base at Table Bay on the Cape. It came to be known as Cape Town. Dutch farmers, known as Boers, came as settlers and were joined by German mercenary soldiers, French Huguenots, and German-Jewish merchants, all looking for a better life. They found good land as they migrated along the coast to the east and then to the northeast. They killed the Hottentots who opposed them. They hunted Bushmen for sport. None of the fighting involved large numbers of people until about 1770, when the Boers reached the Great Fish River. There the white migrants moving north met black migrants moving south. Those African people, the Nguni, were the southernmost extension of many millions of Bantu-speaking Africans. Behind them to the north, all the way to Lake Victoria and even farther, people like them farmed and herded cattle, sheep, and goats. Perennially searching for better land for farming and grazing their animals, those Africans had been moving south in small family groups for centuries. They entered Zululand around 1400 or perhaps even earlier. When some of the Bantu-speaking people collided with the Boers, fighting was inevitable.

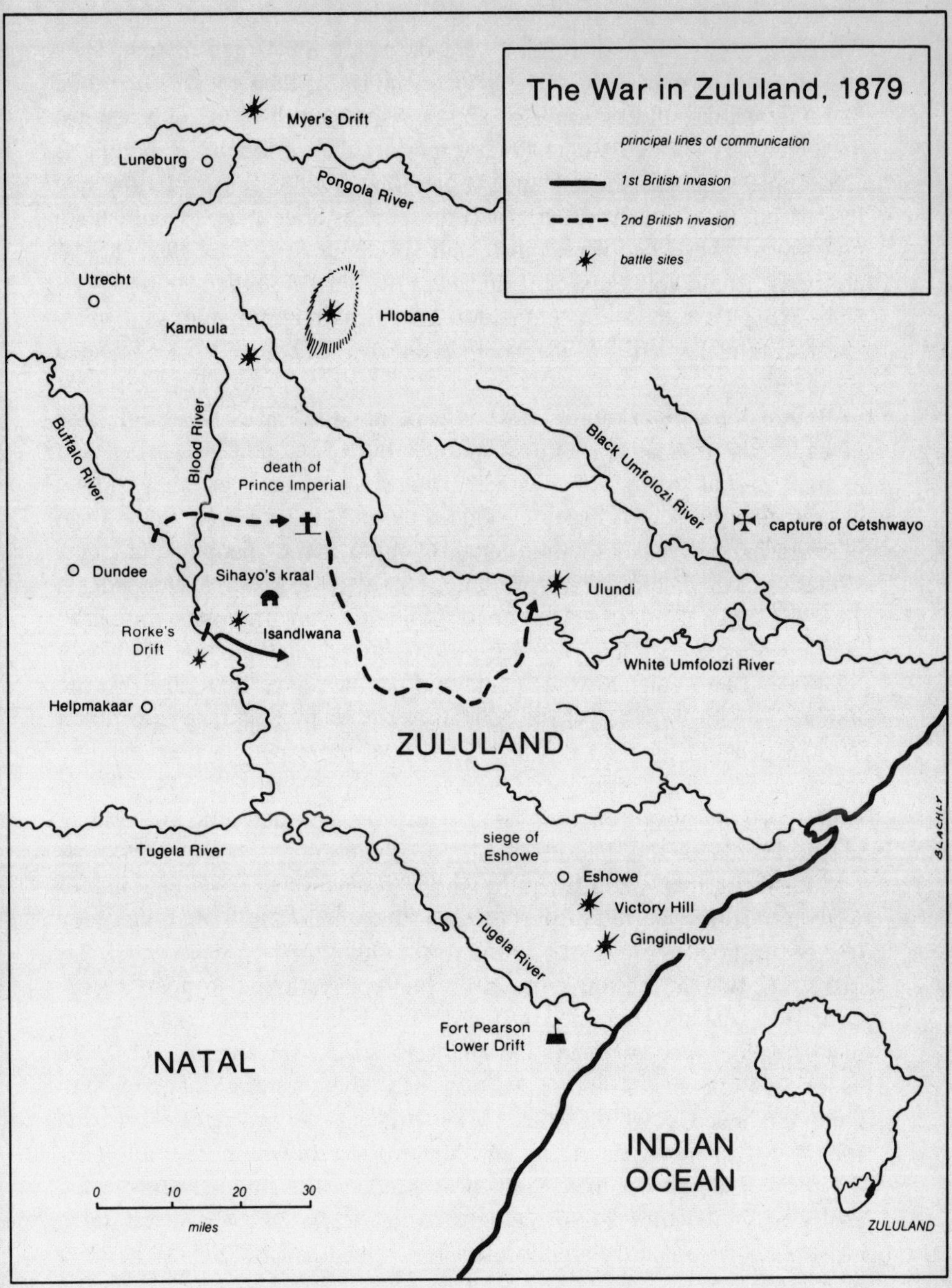
The War in Zululand, 1879
principal lines of communication
1st British invasion
2nd British invasion
battle sites
Myer's Drift
Luneburg
Pongola River
Utrecht
Hlobane
Kambula
Buffalo River
Blood River
death of Prince Imperial
Black Umfolozi River
capture of Cetshwayo
Dundee
Sihayo's kraal
Ulundi
Rorke's Drift
Isandlwana
White Umfolozi River
Helpmakaar
ZULULAND
BLACHLY
Tugela River
siege of Eshowe
Eshowe
Victory Hill
Gingindlovu
Tugela River
Fort Pearson Lower Drift
NATAL
INDIAN OCEAN
0 10 20 30
miles
ZULULAND

While the Boers were fighting to expand their lands by displacing African peoples, British sailors were defeating the Dutch at sea. They took Cape Town in 1793, lost it again in 1802, then took it for good in 1806. British soldiers, sailors, and colonists joined in the fight against the Nguni. A serious student of the period characterized the Nguni as "an aimless people, happy and careless, with little sense of time and less of purpose."[7] The Boers, and the British after them, would learn otherwise. These people needed land for their crops and their herds, and they would fight to get it and keep it. They fought in nine major wars against white soldiers, including British Imperial troops, the last war taking place in 1877–78, just one year before British troops invaded Zululand.

Before the Zulu Empire came into being, the Zulus were only one of hundreds of related Bantu-speaking groups in southeast Africa, and a small one at that. Along with the other Nguni peoples, they slowly migrated to the south, herding their cattle and shifting their fields from place to place. At the southern edge of this wave of people, the Boers slowed and then stopped the migration. To the west was the formidable 10,000-foot Drakensberg (Dragon's Mountain) range, no place for cattle-herding people. To the east was low-lying swampland that was poor for grazing and unhealthy for cattle and people alike. Beyond it lay the Indian Ocean, and the Nguni peoples were pastoralists, not seafarers. With expansion blocked on three sides and more people pressing into the area from the north, there was growing pressure for land. Groups split apart as various factions sought to improve their grazing land or to find farmlands that had not yet been exhausted.

Sometimes the Nguni tribes fought with each other, but their battles were more like spectator sports than killing matches. Sometimes they fought by shouting poetry back and forth. Other times, by prior arrangement, the two sides would line up a hundred yards or so apart before each side sent its champion forward. The rest of the warriors (not to mention older men, women, and children) watched, cheered, and jeered as the two opponents threw spears at each other, fending them off with their toughened cowhide shields. Sometimes other warriors joined the fray, but if a few men were killed, their supporters would flee, dropping their spears as an accepted sign of surrender. The winners took some captives, whom they exchanged for cattle. It was all very exciting to be sure, but really a relatively bloodless way to spend an afternoon at war.

Shortly after 1800, in an area north of Natal that later became known as Zululand, a chief of one tribe, the Mthethwa, had unusual success at this form of warfare. His name was Dingiswayo, and over the next few years, he conquered thirty or more tribes. Early European commentators on Dingiswayo speculated that his military innovations came about as a result of contact with British or Portuguese traders or that he somehow saw British troops drilling in Cape Colony; it has even been suggested that he was white himself.[8] There is no basis for that sort of speculation. Dingiswayo was an African whose men fought traditional battles with little bloodshed; as before, the losing tribe continued to occupy its territory and manage its affairs. What Dingiswayo added to the traditional pattern of warfare was his insistence that the young warriors of the defeated tribes had to serve in his army when needed, and he organized these men into units, called regiments by Europeans, ready for easy mobilization and control.

One of the tribes Dingiswayo conquered was the Zulu. One of the Zulus was a brave, tall, powerful warrior named Shaka, who soon rose to the command of a regiment and, while still very young, to the command of Dingiswayo's entire army. By then all that had changed was the size of the army and its organization into more or less formal units, but Shaka changed the tactics and weapons of that army and, with those changes, the course of African history. No longer would warriors stop at a distance from the enemy and throw spears, which could fairly easily be blocked with shields or avoided. Shaka replaced light throwing spears with short-handled, heavy-bladed spears useful only for stabbing. Shaka's idea was that any coward could throw a spear from a distance, but only brave warriors could rush forward close enough to their enemies to stab them to death. Men brave enough to fight at close quarters would win battles. To make sure that his men could cover ground rapidly, he made them toughen their feet so they could charge without sandals. As a result they were able to run faster than their enemies. He also introduced new techniques for using the shield to throw an enemy off balance before stabbing him and he organized his army into a crescent formation, a main body of men preceded on each flank by two horns that rushed forward in an encircling movement.

Although Shaka's armies did not win every battle, his innovations allowed them to defeat most of their enemies with relative ease. However, unlike Dingiswayo, Shaka would not settle for bloodless victories. He wanted to obliterate his opponents, and his armies killed in terrible numbers. From the handful of deaths characteristic of earlier battles, the toll rose astonishingly. In 1813 the battle of *Um Mona* left almost seven hundred dead, a number that was matched in several other encounters. By 1818 Dingiswayo's brother-in-law, Zwide, chief of a large neighboring tribe to the north called the Ndwandwe, had borrowed many of Shaka's military innovations. Zwide captured and killed Dingiswayo, then attacked the Zulus. His army was large, but it had not fully mastered the Zulu way of making war. In 1818 Zwide attacked the Zulus at Qokli Hill with an army of 11,000 men against the Zulus' four thousand or so. Led by their new king, Shaka, the Zulus won, killing more than seven thousand Ndwandwes with a loss of 1,500 of their own warriors. A year later, 18,000 Ndwandes—a truly immense army for the time—attacked 10,000 Zulus. All but perhaps one thousand of the Ndwandes were killed at a loss of five thousand for the Zulus. The death toll of about 22,000 men was an appalling slaughter for any battle, at any time. In 1826, when the Ndwandes sent their rebuilt army of 20,000 men against him, Shaka put 40,000 men in the field. In the ensuing battle, which was witnessed by a British trader named Fynn, perhaps five thousand Zulus died, and some accounts say that only one thousand Ndwandwes escaped.[9] A thousand survivors out of 20,000! These round numbers are rough estimates, of course, and they may be greatly exaggerated, but there can be no doubt that Zulu warfare had become very deadly. The Ndwandwes would attempt no more wars against the Zulus. They fled to the north, one branch conquering Barotseland, more than 1,000 miles to the northwest, and another traveling all the way to Lake Victoria, more than 2,000 miles to the north. The shock waves of displaced people who adopted Zulu military tactics affected half the continent.[10]

Although shipwrecked British, Dutch, and Portuguese sailors had taken African wives and had prospered in Natal for several hundred years; no European colony existed there until 1824, when a motley assortment of traders, merchants, and former Royal Navy officers set up a trading post called Port Natal. Trade in Natal itself was not profitable, because almost the whole area had been depopulated by the raids of Zulu armies. So, ignoring warnings about the cruelty of Zulu King Shaka, the Englishmen set out to trade with the Zulus. Thanks to their courage, intelligence, and great good luck, they were protected by Shaka, and their trade flourished. Even so, as late as 1835, when the first British missionary arrived, Port Natal was nothing more than a collection of small mud huts with grass roofs and dirt floors. The missionary, the former Royal Navy Captain Allen Gardiner, was shocked to find his countrymen living with African women and, worse, fathering children. Appalled by that sinful state of affairs but unable to bring it to an end, Gardiner went off to tell the Zulus about God. He was soon followed by American missionaries, who, with wives in tow, established mission stations among the Zulus. Two years later, a large contingent of Boers who were ''trekking'' north to escape British rule in Cape Colony arrived in Natal.

Although Shaka was assassinated by two of his brothers in 1828, the Zulu army thrived. It carried out expeditions against distant neighbors, wreaking terror and returning with many cattle. The Boers, in search of land and freedom from British rule in Cape Colony, were more difficult opponents. Always hungry for land, the Boers began to negotiate with Dingane, the new Zulu king. Dingane was rightly fearful that the bearded white men with their horses and guns would drive the Zulus out of their best land, so under the guise of friendship he induced the Boers to come unarmed to a conference. At Dingane's command the Boer men were seized and killed, followed by their women and children, more than six hundred in all.

In the following years, Zulus and Boers fought several battles. When caught on open ground, despite their guns, the Boers had little chance against the Zulus. When the Boers were able to circle their heavy wagons into a defensive *laager,* however, it was the Zulus who had little chance. In one battle in 1838, more than 12,000 Zulus attacked a fortified Boer laager. When their headlong attacks ended after about two hours, more than three thousand Zulus lay dead. Although many Boers had blistered hands from their red-hot rifle barrels, only three Boers had been killed. So many bodies fell or were thrown into a nearby river that it ran red, and it has ever after been known as the Blood River. In 1838, when an army of Africans from Natal led by a few Englishmen marched against them, the Zulus destroyed the army and burned Port Natal. British troops from Cape Colony arrived later that same year, and there was no further fighting. With them came Theophilus Shepstone, who was to play a critical role in the Anglo-Zulu War four decades later.

The Zulus then fought less against their neighbors, but their army grew as the Zulu population increased, and various Zulu factions fought among themselves. In 1856, there was a tremendous civil war between two sons of Zulu King Mpande, who had succeeded Dingane. Each prince intended to be king after Mpande (known as Panda to the British in Natal) eventually died, and each had built up a large following. One of the brothers, Mbulazi, had about seven thousand warriors in his faction; his older brother, Cetshwayo, had 20,000 men in his *uSuthu* faction. Cetshwayo's men attacked and killed virtually all of Mbulazi's warriors and more than 20,000 of his women and children as well. There were several British eyewitnesses to (and participants in) the battle, and there can be no doubt that the killing was ghastly. When the battle was over, Cetshwayo held *de facto* power as the Zulu king, although his father nominally held the throne until his death in 1872. The battle cry of his army continued to be "uSuthu!" The British would hear it often in 1879.

In 1844, Natal became a British Crown Colony, separate from Cape Colony, but the success of its future depended on white settlers. Fortunately for Natal, the Zulus remained at peace with Natal, and the colony's population began to grow. Displaced Africans returned, and British immigrants, lured by the offer of rich land at a penny an acre, poured into the colony. The best land, needless to say, went to those white settlers.[11] Along the hot and humid coast, vast tracts of land were planted in sugarcane, and sugar soon became Natal's main industry.

As the sugar crops flourished, the white plantation farmers found themselves increasingly short of labor. African men could not easily be induced to work in cane fields—for them, farming was women's work—so the newly rich sugar estates began to import indentured Indian laborers. Natal sugar farmers believed that Indian workers were stronger, cheaper, and more honest than Africans. Nevertheless, the Indian men, who came to Natal without women, were treated virtually like slaves, being flogged for any misdeed. To the dismay of the British settlers, when the Indians' five-year period of indenture expired, they moved into small businesses and soon monopolized the fishing industry. In 1879, at the start of the Anglo-Zulu War, there were almost as many Indians in Natal as whites (20,000 Indians and 23,000 whites), but they took no part in the war. In fact, contemporary accounts of the war did not mention their existence.[12]

The sugar plantations continued to draw indentured Indian laborers, but it was not "King Sugar" alone that demanded workers. After the discovery of diamonds in the vast Kimberley fields to the west of Natal in 1867, there was an urgent need for more workers, especially in the sugar fields, which were having trouble competing with the diamond mines. Africans from all over southern Africa began to make their way to the diamond fields. Later, when gold finds began to be reported, even more labor was needed, and still other mineral wealth was rumored to exist in the lands to the west and north of Natal. First in Natal and later in London, the idea grew that Durban, the only port in southeastern Africa, could be the funnel through which immense wealth could flow to England.[13] From Mombasa on the east coast to Kinshasa on the west, the riches of Africa could be funneled to Durban and then, of course, to England. It was a grand imperial vision, worthy of Cecil Rhodes, and it provoked the Fourth Earl of Carnarvon, Secretary of State for the Colonies in Disraeli's new British Government, to write that Britain should declare its own Monroe Doctrine over this land of treasure.[14] Lord Carnarvon spelled it "Munro," but everyone knew what he meant.

One of the problems with this funnel-shaped sphere of influence was that the Boers and Zulus were in the way; they were also armed and independent. They could be a military threat to the still small white population of Natal. Another threat came from the 300,000 or so African residents of Natal, crowded onto the least desirable lands, where their discontent grew. The whites were unwilling to give up the rich lands they had reserved for themselves, so they looked elsewhere for a solution. Some of them saw Zululand as the answer to their problem. If the Zulus could be pacified under a British government, many of the African residents of Natal, who provided no useful labor to the British, could be repatriated to Zululand, where many of them had originally lived. For several reasons, then, the Zulus and the Boers would have to be pacified. If there could not be a peaceful confederation of the South African populations under British rule, then there would have to be a confederation by force. Plans were laid to annex the Boer-populated Transvaal to the north and west of Zululand, and in 1877 annexation took place. Behind the relentless leadership of Sir Theophilis Shepstone, who had been Secretary for Native Affairs since 1846, Natal also attempted to extend its control over the Zulus. Despite Shepstone's considerable intellectual powers, his ability to speak Zulu, and his talent for duplicity, he failed to accomplish much. Even his self-proclaimed crowning achievement of taking a delegation from Natal to Zululand in 1873 to carry out a British-style coronation of the new Zulu king, Cetshwayo, proved to be a farce.

Shepstone hoped that by taking a delegation from Natal to Zululand and by placing a cheap tinsel crown on the new Zulu king's head, he could persuade Cetshwayo to accept at least some degree of indirect rule by Natal. In fact, Cetshwayo agreed to allow the ceremony to take place at all only because he decided that the visible support of Natal with its British troops would strengthen his claim to the Zulu throne. Several contenders were actively challenging his right of succession, including his brother Mbulazi, who was rumored to be living in Natal.[15] Two other claimants, his half-brothers Zibhebhu and Hamu, were to play prominent roles in the Anglo-Zulu War. Cetshwayo got what he wanted from Shepstone and, in return, ceded none of his autonomy. It was clear then, even to Shepstone, that Cetshwayo could not be controlled by diplomatic trickery. Force would be required. Shepstone fumed and schemed. He easily convinced General Sir Garnet Wolseley, who began to govern Natal in 1874, that the Zulus were a menace to Natal and that force would be necessary to deal with them. He added that no great amount of military force would be required; a minor show of British force and some flag-waving would suffice. Wolseley was soon telling everyone that British troops would have to subdue the Zulus.[16]

Lord Carnarvon was concerned that his dream of confederation with its cornucopia of African wealth funneling through Durban to London was falling behind schedule. He persuaded Sir Henry Bartle Frere, one of the British Empire's most distinguished colonial officers, to become the Governor of Cape Colony with a mandate to achieve confederation. Carnarvon promised Frere that success would bring him the Governor-Generalship of the new Union of South Africa, a handsome salary, and, not least, a peerage. Frere, who was greatly respected for his service to the British Raj in Bombay, was neither wealthy nor a peer, so he accepted and began his campaign to destroy Zulu power. He was helped by the outbreak of what was known as the Ninth Frontier or Kaffir War. In 1877, two large tribal groups to the south of Natal—the Gaikas and Gcalekas—rose against British rule. Although the fighting lasted into 1878, it was never a very serious war, and the British and White colonial troops, with their African allies, suffered few casualties in suppressing the rebellion. Nevertheless, the uprising renewed the ever present specter of an African rebellion in Natal, where Africans were acquiring rifles at an alarming rate. Even worse, it was widely believed in Natal that the Zulus were instigating an uprising by the Africans there.[17] Natal newspapers began to carry editorials like this:

> The Zulu question is the keystone of the arch of South African politics . . . there is a strong feeling both in Natal and the Transvaal, that it would be well were the Zulus shown, by strong measures, that the British government is supreme in South Africa, and means to remain so. It is believed that an effective demonstration of British power will be required before the Zulu power shall cease to be a disquieting and disturbing element in South-East Africa.[18]

Frere increased his campaign to justify war against the Zulus by disseminating atrocity stories about Cetshwayo, whom he depicted as a despotic savage who was planning to send his maniacally bloodthirsty soldiers—Frere called them "celibate manslaying gladiators"—to slaughter the helpless residents of Natal. Some of the atrocity stories came from panicky border agents, many came from Shepstone, and some of the most lurid came from a missionary named Robert Robertson (known to the Zulus as the "Fat Parson"), who later admitted that he had fabricated the stories, probably to ingratiate himself with the authorities in Natal who were distressed by his heavy drinking and his large harem of Zulu women.[19]

While rumors spread, Frere was building up British military force in Natal. The man who commanded the British during their war against the Zulus was Lieutenant General Frederick A. Thesiger. Tall and thin, a former Grenadier Guardsman and the son of a Lord High Chancellor, Britain's highest judicial officer, he was known as "Fred" to his friends even after he inherited his father's title—Second Baron Chelmsford—while on board the steamship *America* sailing to Natal to take command. Lord Chelmsford was an aristocrat, but unlike General Wolseley, who would succeed him, and many of the officers whom he would soon lead against the Zulus, he was not a war-lover. The private soldiers called him "that old fool" (he was all of fifty-one-years old, and his beard was still black), and some officers agreed that he was a hapless general, but most of his officers respected him as a gentleman and defended him against criticism long after the war. There was a lot of criticism, because he was neither a very good general nor a lucky one, and his efforts to defend himself against his critics were both self-serving and unsuccessful.

But all that came later. Lord Chelmsford had been in command of Imperial forces in South Africa since March 1878. Earlier he had seen combat in the Crimean War and in India, and he had held a number of staff positions. He was known in the army as a competent general, careful—too careful, some thought—but generally "sound." Unlike many other foppish and high-living generals (some of whom he would command against the Zulus), Chelmsford was down to earth. A teetotaler in a hard-drinking army, he lived simply. He led British troops during the Ninth Frontier War in 1878, and while no great generalship was required to defeat the not-very-military Gaikas and Gcalekas, at least he had won within reasonable time without suffering many casualties. Now, Frere called him to Natal to prepare for war against what he called the Zulu "incubus." Aided by a small staff (Chelmsford was a general who liked to do everything himself), he set to work planning for the war that Frere was determined to make inevitable.

The Zulu Kingdom extended over an area about the size of the state of Georgia. Parts of Zululand were mountainous and heavily forested, but much of the country, including the districts closest to Natal, was relatively open grasslands. It was easy country for a man to walk over or to ride across on horseback, but it was cut by some sizable rivers, many smaller streams, and innumerable deep gullies and ravines called *dongas*. To reach the Zulu king's royal homestead at Ulundi (his "capitol," as the British said), Chelmsford's army would have to traverse 75 miles of that kind of terrain. There were no roads and no maps, but Lord Chelmsford planned to bring the Zulus to battle by marching on Ulundi.

Ulundi was King Cetshwayo's principal residence, but it was not his only one, and it had no strategic or symbolic significance for the Zulus. It was a dusty conglomeration of a thousand or more round, thatch-roof houses arranged in concentric circles and linked by lattice-like fences. Cetshwayo's "palace" was a little larger than the other houses, but it was hardly splendid. It had the same mud walls and dirt floor as the other houses and was lighted by the same 10-inch candles made of cow dung and fat. The king kept some of the many gifts that European visitors had given him, including a trunk filled with old English and Dutch newspapers, an iron box stuffed with used bootblacking brushes, and a photograph of the "Tinsel Crown" Coronation ceremony, but he had nothing that the British would consider of value. The wealth of his kingdom was its herds of cattle, not its easily replaceable dwellings. It made little sense for Chelmsford to march on Ulundi as if it were the nerve center of the Zulu Kingdom. Chelmsford's goal was to bring the Zulu army to battle, but if the Zulus would not fight before the British reached Ulundi, there was no reason why they should fight *for* Ulundi. Still, Chelmsford could think of no other plan, so he would march on Ulundi. Cavalry could easily have ridden to Ulundi in two days. But almost all of the British troops were infantry, not cavalry, and like European and American armies before and since, they could not march to war without tons of supplies. Transport would be a recurring nightmare for Chelmsford.

If the men of a British infantry battalion had been forced to carry all of their supplies on their backs, they could have carried only enough food and water to last two or three days and enough ammunition for one reasonably hard battle. Their rifles alone weighed 10 pounds, and with seventy rounds of ammunition, water, and two days' supply of tinned rations, each man would have to carry about 60 pounds.[20] Chelmsford expected his campaign to last six to eight weeks, not a few days, and so the British army needed transport, and it could move no faster than the hundreds of wagons that carried what it needed. Built like the "prairie schooners" that American pioneers used when they crossed the Western plains, the wagons would be loaded with food, water, ammunition, and tents. The tents for a single battalion of approximately eight hundred men weighed more than 9 tons, and a single battalion of British troops ate at least a ton of food a day. The wagons would also carry medical stores; wood for cooking fires, since much of the invasion route was treeless; camp kitchens; casks of rum; bottles of Bass beer, porter, rum, gin, whisky, and champagne; engineering equipment of all sorts; blacksmiths' tools and supplies; and all manner of desks, cots, changes of clothing, spare boots, books, and other impedimenta that gentlemen officers carried into battle in those days.

Each wagon was pulled by a team of fourteen to eighteen oxen or, sometimes, about the same number of mules. On level ground, a lightly loaded wagon might cover a maximum of 10 miles in a day, but there was little level ground in Zululand, where wagons had to ford rivers, cross deep gullies, and climb steep hills. Lord Chelmsford learned that draft animals would quickly become exhausted and, if not allowed to rest and graze, would collapse. He was warned that wagons would break down too. To his dismay, he also learned that there were too few wagons and teams of oxen in all of Natal to supply his army's needs. Chelmsford was not pleased to discover that the good citizens of Natal were unwilling to sell or even rent their teams and wagons for anything less than a king's ransom. He sent officers all over southern Africa in search of transport. Slowly, teams of oxen arrived in Natal. They soon overgrazed the grass and had to be moved to other areas, where many sickened and died. Transport was General Chelmsford's greatest headache as he prepared to invade Zululand, and it would remain so throughout the war.

Supplies were not a great problem. Natal had no harbor, and so ships had to be off-loaded onto small boats, which sometimes capsized in the heavy surf, but substantial supplies of ammunition and food were available. Chelmsford was worried, however, about the numbers of troops available to him. London refused to send any additional troops to Frere. The Government faced the possibility of a war with Russia over Afghanistan, so Frere's plans in Africa had become less attractive to London. Chelmsford had to make do with the forces already available in southern Africa: ten battalions of Imperial infantry, each with about eight hundred men, and several batteries of artillery. Unfortunately for Chelmsford, there was no British cavalry in all of Africa. Fortunately, there were many white colonists in South Africa who were willing to volunteer. Many were former British army officers, and all were experienced horsemen, familiar with firearms and used to living out of the saddle. Chelmsford was able to raise a force of one thousand volunteer white horsemen that included everything from British gentlemen and European noblemen to teenaged drifters who spoke only French, German, Portuguese, or Dutch. Chelmsford also recruited more than nine thousand Africans, whom he formed into units under white command. The Africans were not expected to stand up to a Zulu charge, but other Africans had proved valuable as scouts in the Ninth Frontier War. On the eve of the war, Chelmsford had almost 17,000 men at his disposal.

General Chelmsford believed that all his forces combined into one massive column would be so formidable that the Zulus would never dare to attack them. Because his primary strategy was to entice the

Zulus to attack, he decided to divide his forces into three columns, which would invade Zululand separated from one another by about fifty miles before converging on Ulundi. Chelmsford left one of his battalions, the 88th Connaught Rangers, known as "wild Irishmen," in Cape Colony to deal with whatever might arise to the south, and he sent another, the 80th Regiment (some British regiments had only one battalion, but others had two), to the town of Utrecht near the northwest corner of Zululand, where it could keep an eye on the Zulus as well as the Boers in the Transvaal. He created another force of African horsemen and infantry under the command of Colonel Anthony Durnford, which was to remain in Natal guarding places where the rivers could be crossed against a possible Zulu invasion.

Chelmsford divided the remainder of his forces into three columns of approximately equal strength. The "left column," commanded by Colonel Evelyn Wood, was built around two infantry battalions, one from the 13th Regiment and the other from the 90th. The volunteer horsemen assigned to Wood's force were commanded by the redoubtable Colonel Redvers Buller. Wood was directed to march south from the northwest corner of Zululand before swinging to the east to join Chelmsford at Ulundi. The "right column" was commanded by Colonel Charles Pearson, who also had two battalions of Imperial infantry, from the 3rd and 99th regiments. In addition to volunteer horsemen, Pearson had several hundred battle-hardened sailors from Royal Navy ships offshore. Pearson would cross the Tugela River near the coast and march parallel to the coast before turning northwest toward Ulundi. The "central column" would be led by Chelmsford himself. Its main strength came from the first and second battalions of the 24th Regiment. This column would ford the Buffalo River on the western border of Zululand and drive east to Ulundi. Each of the three columns had a battery of artillery as well as a large contingent of African troops, and each column, Chelmsford thought, was strong enough to destroy any Zulu army that could be sent against it while appearing to be small enough to tempt the Zulus to attack.

Chelmsford had been warned repeatedly that the Zulus were much more formidable that the "Kaffirs" he had defeated so easily a year earlier. He listened politely but remained skeptical. He was not worried that any of his three separate columns would be too weak; he feared only that the Zulus would not face his men in open battle and that he would be forced into a guerrilla war that his immobile, supply-hungry troops could not win. Although Chelmsford did not believe what he was told about the Zulus, he did attempt to collect information about them. As a result of his intelligence system, British officers from Lord

Chelmsford to his youngest subaltern probably knew more about their enemy than any colonial army before them ever had. British traders, missionaries, and government officials had fifty years of firsthand knowledge of the Zulu army. The British also had many spies in Zululand, and hundreds of Zulus were fighting on their side. A British trader named John Dunn knew King Cetshwayo and the Zulu army intimately. In fact, Cetshwayo had given him a district and a small army of his own. A British border agent named Fynney, who like Dunn spoke Zulu well, provided Chelmsford with details of Zulu tactics as well as a regiment-by-regiment description of the entire Zulu army. It wasn't completely accurate, but it was close enough to help. Chelmsford gave a copy of the information, along with a map of Zululand, to all his officers, including the junior men. Some of the Boers also helped. A few rode with the British as scouts, and several warned Chelmsford and his aides about Zulu military prowess. The Boer leader Paul Kruger, who had personal experience fighting against the Zulus, warned the British always to scout miles ahead and never to camp without forming a defensive laager. Chelmsford only seemed to listen, and most of his staff officers ignored Kruger's advice. They had beaten the ''Kaffirs'' in 1877–78 without laagers, and they would do the same to the Zulus. What really gave them concern was to hear from old Zulu hands like Sir Theophilus Shepstone that King Cetshwayo was a coward who would not stand against them. They wanted the Zulus to fight, and their only worry was that they would not.

Delighted by the opportunity for glory, British officers were more than willing to accept the challenge of invading Zululand. For example, Major (later General Sir) Francis Clery, adjutant to Colonel Glyn of the 24th Regiment, wrote in 1878 that the Zulus had been ''very 'cheeky' for a long time, and unless they knuckle under now it is thought that it is time to have it out with them.''[21] Colonel John North Crealock, Chelmsford's military secretary, added that the time had ''come for the Zulus to be taught that the white man was the better man.''[22] Several other officers wrote that Africans in Natal had told them that only after the British had defeated the Zulus would the Natal tribes accept British rule. Captain (later General Sir) Henry Hallam Parr recalled the sense of ''sullen expectancy'' on the part of Africans throughout South Africa who believed that their acquisition of guns would enable them to defeat the British:

> ''Yes, you have beaten us,'' an old Galeka warrior said. . . . You have beaten us well, but there,'' said he, pointing eastward—''there are the Ama Zulu warriors! Can you beat them? They say not! Go

and try. Don't trouble any more about us, but beat *them*, and we shall be quiet enough."[23]

It was a challenge that would dominate British thinking until the end of the war.

Frere had hoped that a British Boundary Commission, which had been appointed to investigate a dispute between the Zulus and Boers concerning borderlands in northwest Zululand, would find in favor of the Boers, giving him a reason for military intervention. To Frere's dismay, late in 1878 the commission upheld the Zulus' claims, not those of the Boers. Frere squelched the report and continued his preparations for war. Because Britain was faced with the growing possibility of war against Russia, Frere's new superior, Colonial Secretary Michael Hicks Beach, urged him to exercise restraint, acknowledging to others as he did so that he had lost all control over Frere and his plans for a Zulu war. Frere had cynically timed his ultimatum to expire in mid-January, because that was the time of the year when the Zulu harvest usually took place and Frere had been led to believe that many Zulu men would be too busy harvesting their crops to join their regiments. Somehow Frere failed to understand that the harvest was primarily the work of women, not men. What is more, the rains were so late in 1879 that the crops would not be ripe until late February. All Frere's scheming had managed to achieve was to send Chelmsford's army into Zululand at the height of the rainy season. It is one of the war's many ironies that Chelmsford's supply wagons spent more than a week stuck in the mud in Zululand. As a result they got no farther than Isandlwana before the newly mobilized Zulu army met them. But for the mud, the battle would not have been fought at Isandlwana and the outcome might have been different.

On January 4, 1879, Frere declared that he "had exhausted all peaceful means" in dealing with King Cetshwayo's "grinding despotism," "atrocious barbarity," and "faithless and cruel character." Frere had never met Cetshwayo, nor had he ever visited Zululand, but ever sanctimonious, he now wrote to Colonial Secretary Hicks Beach that war would begin on January 11, adding, "Of the perfect justice of our cause, I think you can have no doubt . . . by God's help we can relieve South Africa of the Zulu incubus." Frere blithely assured the Colonial Secretary that the war would be an easy one: "Their courage is the courage of maniacs and drunkards, of wild beasts infuriated and trained to destruction, and once cowed they will not rally."[24] Frere's words would come to haunt him.

Frere could be certain that war was inevitable, because he had sent Cetshwayo an ultimatum that he admitted to his superior Hicks Beach would be "impossible" for the Zulu king to accept.[25] To make doubly certain that King Cetshwayo could not comply, Frere also set an impossibly short deadline. And so the British troops marched into Zululand. Modern historians have interpreted the causes of the war in economic terms, arguing that the expanding needs of white capitalism for Zulu labor as well as free passage for other African labor through Zululand made war inevitable. It is obvious that there were economic motives for the war, and they were important, but as much as anything the war was fought because British colonial officials could not tolerate the existence of a powerful African State on the border of their dreamed-for South African confederation. From their perspective as agents of imperial progress, it made perfect sense for Britain to annex native states, by force if need be. They said, and no doubt believed, that everyone would be better off when British rule was established. Frere precipitated the Anglo-Zulu War by misrepresenting the dangers that armed Zulus might pose to Natal and by delivering an ultimatum to the Zulus that amounted to a demand that they disband their army and surrender to British rule.[26] Frere complained that only about half the white colonists in Natal supported "his war." He was quite right. Just before the war, a Natal newspaper characterized Frere's ultimatum as a demand that the Zulu people commit "self-emasculation."[27]

Frere was not terribly concerned about the lack of enthusiasm for "his" war among the residents of Natal. He represented Carnarvon, Froude, and others of great stature in London who planned the advance of empire. He was their agent, not Natal's, and so the war began. Frere declared it the perfect colonial war, one that protected the colonists in Natal while bringing God and good government to the benighted and oppressed natives of Zululand. No doubt most good Britons believed Sir Bartle's self-righteous declarations, and so did most of the British officers who fought "his" war. They did not know that Frere had knowingly lied about King Cetshwayo and had intentionally presented him with an unacceptable ultimatum to justify the calculated destruction of a sovereign state. The war lasted six months. After seven major battles, with great loss of life and destruction of property, the Zulu state met a tragic end, but so did Frere, who misjudged the Zulus' will and ability to resist. After the war, London recalled him in disgrace.

In 1879 the Zulu army had retained the tactics, weapons, and discipline that had allowed it to defeat other African armies. The army was large, between 40,000 and 50,000 men served in royal regiments, ready to fight at their king's command. This time they would not fight other Africans, they would fight the British, the "red soldiers." King Cetshwayo was determined to preserve his kingdom's independence, but he was at peace with the British in Natal, whom he had consistently treated with deference. Cetshwayo had no reliable information about British intentions, and he was confused by Frere's duplicity. Nevertheless, when Frere gave the Zulu king his insulting ultimatum, Cetshwayo and his counselors tried to formulate a reasonable response. Cetshwayo made substantial concessions, but the British were bent on war. Early in January 1879 three strong columns of British troops and their native allies invaded Zululand. Not until the invasion was under way did Cetshwayo mobilize the Zulu army.[28] The king ordered his army to repel the central column of the British force but not to invade Natal; he sent smaller forces to delay the other two British columns marching into his country.

# Chapter 2

# "Celibate Man-Slaying Gladiators"

Many British officers in Natal shared with Sir Bartle Frere (not to mention many modern writers) basic misconceptions about the Zulus. We have already seen that most of them believed that the Zulus would not stand and fight. Another important set of misconceptions the British had about the Zulus involved King Cetshwayo. They believed that like King Shaka before him, Cetshwayo was a bloodthirsty monster who possessed absolute authority over a monolithic Zulu kingdom. The British also believed that King Cetshwayo commanded a professional army, like their own, that was disciplined to follow the orders of its officers and king without question. But they also believed the Zulu army's zest for combat, unlike their own, came not from higher motives such as duty, but from sexual frustration. The reality, as a few British Government officials, missionaries, and traders knew, was altogether different.

Cetshwayo was not cast in the same mold as King Shaka. He did not use terror to enforce his will and rarely ordered executions, even for serious crimes. What is more, he had never ordered his army to war during the more than twenty years he had been in power. In fact, his powers as king were so limited that he could make few important decisions without the approval of his major chiefs and counselors. Those men represented powerful and often largely independent districts within Zululand. They acknowledged a tenuous allegiance to the king, but the most prominent men of each district largely ran their own affairs, including punishing capital offenses and deciding whether to join the king in a military campaign. Some districts were remarkably independent, and at least one large tribal group within Zululand, the Cube, never conquered by Shaka's armies, remained almost wholly independent. Another district, led by Cetshwayo's obese half-brother, Hamu, was actively seeking to overthrow him. Still another, led by Zibhebhu, was subversive. At best, the Zulu Kingdom was a loose confederation of districts and tribes that was sometimes united by similar customs, symbols, and economic interests, and sometimes divided by political or economic circumstances. Shaka had held this fragile collectivity together by his political genius, which included the strategic use of terror, but eventually even he was assassinated. Zululand had been on the edge of civil war ever since Shaka's death. Subsequent Zulu kings stayed on the throne not by their exercise of absolute authority but by their political ability to balance opposing factions. No Zulu king, least of all Cetshwayo, was secure in his power.

King Cetshwayo did have considerable power over various military forces, but he had no standing army mobilized and ready to carry out his orders. Instead, Zulu men formed a militia, ready and able to fight if need be, but when called up to serve the king, their duties were most often primarily economic, not military. What is more, many Zulus of military age never served the king directly. Large numbers of men remained in their home districts, where they worked or fought for their *induna* or chief. When Zulus did fight, they were ferocious warriors, but it would take a charter member of the Flat Earth Society—or a Victorian British army officer—to believe that those men fought because they were sexually repressed. To understand how and why the Zulus fought against the British as they did, we need to set aside these and other misconceptions by examining some of the realities of Zulu life in the 1870s.

Shortly after the British defeat at Isandlwana, the British magazine *Punch* lampooned Sir Bartle Frere's already famous description of the Zulu warriors as "celibate man-slaying gladiators" by printing a letter they imagined Frere might have written to Queen Victoria reporting the extent of the British losses in the battle and asking for reinforcements. It closed with the following postscript: "P.S.—It would be better, if possible, to send out only unmarried men. I find there is something to be said for a force of celibate man-slaying gladiators, after all."[1]

The sharp edge in *Punch*'s satire was aimed at Frere's decision to invade Zululand, not at the idea that the Zulu warriors' ferocity was related to their supposed celibacy. Because Zulu warriors usually were not permitted to marry until their mid-thirties or later, it was widely believed at the time that sexual frustration was the cause of the Zulus' martial spirit.[2]

Shepstone and Frere were not alone in proclaiming those fixed ideas about the "celibate" Zulus. Many of the British officers and men who marched to war against the Zulu armies believed that the Zulus were sex-starved, grizzled veterans who fought savagely in a quest for their king's ultimate but long-delayed reward—the right to take virgin brides.[3] Some even speculated that like Greek soldiers of antiquity the Zulus must be homosexual. So ingrained was the idea that the Zulus' pent-up sexual energy had to be released in battle that it is still repeated in modern scholarly accounts of the British army. For example, in his well-known book *Britain and Her Army, 1509–1970,* the British historian Corelli Barnett wrote that among the Zulus, "the martial spirit was kept high by sexual repression, leading to marked irritability vented on the enemy by means of the assegai [spear]."[4]

Even if one were willing to believe that ferocity in battle could be a product of sexual repression (the same interpretation was applied by the British even to the "Amazons" in West Africa), there are some daunting practical reasons why this thesis did not fit the Zulus. First, more than half of the regiments in the Zulu army were composed of married men, and half of the Zulu warriors who actually devastated the British at Isandlwana were married. In another battle, the savage fight at Rorke's Drift, which will be examined later, *most* of the Zulu warriors who fought so heroically were married men. It would seem a fair assumption that married men, especially men like the Zulus, who were allowed to have several wives, would not be sexually deprived. In fact, it was a Zulu saying that a man who had more than two wives would break his back. The saying does not refer to hard work in the fields.

A second problem with the theory of sexual repression comes from the quaint Victorian assumption that unmarried men were sexually deprived—a charmingly innocent idea, but very wrong where the Zulus were concerned. It is true that many Zulu men did not marry until they were in their thirties, but there was nothing particularly unusual about the Zulu practice of requiring its young men to provide military service for a decade or more before they were allowed to marry. A similar pattern occurred in many parts of the eastern portion of Africa from its southernmost extension all the way north to the Sudan. As young men in most of those societies came of warrior age, they were organized into age groups 18–20. These young men defended the cattle herds of their fathers and other married men against neighboring societies that might attempt to steal them, and now and then they carried out cattle raids against their enemies. Most of the cattle captured in the raids went to married men, who used them to acquire more wives. The warriors were denied the right to marry for ten or fifteen years, or sometimes even longer, and when the older men chose the girlfriends of the younger warriors as their wives, there was resentment. While the young men lived in warrior encampments, usually near their societies' borders with their neighbors, they were allowed to have only limited sexual relationships with young unmarried women. Young couples were supposed to confine their passion to what anthropologists, in a truly Victorian triumph of bowdlerization, call intracrural intercourse—literally, "between the legs." That form of sex was not supposed to include any vaginal penetration, although it sometimes happened. Warriors were not supposed to have affairs with the wives of older men, either, but that happened too. Young men of the east and south African cattle-herding societies often chafed under this system, and sometimes they threatened rebellion when their girlfriends were married off to wealthy older men, but the system survived for many centuries. In some more remote areas it still does.[5]

The Zulu version of this widespread pattern of delayed marriage left neither young men nor young women "sex-starved." Although unmarried men and women were not allowed to have vaginal sexual intercourse (girls were regularly inspected for loss of virginity), they were permitted to practice a form of "between the legs" sex called *hlobonga*.[6] Even young children engaged in hlobonga as freely as they wished. Girls as young as ten often enticed small boys to have hlobonga with them by singing in a seductive manner.[7] Hlobonga was much more than "petting," as some writers persist in calling it. The young couple lay together naked, traditionally with the girl on her right side. Although couples sometimes "lost their heads," especially after a night of dancing, the man was not ordinarily permitted to penetrate the vagina, but he was encouraged to make as much contact with the clitoris and labia as possible before ejaculating on the girl's perineum. A girl who practiced hlobonga expected to have an orgasm, and if she did not, she blamed the man, spreading gossip about his ineptitude, and rapidly found a new lover. Most men apparently succeeded well enough as lovers, because both men and women considered hlobonga to be "very sweet." Hlobonga was very widely practiced, and most young Zulus had not one but many lovers.

Sexuality was central to Zulu life, and so was physical beauty. European visitors uniformly reported that Zulu women were exceptionally attractive, and Zulu men had a very active interest in their women, admiring their beauty, courting them, and talking about them almost incessantly. Huge thighs were admired; some people, particularly in the royal lineage, had such immense legs that they had to put aloe between their legs to prevent chafing when they walked. Zulus believed that breasts and buttocks should be also large but "firm enough to crack a flea on," as they said. Zulu women were no less interested in sex than men. A British officer during the Zulu war reported that he received many shamelessly blunt invitations from Zulu women to engage in sexual intercourse, a phenomenon that Nathaniel Isaacs also reported—disapprovingly, he would have us believe—fifty years earlier.[8] Given their lusty interest in sex, it is not surprising that some unmarried men went beyond hlobongo to engage in vaginal intercourse with married women or the hundreds of concubines in the king's harem. Adultery was a capital offense, and when infidelity was discovered the woman might be executed, as happened just before the Anglo-Zulu War when a chief named Sihayo discovered that two of his wives had taken lovers. The women fled to British Natal but were abducted and returned to Zululand, where they were killed. Those women were particularly brazen; they had previously given birth to illegitimate children by their lovers, yet they continued to maintain their relationships. Although the abduction was a perfectly legal action in Zulu eyes, Frere chose to make it a *causus belli* by insisting that Natal's sovereignty had been violated.[9]

The Zulus knew that adultery had to be practiced discreetly or the penalty could be death, but they knew also that many Zulus were as capable of discretion as they were persistent in their pursuit of married women. Some young women married to older men did not object to the attention of younger men. What is more, in some parts of Zululand, especially in outlying districts far from the royal household, Zulus simply ignored the king's edicts about delaying marriage; young couples married when they and their parents wished.[10] Other men left Zululand to marry, sometimes returning later.[11] It also happened that young women sometimes openly defied their king. For example, in 1878 several hundred young women married young men in an open violation of King Cetshwayo's ban. Christian missionaries, the "Fat Parson" Robertson prominent among them, soon reported that the king had ordered all of those women "slaughtered," and Natal was properly horrified. In fact, as evidence later showed, no more than six, and perhaps only three, women were killed; in all probability those women were singled out for punishment because of some past indiscretion by their families (with or without the king's permission, marriage was always a matter for families to decide). All in all, it seems obvious that unmarried Zulu warriors were not sexually frustrated. In fact, as often as they practiced hlobonga it might be more accurate to say that they were sexually sated.

Zulu men and women *did* want to marry, and men *did* go to war, but they did not marry or go to war for sex. Zulus loved sexual experience, and sex was undeniably their favorite topic of conversation,[12] but the traditional reason for war was *cattle*. Cattle were fundamental to Zulu life. They were the people's most prized possession, and much of their time was spent caring for cattle, naming them, admiring them, making up poems about them, shaping their horns, painting designs on their faces, clipping their ears (it was popular to cut their ears to resemble elephants) and worrying about their welfare. Cattle were considered to be beautiful, and the Zulus had more than three hundred terms for different shades of color among their cattle (an American cattleman would have trouble coming up with more than a dozen or so color terms). Zulus doted on their cattle and sometimes empathized with them. For example, when cattle bellowed, Zulus felt an irresistible impulse to dance. But cattle were much more than ornamental pets. They supplied meat, milk, hides, and milk-curds, a Zulu staple; men without cattle could not obtain wives and therefore could not have children. A man with cattle had power and prestige. A man without cattle had nothing. A brave warrior would be rewarded by the king with cattle, and other cattle might go to the warrior's family. War was important and bravery essential, but the basic reason for life was cattle.

In 1878 there was a severe cattle shortage. Years of drought and disease had reduced the Zulus' herds, and the pressure for war to capture cattle was growing. King Cetshwayo asked Natal for permission to raid the Swazi Kingdom to the north for cattle. Natal, which had an alliance of sorts with the Swazis, refused. King Cetshwayo did not order war. It is worth repeating that the Zulu army had not been ordered to war since King Cetshwayo informally assumed power from his father, Mpande, after the civil war of 1856 (he actually became king in 1872). On the other hand, since Queen Victoria had been crowned in 1837, not a single year had passed without British troops fighting somewhere in the Empire.[13]

Late in 1878, while Frere was fomenting war and Lord Chelmsford was collecting the supplies and transport for his 17,000-man army, the Zulus remained at peace. Nonetheless, the British conceived of the Zulu state as, in Frere's term, an "armed camp" or, in Shepstone's words, a "war-machine." These men imagined a huge standing army, housed in military barracks, ready for war at the king's whim. They said Britain was forced to embark on war to destroy this Zulu "menace." In reality, there was no Zulu standing army. The Zulu population of some 250,000 or so lived in tens of thousands of scattered homesteads or *kraals* (from the Portuguese word, *corral*). More than 90 percent of the population lived in small family groups revolving around a married man, his wives, their children, and perhaps a few older relatives. Most Zulus had little wealth. Their kraals held a few cattle, sheep, and goats, and their fields grew corn, millet, sorghum, melons, pumpkins, and beans. Perhaps 10 percent of the Zulus, including members of the royal lineage headed by the king, and some of the chiefs of the clans and tribes that were amalgamated into the Zulu state fifty years earlier, were quite wealthy. Many controlled vast acreages of farmland, owned thousands of cattle, had dozens of wives, and commanded the labor and allegiance of hundreds or thousands of armed retainers. The most powerful of them, called "the great ones," formed a council of state that shared power with King Cetshwayo. Some also served as military commanders. These men could, and often did, overrule the king.

The Zulu Kingdom they governed had absorbed many different peoples. As a result, there was substantial variation in custom, dialect, and dress among the Zulus, just as there was variation in skin color and body type.[14] But contrary to British belief and Frere's propaganda, nowhere in Zululand was everyday life routinely martial. The day usually began with bathing. Most Zulus bathed at least once a day, with a passion for cleanliness that mystified the bath-shy British. In general, families were at work before daybreak. Boys took the cattle out to graze, women worked in the fields, and married men worked around the homestead or gathered together to discuss the news of the district. Older girls cared for smaller children. Specialists worked with wood, metal, and hides, and some men traveled great distances to trade. Most people worked hard, but they enjoyed life too. There were usually two meals: the first in the late morning, the second late in the afternoon. Most of the time, food was plentiful enough, and so was beer for the men. Most men, including the young men who were performing military service, began the day with beer. Made from millet and slowly fermented, Zulu beer was served hot. A gray, sour, almost bitter brew, it was drunk from large pots with great gusto. In moderation, as it was ordinarily drunk, Zulu beer was nutritious and only mildly intoxicating, but older men sometimes drank huge amounts of it and became decidedly tiddly. Men also smoked *dagga* (*cannabis sativa*) on a daily basis,[15] as the missionary Allen Gardiner noted on a visit in 1835. Although there was a heavy stress on etiquette and polite conduct, when people got together there was much laughter. The Zulus loved to gossip and tell jokes, snapping their fingers sharply for emphasis. Punning was popular, and so was making up funny nicknames. The Zulu language contained at least 19,000 words, and the Zulus loved to use them all in their play with words based on double meanings. Children's games often involved learning the names of hundreds of birds or plants. Children were also taught traditional stories and songs praising their ancestors and chiefs. It was common for a Zulu child to commit to memory stories and praise songs that took a half-hour to recite.[16] Pranks and practical jokes were common too.

There was a dark side to Zulu life as well. Cannibalism was said to be practiced in some remote areas of Zululand; witchcraft was common, and so was the use of poison against one's enemies. Many Zulus were terrified of evil spirits, which sometimes took animal or human form and were commonly believed to be abroad at night. Prominent persons used "tasters" to guard against poisoning and lived in perpetual fear of sorcery. Some sorcerers had to kidnap and sometimes kill children in order to maintain their powers. After describing a case in which a missing boy had been murdered, a Zulu man remembered another episode that illustrates why many Zulus lived in dread of sorcerers:

> The other case is of a boy who was caught on the edge of a field, chasing off birds with two others. Finding him missing, his companions shouted but he did not answer. It so happened that the company of men, etc. . . . were passing by at the time. They came to the bush in which the gardens were, and found the boy in the bush. His penis had been sucked, as also his nostrils, and his ears had been spat into. The men took him out of danger, and he was treated with medicines, and given a purgative, and his penis, which had been swollen, returned to normal size. He recovered.[17]

The ideal Zulu man was not only a brave warrior but a singer, dancer, and punster. King Shaka was all of those and, despite a slight speech impediment that made him sound as though his tongue was too big for his mouth, he was extraordinarily eloquent. So was Cetshwayo. Europeans were seldom able to appreciate Zulu puns, but almost every European who heard Zulus sing was struck by the power and beauty of the men's deep baritone voices, joined by the women's sopranos in melodic choruses. Colonel Anthony Durnford, who would play a pivotal part in the battle at Isandlwana, was in Zululand as part of Shepstone's entourage for the British "crowning" of King Cetshwayo, described a song sung by five thousand warriors: "They sang a war-song—a song without words, wonderfully impressive as the waves of sound rose, fell, and died away, then rose again in a mournful strain, yet warlike in the extreme."[18] Sometimes accompanied by various kinds of musical instruments, Zulus had songs for most occasions: work, courting, drinking, and war. Anyone might create a new song, but there were professional composers, too, and every wealthy and important man employed his personal composer or bard. It was a bard's job to update a man's "praises," verbal recitations of his great deeds. Other men, functioning as national historians, captured historical events in their elegantly composed heroic poetry.[19]

Dancing was also a focus of Zulu life. There were scores of different dances, each with its own name and movements. For example, in ordinary life, one of the favorite games for children was a dance called *umbanga.* Adults would gather to watch while children competed in a dance that called for boys and girls to jump as high as possible and, while still in the air, smack their heels against their buttocks, making a loud clapping sound. Winners received prizes.[20] Dances were frequent, and on more important ceremonial occasions thousands of people would participate, often in elaborate and beautiful dress. Women, their bodies oiled until they glistened, beads and copper arm coils outlining jutting breasts and buttocks, joined men who wore ostrich plumes, feathers, furs, and hides of all sorts in dances that were wondrously athletic and erotic. Sometimes the dancers improvised their movements to synchronize with a song sung by an important man, even King Cetshwayo, who sometimes sang brilliantly at such ceremonies.

When the missionary Allen Gardiner visited Zululand in 1835 to preach the Gospel, he described many dances, including one in which young Zulus danced and sang most of the night: "The lips of many of the bystanders, among whom were several old warriors, were observed to move as they instinctively followed the words of the song, and occasionally forgetting their dignity—for they never mingle with the lads—they would go through the accompaniments with their arms and feet."[21] Gardiner described another dance in which young men danced athletically around young women, who responded by

> . . . bending their bodies forwards to the clap of their hands, stamping with both feet together, and raising their voices to the highest pitch, they fill in their parts, and follow out the chorus with such a degree of continued exertion, as would cause an European female to go upon crutches for the remainder of her life.[22]

Nineteenth-century Europeans were astonished by the athletic agility of Zulu dancers, including women and corpulent older men, just as they were taken by the beauty and sensuality of the dance movements. Often simply watching the women dance drove male European visitors mad with lust. Zulu men themselves were not unaffected either. Anyone who has seen modern Zulus sing and dance, whether in South Africa or on a stage overseas, should have little difficulty understanding something of the effect those dances must have had on the men and women who participated in them (or watched) at the time of the Anglo-Zulu War.

Song and dance provided an exciting climax to a pleasant, if usually routine, round of everyday life. It was a way of life that many Britons did not find alien. Several settled among the Zulus; the trader John Dunn did so with such enthusiasm that he acknowledged 47 wives and 117 children in his will (there were others he did not acknowledge). Dunn became such a favorite with Cetshwayo, mostly by trading guns for cattle, that the king made Dunn the chief of a district near the coast that contained about 10,000 people. The men of that district were Dunn's personal retainers and army, and not subject to military service in the king's regiments. In 1879 some of those men fought with Dunn and the British against Cetshwayo's armies.

While it is true that the Zulu state was not an armed camp, the Zulus *were* an armed people, as their defender, John Colenso, the Bishop of Natal, affirmed. Their kingdom had been built by war, and even though war had been a rare occurrence for a number of years, Zulu martial spirit was very much alive in 1879.

When young men reached their late teens, most of them reported to one of the fifteen or twenty military kraals (*amakhanda*, sing.: *ikhanda*) scattered throughout Zululand to begin their military service. About fifty youngsters from the same district formed an *iviyo* (pl.: *amaviyo,* usually rendered in English as "company") under the direction if not quite command of an older officer, who, like a chief, was called induna. Frequently, girls of the same age were gathered in a nearby kraal as a kind of guild. Both the young men and the young women in those kraals were indoctrinated with the values of Zulu culture. Among other admonitions, they were told to honor their fathers, the great men of their district, and the king, as well as to work hard and avoid quarreling. One man recalled: "There are so many 'don'ts' that I can hardly remember all of them, especially as not many of them were observed generally."[23] There is no doubt that although obedience was stressed and young Zulus usually obeyed their elders, life in a Zulu military kraal was a far cry from the disciplined world of a British regiment. Young men and women were required to work for the great men of their district, but there was plenty of time for courting, and much of their time was spent acquiring love magic and pursuing romance. In fact, the main topic of conversation in a military kraal was romance, not war.[24]

Every few years, the young men in amaviyo throughout Zululand would be summoned to the king's kraal to be inducted into an *ibutho* (pl.: *amabutho*), or regiment, as the British thought of it. For example, in 1873 Cetshwayo called all the companies of young men who were born between 1850 and 1853 to his military kraal to form them into a regiment known as the *Ngobamakosi*. Perhaps as many as six thousand young men aged 20–23 put on distinctive attire, marked by a single red feather in their leopard-skin headbands, and were provided with shields that were either all black or black with single red or white spots. Their name, which meant "bender of kings," referred to their power to destroy foreign kings, not Cetshwayo. Sometimes, smaller groups of young men were incorporated into established regiments that needed to replace losses. For example, some of the young men from the draft of 1873 were incorporated into the *Thulwana* regiment, which was composed of men forty-five years of age or older. That was the regiment Cetshwayo himself had served in, and he wanted to keep it strong. The policy of adding young single men to an older regiment of married men was dangerous. Five years later, the tensions between the young men and the married men of this regiment would erupt into bloodshed when the young women's guild that had grown up with the young men and had served as their lovers was declared ready for marriage to the already married men of the Thulwana. The young women protested, and the young men fought the older ones.

Some young men were not incorporated into a company or regiment at all. The great men who controlled districts wanted troops of their own to provide labor and ensure their protection. Probably no less than 10–15 percent of the military-age Zulu youth stayed in their home districts, where they gave their primary allegiance and their labor to the district's headman, not to the king. Other young warriors belonged to semi-independent localities or tribes, such as the Cube people of the Nkandla forest, who chose not to fight for Cetshwayo against the British, or the Qulusi, whose four-thousand-man army did fight for the king, but only in their own district. In some regions of Zululand, especially near the coast, more young men belonged to local "territorial" units than to the king's "royal" regiments. Although the British believed that all the manpower of Zululand served in royal regiments under the supreme command of King Cetshwayo, in reality probably no more than half of the men of military age in Zululand served in a royal regiment during the war against the British. Others had territorial or tribal loyalties; some ignored Cetshwayo's orders, others were openly hostile to the king, and increasing numbers of young men avoided military service by claiming to be diviners or religious specialists who were exempt from army duty.[25] There were at least 50,000 and perhaps as many as 70,000 men between the ages of seventeen and fifty in Zululand in 1879, but the largest army Cetshwayo was ever able to put into the field was approximately 25,000 men.

By the time Zulu boys reached the age of seventeen or eighteen, most were already physically tough and imbued with the spirit of warriors. As very young children, they learned to throw wooden spears until they could hit a rat or a rolling melon at some distance. They also learned to enjoy stick-fighting, first with light sticks, then with heavier hardwood staves 2 or 3 feet long. Often they fought in teams of ten or more, but sometimes it was one boy against another in response to a direct challenge. The tactics and skills they used were the same as those needed for spear-fighting, and so was the bravery. The fights could be painful, but no one was allowed to flinch, much less to back down. British officers who had endured the bullying and "manly" games at their public schools would have understood. In addition to their athletic dances, young men swam and ran long distances. To run 50 miles in a day was a common feat. When they moved to military kraals, some ran even farther, learning the trails that ran through the plains, mountains, and forests of their homeland. They were also taught to endure hunger, cold, and fatigue; most of all, they were taught discipline. Absolute obedience to their officers was demanded, and sometimes it was given but, again contrary to British belief, sometimes it was not. In Shaka's time, Zulu soldiers were compelled to follow orders. They were capable of remaining absolutely silent under cover while their officers waited for the right moment to order an attack. In 1879 Zulu discipline often broke down in battles against the British.

Most of the fighting against the British was done by royal regiments, that is, regiments that were raised, named, uniformed, and armed by the king. In Shaka's era, each royal regiment had a highly distinctive uniform, and every man in a regiment apparently dressed in exactly the same way. By 1879 there was less uniformity, but members of unmarried regiments still carried black shields, which they would exchange for shields that included more and more white as their regiment grew older (white was the color of purity; black represented defilement).[26] Although regimental uniforms were no longer exactly alike in 1879, they were still beautifully made and visually dramatic. Men wore various kinds of feathers and ostrich plumes in headbands of otter or leopard skin, and some regiments wore earflaps of green monkey skin; their arms and legs were encircled with coils of copper, and there were flamboyant white oxtails around their knees, wrists, and biceps; they wore covers over their loins and buttocks made of many kinds of skin and fur, and their necks and chests were covered with tassels, necklaces, and sometimes flowing capes. Officers were distinguished by leopard-skin kilts or capes and by certain kinds of "royal" blue feathers. When a regiment went to war, it left most of its ceremonial regalia behind, wearing just enough—a feather or plume, for example—to identify it in the swirl of battle, but when the men assembled for ceremonies in their full regalia they were awe-inspiring. Thousands of men—dancing, leaping, and stamping their right feet three times in unison—advanced and maneuvered in military formations. Sometimes they rattled their spear handles against their shields, making a sound like machine-gun fire; sometimes they hissed, sounding like angry bees. They were something to see and to hear, and as they advanced behind their 5-foot-tall shields, razor sharp spears with 18-inch blades in their hands, they were formidable and fearsome.

Like the British whom they were soon to fight, Zulu warriors owed allegiance to their regiments. When the men of a Zulu regiment were gathered together, they ate, drank, and played together, practiced their regimental war cry, perfected their uniforms, and made up new war songs. When all the regiments gathered together for great ceremonies or to prepare for a military campaign, they challenged one another to singing contests, somewhat like the ancient Anglo-Saxon mead-drinking toasts or rival fans at a modern football game or soccer match. Most of the cries and songs were allegorical and metaphorical, referring to past wars. They do not translate at all well into English. For example, men of the *umCityo* regiment (formed in 1867) roared the following: "It is not to be seen; the hornbill is not to be seen. Do you burn the whiskers of the buffalo? Do you burn them? We smash the rocks of the sky!" Men of the younger Ngobamakosi regiment would answer with this: "Iya! Iya! Iya! Oh ho, ho, ho, the lightning of the sky. This sky is dangerous!"[27] Such words meant enough to the Zulus for men to become fighting mad over them, and the king and his counselors often had to restrain them from fighting. Regiments also competed with one another for the king's favor in the skill and precision of their martial dancing; a winning regiment was boastfully triumphant, while the losers were resentful. Regiments competed for girls as well, with predictably bad feelings among the losers. Brawls often broke out, especially between older and younger regiments, and men fought with their hardwood sticks. When the men occasionally went for their spears, there were killings. In one such fight in 1878, sixty or seventy men were killed. John Dunn, who was a witness to the fight, reported that King Cetshwayo was powerless to stop the bloodletting.

Several regiments were such implacable enemies that they could not be allowed to camp near one another or even to take up adjoining positions in a battle. The British would have understood this too. Some of their regiments were also hostile to one another. But the Zulus took their rivalries even further than the British did. After a fight between regiments in 1878, more than three hundred men of a newly formed regiment (*Dluyenge*) crossed over to Natal. When war came, they fought for the British. Hard feelings among the Zulus could be *very* hard. As serious as the competition between Zulu regiments was, rivalries between companies of the same regiment could be even more bitter. A company (iviyo) was composed of about fifty men who had grown up together and were often related. They were usually close friends for life, but they were seldom very close to men from other companies, and a company from the western mountains of Zululand might have nothing but contempt for a company from the coastal area, even though both companies served in the same regiment. Like Texans and New Yorkers in the U.S. army, they were given to insulting one another and often had to be restrained from taking up their spears.[28]

The king usually tried to prevent lethal combat between his regiments, but on the eve of battle he encouraged them to *giya,* that is, to compete with one another by dancing and shouting boasts and insults back and forth until there could be no question that they were ready for war. A warrior named Mpatshana recalled how his regiment was paired off with another at the king's kraal as the Zulus were preparing to meet the British at Isandlwana. A man from Mpatshana's regiment leaped up and challenged a man from a rival regiment by saying that if he did not kill a white man before the other man did, his rival could have his kraal and his sister, too. The other man had to respond in kind, while the men of both regiments watched and remembered. A man who refused to accept the challenge was called a coward. Those who accepted had to prove their valor when the fighting started.[29]

Sometimes a man's boasts so infuriated the men of other companies that they tried to take vengeance. For example, before the battle at Isandlwana, a man of the newly formed Ngobamakosi had boasted that he would be the first in the regiment to kill one of the enemy. True to his boast, when the Ngobamakosi charged the British lines, this man—named Ntobolongwana—sprinted ahead of the other warriors, but instead of killing a "red soldier" he was knocked down by a rifle bullet that shattered his jaw. Men from the rival company of the Ngobamakosi, whom he had challenged and insulted, were on the verge of spearing him to death when he was rescued by his relatives.[30] Rivalry could drive Zulus to great feats of courage, but it could also be divisive, and in the war against the British it would several times lose battles.

The Zulu army was not the perfectly disciplined "war machine" that the British had conjured up (and that recent writers continue to imagine),[31] but Zulu warriors were trained to fight and they were very good at it. They were big men, some as tall as 6′5″, and very few were shorter than 5′8″. They were too large to wear British uniforms, as Colonel Evelyn Wood discovered when he tried to outfit some of the disaffected young Zulus who had volunteered to fight for the British. Although several British officers noted that the Zulus did not have large biceps (the same observation was made by the U.S. soldiers who fought the Plains Indians, such as those who defeated General Custer) and that British soldiers appeared to be more muscular, all agreed that most Zulus were large and powerful men, even if they tended to become paunchy. Older men frequently became decidedly stout, but they were remarkably nimble. Like younger men, many of them could jog all day or, as was also common, all night, and still fight at the end.

The English trader Henry Francis Fynn, who lived among them during King Shaka's reign, was an enormously brave, or foolish, man himself, who sometimes faced down Shaka. He wrote that the Zulus were "daring" in battle but not "brave." He believed that if their initial charge—the charge that had devastated their African enemies—were repulsed, they would falter. Fynn had seen the Zulus repulsed in battle, and so had another trader, Nathaniel Isaacs, who fought alongside the Zulus in the years just after Shaka's death.[32] Contrary to many recent accounts, the Zulus of Shaka's time were not invincible; they did sometimes lose battles and run away.

Still, the Zulus had not won their empire without displaying great bravery. Shaka had seen to that by rewarding his bravest warriors and killing the cowards, but we should keep in mind that there *were* cowards for Shaka to punish. A common term for a coward was *isiboto* (weak-footed person) referring to men who lagged behind. Not all Zulus were somehow born mindlessly brave, as the British imagined. The men of Zulu regiments had been taught all their lives to attack and, if necessary, to attack again. To fight a defensive battle was thought to be cowardly. When the British invaded, the royal regiments were ordered to attack. Small groups of Zulus who fought in their own districts might resist by guerrilla tactics, and even the royal army might lie in ambush before it attacked, but the king's army, called an *impi,* was trained for one thing: to attack. With extremely rare exceptions, the Zulu army used only one tactic in their attacks: the "charging buffalo" formation. Developed by Dingiswayo and refined by Shaka, it was a version of a classical "pincer" attack, like those used so often by European armies in World War II. It was also used by the Zulus in hunting and may have derived from that source. In the charging buffalo formation, a large body of men made a frontal attack while two large flanking columns attempted to envelop the enemy. Another large number of men remained in reserve awaiting orders to exploit a weakness in the enemy's defenses. Predictably, the Zulus conceived of this formation in cattle terms. The central force was the "chest," the flanking columns were the left and right "horns," while the reserves were the "loins." In Shaka's times the men of the loins sat with their backs to the battle so they would not become excited and charge before they were ordered to do so. Using their enveloping tactic, the Zulus first jogged, then sprinted forward to close with their enemies, stabbing with their heavy spears, usually called *assegais,*[33] and sometimes, but not always, throwing the lighter spears they also carried. They also smashed heads with wooden clubs. The Zulus did not use bows and arrows in warfare, and although Zulu specialists knew many deadly poisons, they did not poison their spears. There were a dozen or so kinds of spears, but the main weapon was a short, heavy-stabbing spear usually known as the *iklwa* for the sucking sound it was supposed to make as it was pulled out of an enemy's body. There were also many kinds of hardwood clubs, some of which were designed for throwing. Many men could hit birds in flight with these weapons, but the clubs were seldom thrown in warfare.

Zulu tactics were designed for the rapid charge and the spear thrust, but Zulus had been acquiring guns since the 1820s, and beginning in the 1860s they imported them by the thousands. In the late 1870s, 20,000 guns each year passed through Portuguese Mozambique, the majority of them headed for Zululand. Most of them were poorly made, obsolete muzzle-loaders, but in later years some Zulus had purchased modern breech-loading rifles.[34] By 1879 most Zulu warriors had rifles. However, the Zulus did not change their tactics to make effective use of rifle fire. They slowed their charge at a great distance from their enemies, fired once or twice, then usually left their rifles behind when they charged. With the exception of a few men who regularly used their rifles for hunting, most Zulus were terrible marksmen. They almost invariably fired much too high, because they set their sights as high as possible to give their bullets "strength." As we shall see, if they had been even moderately accurate marksmen, they might well have won the war.

Zulu tactics were designed to destroy the enemy quickly. A Zulu army, especially a very large Zulu army, could not stay in the field for more than a few days. Shaka had insisted that his armies travel with only small supplies of food. That way, they had to conquer their enemies or starve. Even in 1879, if a Zulu army could not defeat its enemy in a day or so, hunger would usually compel it to withdraw. When a Zulu army was on campaign, its scouts went well ahead, sometimes on horseback. The army was accompanied by boys (*udibi*) who carried a little food as well as the warriors' sleeping mats. Chiefs might be accompanied by girls who carried food and beer for them (rank had its privileges). Sometimes a few cattle were driven along with the troops, but Zulu troops often covered 40 or 50 miles in a day, and cattle could not keep up. If there were a kraal nearby when the army camped, its men would eat; if not, they went hungry. A Zulu army was expected to win a quick victory, then feed itself on the enemy's cattle. Since the primary purpose of Zulu war was to capture cattle, their raiding tactics made a virtue of a necessity. But there was another reason why battles had to be ended quickly. While a Zulu force was in the field, the warriors' own cattle, as well as their wives and children, were vulnerable to enemy raiders.[35] Their wives were also vulnerable to the attentions of Zulu men who remained in the area. Zulu warriors were anxious to return home.

Because battles had to be ended quickly, there was no tolerance for cautious warriors. For a man to lose his shield or his spear was disgraceful, and to return from battle with a wound in the back was worse. In Shaka's time, either could have meant a death sentence. Men who were identified as cowards were lined up before Shaka with their left arms raised; an executioner slowly pressed his sharp spear point into the man's armpit. If the man flinched, the spear was driven into his heart, but if he bore the pain bravely, he might be spared.[36] In more recent times, the result of cowardice was humiliation and disgrace rather than death. After a battle, Zulu regimental officers (the indunas) decided which of their men deserved honors. Zulus of the time said that most indunas were niggardly in the extreme, being reluctant to create new heroes whom the king might prefer to themselves. Nevertheless, they did put some men forward for special recognition. In addition to awards of cattle for exceptionally brave men and their families, the king might choose to award a very special spear, a beautifully carved necklace of beads made of wild olive wood, or brass armlets or collars. For heroes who had killed enemies, distinctive necklaces of willow sticks representing the numbers of "kills" a man had were awarded.[37] Cowards might no longer be killed, as they were in Shaka's day, but they were identified, and women still took it upon themselves to shame a man who was not brave. They did it with characteristic drama, sometimes stripping themselves nude in public to mortify a man who had behaved badly. And when a man who had shown cowardice in battle was being served roasted meat in public, he would be terribly humiliated by having his meat dipped in cold water just before it was handed to him.

As brave and determined as the Zulus were in war, they were paradoxical too. They killed their enemies with relish and did not shrink when asked to strangle a woman "until her eyes popped out." When ordered to do so, they could "send home" the infirm elderly or the very sick by burying them alive or, as was also considered merciful, by spearing them under their upraised left arms.[38] They sometimes killed cattle—their great love in life—so cruelly that the British were appalled.[39] For example, to make a magically protective shield, it was necessary for the ox to be skinned while it was still alive. A cow's death had to be prolonged so that its bellowing could communicate human good wishes to the ancestors.[40] Yet Zulus were also kind to some animals, such as field mice, which chewed on people's toes while they slept, saying that they were simply poor little animals trying to find food.[41] They were also kind to their dogs. Older regiments wearing the shiny black headring (*isicoco*) that symbolized their married status sometimes fought more recklessly than young unmarried men did. Yet they also had tender feelings, compassion, and empathy for others. And warriors who killed in battle without a second thought recoiled in horror when they encountered death that was not of their own making. The great Shaka embodied this paradox. He could order women and children to their deaths without concern, yet he could also be extraordinarily compassionate to people who had been kind to him as a boy.

A short sketch like the foregoing runs the risk of giving a reader the impression that Zulus were rather simple folk whose interests in life did not go much beyond war, cattle, sex, dancing, music, and a good laugh. All of these were important, but individual Zulus were much more complex people than that brief list of interests suggests. For example, many modern writers, including anthropologists, have indulged themselves in fanciful interpretations about King Shaka's personality, declaring him to be, among other things, a latent homosexual and a psychotic.[42] While it is true that Shaka was an autocrat who used ghastly terror to maintain his hold on Zulu obedience, he was more than just a monster, and he was almost certainly *not* homosexual.[43] He had a keen sense of humor, was enormously eloquent, and could express great love not only for his mother and grandmother but for otherwise powerless people, such as the physically handicapped. And while it was true that Shaka's needs were attended to by a large retinue that, among other things, bathed him, carried his urine pot away, and wiped his regal anus, sometimes members of his court defied him with impunity. Shaka once joked about an occasion when his harem girls were so angry with him that they refused to light his fire as they were supposed to do. Shaka started the fire himself and laughed about it.[44] Some of Shaka's great chiefs treated him virtually as an equal, and even some low-ranking Zulus remembered him fondly, recalling such homely things as the fact that Shaka's nose was unusually wide and always sweated copiously.[45] Zulu warriors who seemed obsessed only with war, cattle, or women were also naturalists, poets, fathers, gamblers, and generous friends. They were warriors to be sure, but like Shaka most of them were also complex and contradictory people.

If women appear at all in the many accounts of the Anglo-Zulu War, they do so fleetingly. Zulu society was male-dominated, and women rarely took an active part in war. Women were nevertheless economically powerful and politically influential. Women were far more than men's sexual partners, wives, or mothers.[46] They directed household life with an iron hand, even including cattle management when necessary (women put on men's clothing to herd cattle). Women were enormously articulate, and few men willingly crossed them. They played crucial roles in their society's religious and ceremonial life, and many women, particularly favored wives, had tremendous influence over their husbands' political behavior. Women of high rank sometimes exercised great power. For example, Princess Mkhabayi had great influence over Shaka and later became so powerful that her nephews Dingane and Mpande, both Zulu kings, were terrified of her. It is said that she lived to be one hundred and cut her own throat after the British burned the royal kraal at Ulundi.[47]

Many women were feared because they were thought to be able to smell out evildoers; no people had greater power in Zulu society than such women, who parlayed their talents into a profitable system of extortion. If they were not paid off, they would denounce someone, especially someone wealthy. Even young women had influence, using their beauty to taunt men to fight for the right to possess them, or to shame men whom they deemed cowards. Young women could prevent a regiment from going to war by stripping naked and standing before it.[48] Although their influence was usually felt behind the scenes of battle rather than in actual combat, Zulu women, like their British counterparts, played a part in this war.

British officers, like Colonel Arthur Harness, who was in command of British artillery at Isandlwana, often wrote that the Zulus who attacked them had "no fear of death."[49] Although bravery in war was praised and rewarded, and although Zulus sacrificed their lives in battle, Zulus emphatically *did* fear death in ordinary life and in war. Unlike many

Christians and Muslims, they had no belief that death in war would lead to Heaven or Paradise; in fact, their ideas about life after death were decidedly vague. Life was thought to continue, but people were not sure just how or where life would go on. Their ancestors were venerated and sometimes feared, but while some people thought they lived in the sky, others insisted that if they were anywhere at all it was in the center of the earth. Zulus had a concept similar to our notion of ''soul'' (*isithunzi*), but before Christian influence, only great men or kings were buried. Everyone else was simply thrown into the bush and abandoned.[50] Death promised no rewards, only the need for survivors to protect themselves against the dangerous pollution it brought to all who were close to the deceased.[51]

The first thing a child received in life was an amulet to protect it against danger. The growing child would be told to avoid certain foods and places, while following other rules and taking various medicines that strengthened it against possible harm. Zulu doctors employed a large number of more or less effective herbal medications, some of which were used successfully by early European travelers. But Zulu medicine was less than perfect, and the Zulus eagerly sought Western remedies. Shaka continually badgered Fynn and Isaacs for better medicines, especially a potion to prevent his hair from graying (he was given hair dye). Once when Isaacs, who was Jewish, was called upon to treat a man with a very sore throat, he prescribed chicken soup. The man died. Much of Zulu medicine was focused on the rectum. For example, when a child was only three months old, a specialist used the stalk of a shrub to induce plentiful bleeding from the infant's rectum.[52] The treatment was intended to promote health and prevent lechery. In addition, enemas were a favored restorative. The patient knelt in a shallow stream and used a cow's horn with an opening in the tip to induce medicine into the rectum. When British troops first saw a dozen or so naked Zulus in a stream poking horns into their upraised rectums, they were, to say the least, amused.[53]

As life went on, men and women continued to do various things, and avoid doing others, in an unending effort to protect themselves against evil spirits, malign ancestors, or the hostility of sorcerers and witches. Witches were so feared that they were not subject to trial within the Zulu legal system. Unless they could flee to a sacred place where they could achieve temporary refuge, a person accused of being a witch was simply killed, usually by having a thick stake driven up the anus.[54] Zulus believed that life was dangerous, and they took every possible precaution against its dangers. The services of specialists against danger were in constant demand. Sometimes danger became so acute that the army was assembled and, while ritual specialists gave the king protective medicine, which he spat into a fire of specially prepared wormwood, chanted something that sounded like "ooh, ooh, ooh" in order to drive away all evil spirits, pestilence, and disease.

The army in particular was in need of regular protection and strengthening. It was fed specially prepared foods and provided with powerful medicines while it carried out all manner of rituals that involved everything from feasting to fasting. Zulu warriors might appear to have thought of themselves as invincible, as most Europeans observers wrote, but in fact they were taking no unnecessary chances. No matter how urgent the king's orders to mobilize might be, no man would report for military duty before he had visited his homestead to pray to his ancestors for protection. Warriors also took with them various charms to protect them against enemy action and others to render their enemies foolish or feeble. They observed numerous food taboos. Ritual specialists carried out complex magical procedures to weaken the enemy still further, and, finally, the Zulu army had to be ritually "strengthened" (the British called it "doctoring"). A special bull was magically prepared, then after it was wrestled to the ground and killed by men of the king's favorite regiment, was slaughtered and fed to the army in tiny strips. Later the men marched by a pit 6 or 7 feet deep surrounded by materials of great religious significance. After taking an emetic substance that was handed out like wafers at communion, each warrior vomited into the pit. Some of the vomit was collected and bound up in a python-skin coil shaped like a rubber tire. This coil, known as the "national coil" (*nkatha yesiwe*) was the Zulus' most powerful supernatural possession. It symbolized strength and unity. Every year at the national first fruits ceremony the coil was opened, and fresh vomit was added. During the war the British burned the kraal where the coil was kept. If they noticed the coil, there is no record of what they thought. Sometimes doctors cut small incisions into the flesh of the soldiers, rubbing protective medicine into them as a kind of inoculation against death. The most potent protection was human flesh, which was cooked and served to the troops before battle. Zulu warriors did not believe in spending the night before battle in the arms of their wives or lovers. After more prayers to their ancestors, the troops took final precautions by avoiding the weakening influence of women.

Before the men set off to war, they were cleansed again in a mass ritual conducted with great ceremony and flourish by a ritual specialist. If circumstances permitted, just before they went into combat they were ceremonially protected by yet another solemn ritual involving fire and liquid. The same specialists who purified and protected the troops just before battle did so again if they were wounded; in addition to practical medical treatment they employed all manner of ritual procedures, including more emetics. Emetics would not be exactly the treatment of choice for wounded men, one would think, but some Zulus survived horrendous wounds nevertheless. A warrior who killed an enemy was polluted too, and he was required to slit open his victim's abdomen to release his spirit; if he failed to do so, he ran the risk of going insane. That is why the British dead at Isandlwana had been disemboweled. He also had to wear some item of his victim's clothing. Even if the dead man wore nothing more than a small penis cover, his slayer removed that and wore it. Many British uniforms would be worn in Zululand. Before returning to ordinary life among other Zulus, he also had to wear a sprig of wild asparagus in his hair and have sexual intercourse (between the legs was acceptable) with a woman who was a stranger to him or, if necessary, a boy. It was called "wiping the hoe" and it was done because it was thought better to pollute strangers than relatives. Through the entire process of preparing an army for battle and returning warriors from it, women went through an elaborate set of ritual practices intended to ensure the safety of their husbands, sons, or lovers. They marked their faces in black, wore some of their clothing backward, beat large stones together, and, most difficult by far, avoided all quarreling.[55]

Those practices were not just ideals that were seldom actually carried out. When King Cetshwayo mobilized his regiments after the British invasion, the protective rituals were carried out by ritual specialists—"war doctors" would be a loose translation—from the royal lineage. The preparations lasted three full days. First, every man in each of the mobilized regiments—more than 20,000 men in all—marched up to the vomiting pit (it conformed to tradition by being only 18 inches in diameter but 6 or 7 feet deep). Three or four at a time, the men approached the pit, took the emetic substance from the war doctors there, and vomited. They then marched off to wait and fast until everyone finished. The procedure took an entire day, and while it was intended to purify the men and unite them spiritually and emotionally, it must have been an astonishing spectacle to see and hear—20,000 men lining up to vomit.

Next, a few men from selected regiments were honored by being assigned the task of killing the bull. This one, as described by Mpatshana, who was there with his regiment, was a huge black beast and very fierce. Most accounts of Zulu ritual say that Zulu warriors threw themselves at such a bull, killing it with their bare hands. In this instance, fanatic heroism had to wait. Not until the bull had been run in circles in a large kraal for three hours did the warriors risk trying to seize it, but when it was finally exhausted dozens of men wrestled it down and killed it by twisting its horns until its neck snapped. Strips of meat from the bull were cooked, treated with magical preparations, and tossed to the regiments as they stood in military formation. Men took a bite then tossed the strip in the air for someone else to catch, and so it continued for hours. Later, each man was "strengthened" with a kind of soup made from, among other things, human flesh, especially the penis, rectum, right forearm and cartilage from the breastbone. Each part of the body had magical significance involving strength, throwing ability, impurity, and so on. This time, the flesh is said to have come from a white man named E. O. Neal.[56] After the men were strengthened still further by standing in the smoke from ritually prepared fires (those with guns held the barrels over the smoke to improve their aim), they were sprinkled with more magical substances to assure their power and safety. Only after three grueling days of these and many other preparations were the Zulu armies ready to march to battle.

After their crushing defeat of the British at Isandlwana, Zulu survivors dutifully slit open the belly of the dead men and then stripped off and donned their clothing. The returning warriors underwent many days of cleansing before they were free enough of their contagious pollution to be permitted to present themselves to King Cetshwayo at the royal kraal. Only then were they allowed to recount their deeds and receive honors from the king. Not all of these and many other ritual practices were observed before and after every battle against the British. Sometimes there was simply no time. But the serious attention that Zulus gave to magical and religious protection against injury or death could hardly have been exceeded by *inept* warriors. The Zulus were among the best warriors Africa had ever seen, but they did not rely solely on their skill or courage. Far from being fearless, as the British thought in 1879, the Zulus feared death enough to take every precaution against it.

Another of the British misconceptions about the Zulus was their insistence that King Cetshwayo was a despot who was capable of the kind of enormous bloodletting in which King Shaka had indulged.[57] That view of Cetshwayo was created in part by sundry American, British, Norwegian, and German missionaries in Zululand, who exaggerated every act of Zulu violence into wholesale massacre. It is worth noting that no missionary in Zululand was ever harmed, not even *during* the Anglo-Zulu War, and that several were strong advocates for the Zulus. The perception of Cetshwayo as violent and tyrannical was also insisted upon by Sir Theophilus Shepstone, who had once been Cetshwayo's advocate. Ever since Cetshwayo rejected Shepstone's self-proclaimed stewardship over Zululand, Shepstone had been decidedly peevish about the Zulu king, whom he increasingly described as a tyrannical killer who oppressed the Zulu people. Shepstone's new opinion was a true about-face, since he had written in 1873 that Cetshwayo was "in every respect far above any native chief I have ever had to do with. I do not think that his disposition is very warlike."[58] Shepstone's change of heart had to do with Sir Bartle Frere's plans for a war against the Zulu, which were well-served by outcries that Cetshwayo was a monster. Frere himself was quick to tell everyone who would listen that Cetshwayo was "an ignorant bloodthirsty despot."

Cetshwayo was undeniably ignorant from the British point of view. He did not understand worldly affairs outside Zululand. For one thing, he was unable to understand why the British, whom he had never attacked, felt privileged to dictate to him about the laws of his own kingdom. As for being bloodthirsty, he sometimes carried out capital punishment as called for by Zulu law, but almost all capital sentences were made by the chiefs of districts, not by the king. Clearly, Cetshwayo imposed no reign of terror on his subjects, as Shaka had done. He was simply not a despot. He could not even make a major decision without the approval of the wealthy and powerful men who made up his council of state. Even Shaka had sometimes been constrained by his counselors, and the young King Cetshwayo was very much limited in his freedom of action by those tremendously influential older men. What is more, as we noted earlier, some portions of the Zulu empire were inclined to ignore the king's orders even when his counselors supported him.[59]

When the execution of the two adulterous wives of Chief Sihayo gave Frere a pretext for war, the counselors joined Cetshwayo to ponder Frere's ultimatum. Stripped of its more opaque language, Frere's four thousand-word ultimatum (which was read to the Zulus by Shepstone in his fluent but heavily accented Zulu) called for the Zulus to pay large fines in cattle and to turn over Sihayo's brother and three sons for trial by the British. Some counselors who resented Sihayo's extensive trade relations with Natal were willing to hand the young men over, but others were not. But the crux of the ultimatum came next. The Zulus were given only thirty days to disband the army, allowing its men to return to their homes, and abolish the Zulu military system (the British would defend Zululand in the future), and every Zulu was to be free to marry on reaching maturity.

Cetshwayo and his Great Council met to consider their options. Baffled, they agreed to pay the fines and tried to stall for time. The other demands were obviously impossible to meet. The army could not be disbanded, because it was not mobilized (even after Frere's ultimatum, the army was not assembled). The Zulu king and his counselors could hardly end the Zulu military system and allow everyone to marry without changing virtually every aspect of Zulu society. To do so would not only be self-emasculation, it would be self-destruction. For one thing, there weren't enough cattle to allow everyone to marry; to acquire more cattle, the army would have to go to war. Moreover, when a regiment was summoned for duty, it was primarily engaged in important economic production and police work. The Zulus began to see Frere's demands for what they were: an excuse to invade Zululand. Rumors spread that the British would force Zulu men to become laborers in Natal and would take Zulu women for their pleasure. Still, Cetshwayo and his counselors chose restraint, sending messengers to Frere asking for more time. As King Cetshwayo said later, he felt like a man trying to "ward off a falling tree."[60]

Frere had no intention of negotiating. Frere's ultimatum did not expire until January 11, but patrols under the command of Colonel (later Field-Marshal Sir) Evelyn Wood rode through Zululand as early as January 8, and Wood's entire column invaded on January 10. Before dawn on Saturday, January 11, 1879, Chelmsford's central column waded across the cold Buffalo River into the Zulu Kingdom. Only then was the Zulu army mobilized. Eight days later, when the Zulu army was ordered to confront the invading British columns, at least 10 percent of the Zulu soldiers had not yet reported for duty, but those who did report assembled at the king's kraal. Young bachelors joined married men in their forties and fifties. The Zulu army was ready to fight for king and country, for glory and booty, to protect their property, and because, at bottom, they were being attacked.

# Chapter 3

# The "Red Soldiers"

The Zulus called them the ''red soldiers'' because of their red tunics; the British soldiers sometimes called themselves ''red backs,'' because they were often flogged until their backs were bloody. Their European opponents in earlier wars were often impressed by the bravery of the British infantrymen, although rarely by the intelligence of their officers. It became a common joke to refer to British soldiers as ''lions led by donkeys.'' It was a joke enjoyed more by British soldiers and civilians than by British officers. Nevertheless, the British army that invaded Zululand was the best of its kind in the world. The massive German, French, and Russian armies were organized to fight in Europe against one another, and each army had close to a million soldiers. Even the Italian army, which the British thought of as faintly ridiculous, had more than 600,000 men. At the time of the Zulu War, the British army numbered only 186,000 officers and men. The British had begun to worry about the need to develop an army that could wage war on the Continent if need be, but their army was still small, and it was experienced in fighting small colonial wars throughout their vast empire. British volleys of rifle fire, their cannon, their cavalry, and, perhaps as much as anything else, their discipline had defeated rebellious ''sepoys'' in India, Sikhs in the Punjab, Afghans, Maoris, Chinese, Burmese, Canadian rebels, and sundry tribes of Africans.

Hollywood's image of the nineteenth-century British colonial army included tall, aristocratic officers who displayed reckless courage and ramrod-straight sergeants who screamed orders at the illiterate, tough men in the ranks, who stood firm against their savage enemies. Unlike most of Hollywood's images, this one was very largely accurate. The British officers who fought the Zulus were from the ruling class, and many were from the very best families, including the nobility. The men in the ranks were still recruited from the very lowest classes in Britain. But there were changes, too. By the time of the Zulu War, many young recruits were entering the ranks, replacing the tough veteran soldiers of years past. Earlier in the century, when British infantry marched past the Duke of Wellington before the battle of Waterloo, he was quoted as saying, "I hope that the French are as frightened of these men as I am because by God they terrify me." Many men just as tough were still in the British Army, but Wellington would not have been terrified by the beardless boys who filled the ranks of many regiments in 1879, including several that fought against the Zulus.

In 1879 the British public still looked on private soldiers as social outcasts, but their contempt for soldiers had moderated somewhat over the years. Although a single woman who was seen with a private soldier would still be likely to lose her reputation, signs warning soldiers to stay off the sidewalks were disappearing in English towns. Still, for a son to "go for a soldier" or to "take the Queen's shilling," as joining the army was called, could ruin a family that had any pretensions of social respectability.[1] When William Robertson (who later became a field marshal and Chief of the British Imperial General Staff during World War I) enlisted in the ranks in 1877, his mother said that she would rather bury him than see him in a red coat.[2] Although the term of enlistment in 1879 had been reduced to six years, followed by six more years of reserve duty instead of the eleven years plus ten more that soldiers used to serve before the army reform of 1870, the army was still chosen mostly by young men who were hungry, cold, drunk, or running from the law. The great majority of recruits were common laborers, and many were both unemployed and unemployable. Once in a very great while, a gentleman would enlist as a private soldier, usually to escape a gambling debt, the police, or a woman.

Photographs taken in Natal in 1879 show pleasant-looking young men in the ranks. A few who had bushy black beards looked more like the men who were pictured in American Civil War photos than men of today, and most of the men of the 1st Battalion of the 24th Regiment—the men who died at Isandlwana—had beards. But in more recently recruited units such as the 2d Battalion of the 24th and the 90th Regiment, which made up part of Colonel Wood's "left" column, the soldiers were mostly clean-shaven. Moustaches were considered masculine by the British then, as they still are. Soldiers were not only encouraged to grow moustaches, there was actually a regulation forbidding men to shave their upper lips, but many soldiers in surviving photographs were too young to grow a visible moustache. Those young men looked like the teenagers whose faces smiled out of American high school yearbooks a century later, except that the British soldiers did not smile when they were being photographed. It was not done in those days.

Most of the men in the ranks were not very large. Not only were most of them smaller than the Zulus, they were smaller than the British soldiers who fought against the American Revolution more than a century before. Some regiments recruited only tall men. The average in three regiments of dragoons (mounted infantry selected for their size and strength) was between 5′9″ and 5′10″, and some guardsmen were even taller.[3] But in ordinary British infantry regiments, most soldiers were not very tall. In 1878, the average height of the British army as a whole, including the taller dragoons, lancers, and guards, was just about 5′7″. Infantry regiments that recruited men from the urban poor of the economically depressed industrial centers or from Welsh coal-mining areas had many soldiers who were under 5′6″, and a good many of the younger men weighed as little as 115 pounds.[4] By 1900, the recruiting standard was lowered to 5′3″.

Despite appalling hygienic practices, such as serving food in hastily rinsed wooden urinals, the men in the ranks were reasonably healthy, and most of them were no longer totally illiterate, as they had been in earlier decades. Although there was no educational standard for enlistment by 1878, many soldiers could read and write a little; as their letters home during the Zulu war showed, some wrote fairly well and were reasonably well informed.[5] A few decades earlier, when the army was largely illiterate, many of its recruits were Irish, escaping the terrible famine of mid-century, but by the time of the Zulu War, Irish recruitment had fallen off. Nevertheless, 22 percent of the army in 1878 was Irish, and some units, like the 88th Infantry (the Connaught Rangers), who were left in Cape Colony at the start of the war but would later fight the Zulus, were entirely Irish. In the same year, 8 percent of the British army was Scottish. The numbers of Welsh soldiers were not systematically recorded, but in some regiments, like the 2d Battalion of the 24th Regiment, which recruited heavily in Wales, it is likely that most of the soldiers were Welsh.[6] Although it was common at the time of the Zulu War to refer to the British army as the "English" army, it is probable that no more than half the men in the army, if that many, were English.

A British army recruit in the late nineteenth century, like his predecessors, did not really join an army, he joined a regiment. General Sir Garnet Wolseley was fond of declaring that for a man in the ranks his regiment was his "mother," his "mistress" (Wolseley did not say exactly what he had in mind here, although he wrote in his journal that monogamy was unnatural and he took a mistress himself when he served in India), and his "country." Whether most soldiers actually felt what Wolseley thought they did is unknown, but they were certainly never allowed to forget that they were part of a regiment, owed their lives to it, and drew much of their reason for being alive from being a part of it. Men fought and died for their regiment. They charged to the order of "forward the 24th" or whatever the regiment's number was. They were not ordered to charge for England or even for the Queen, and so it has remained, if we can believe an unbroken chain of British officers, all of whom have insisted that British soldiers fought primarily for their regiments. After World War II, Field Marshal Viscount Bernard Montgomery warned politicians to keep their hands off Britain's "outmoded and costly" regimental system: "We must be very careful what we do with British infantry. . . . Their fighting spirit is based largely on morale and regimental *esprit de corps*. On no account must anyone tamper with this."[7]

It is no more demanding to be a recruit in the United States Marines today than it was to endure training as a private soldier in a nineteenth-century British regiment. Training consisted of endless drill (mostly marching to the orders of terrifying noncommissioned officers), and learning absolute obedience to commands. Men quickly learned that they existed only to serve the regiment. Discipline was always tough, and sometimes it was savage. There were many ingeniously painful methods of physical punishment, but the preferred method of punishment throughout the nineteenth century was flogging. Before the Crimean War in 1854, men were rather commonly sentenced to receive several hundred lashes. Men were known to live through eight hundred lashes, and even sentences of as many as two thousand lashes were inflicted.[8] But after the Crimean War, regulations specified that no more than fifty lashes could be given. After fifty strokes "well-laid on" with a cat-o'-nine-tails, a man's back could be turned into a mass of red jelly, and as late as 1867 a soldier died after receiving "only" fifty lashes. In actual practice, it will come as no surprise, punishment was not always limited to fifty lashes.

Whatever the number of lashes, flogging had to be witnessed, often by the entire regiment. Some men could bear hundreds of lashes without screaming, but most men were not nearly that tough. A man usually bore the first several lashes in silence, and the men in the ranks might even laugh if, as sometimes happened when the blows fell on a man's bare buttocks, he developed an involuntary erection,[9] but as the number of blows mounted, many victims screamed and lost control of their bowels before passing out, only to be revived before the flogging continued (a man could not receive his punishment while he was unconscious). Men in the ranks sometimes fainted. General Sir Bindon Blood, who fought against the Zulus, recalled seeing one hundred men faint while witnessing the flogging of two of their fellow soldiers. Many officers were unable to watch as well.[10] As a young lieutenant (later Field Marshal Lord) Francis Grenfell witnessed punishment in the 60th Regiment, which was later to fight the Zulus: "The man was given a bullet to chew, and received fifty lashes, and I think on the whole he minded it less than I did."[11] Despite the fact that many senior officers, including Lord Chelmsford and Wolseley, believed that flogging was indispensable, and despite the fact that most officers seemed quite capable of witnessing flogging without fainting, the practice was greatly curtailed until the Zulu War began. In 1879, 545 British soldiers were flogged; the largest number of men flogged in any one of the previous fifteen years was 233, and in some years only a handful of men were flogged.[12]

Every conceivable detail of a soldier's life was regulated in minute detail, and the regulations were enforced. Even without flogging, discipline was strictly maintained by fines, extra duties, and other punishments, which were sometimes as creative as they were arbitrary. Captain Thomas Lucas reported that the 5′4″ colonel of his regiment in the 8th "Kaffir" War in South Africa once became outraged when a soldier's hair was not cut short enough to suit him. The colonel sentenced the man to be confined and have his hair cut every two hours "for the rest of his natural life." Lucas commented that the colonel *may* not have had the punishment carried out.[13] Even brutal and capricious discipline rarely drove the men in the ranks to rebellion, but there were occasional explosive outbursts of indiscipline that the army chose not to advertise. For example, some officers in Wellington's army were shot by their men, and during the Anglo-Zulu War, drunken soldiers on a troop ship attacked a group of uniformed officers.[14] But that kind of rebellion was uncommon. Some men complained and a few deserted, but the majority bore their lot stoically. Many even approved of tough discipline. Private soldier Stephen Graham wrote about his years as a "ranker" in the Guards: "The sterner the discipline the better the soldier, the better the army."[15] Graham's use of language was not typical (he was a gentleman who chose to serve in the ranks), but his attitude was widely shared.

Physical training was imposed with exceptional rigor. Men were routinely put through a variety of body building exercises; after only three months of training soldiers were expected to be able to do ten pull-ups on a horizontal bar and to run a mile in under seven minutes. Apparently they could. Recruits measured before and after training in 1869 showed remarkable increases in their physical performance and in the size of their muscles,[16] but as their officers never tired of lamenting, the men's interests did not lie in physical fitness. At every opportunity, especially on pay day, most of the redcoats went in search of strong drink and women. They were, as a saying at the time went, "filled with beef, beer and lust." The army no longer provided its men with vast quantities of rum every day, as it had, for example, during the American "Rebellion," when rum was the single largest expense borne by the British army.[17] Most British soldiers a century later still answered a bugle call to receive their daily rum ration of half a "gill" (2 fluid ounces), but for serious drinking they spent their off-duty hours in the many bars that surrounded military camps, where they drank so often and so heavily that drunkenness was the most frequent reason for punishment in the British Army. In 1880, fully 28 percent of the men in the army were fined for drunkenness. When in their cups, the redcoats fought (75 percent of all crime in the army was reported to be alcohol-related) and looked for women. No halfway decent woman would have anything to do with drunken redcoats, but most bars doubled as whorehouses, and there was no shortage of prostitutes. The redcoats were relentless in their whoring. Although 13 percent of the men were married and may have been less avid in their search for prostitutes than single men, venereal disease was the army's main health problem. Every year, even the relatively well-behaved Guards Regiments had a minimum of 10 percent of their men hospitalized for the treatment of venereal disease, and in some regiments during any single year over more than half the men were hospitalized with a venereal infection.[18] Men who reported sick with venereal disease were liable for fines, and most men medicated themselves when obvious signs of gonorrhea or syphilis appeared, so it must be assumed that many men with venereal disease were not hospitalized. Instead, they went to the far reaches of the empire, where in addition to maintaining the *Pax Britannica* they spread the "pox," as venereal disease was called.

Conditions in the British army changed somewhat from year to year in the 1870s, and no two regiments were ever quite the same. Still, the troops who assembled in South Africa to fight the Zulus were a fair cross-section of Britain's late Victorian army. Even an elite Guards regiment (1st King's Dragoon Guards) was represented, and the Guards rarely left England to fight in colonial wars. The regiments that fought the Zulus were like the army itself: Some were filled with veteran soldiers, others were mostly boys. The 24th Regiment was the best-known. It was an old regiment that dated back to 1689; it had once been commanded by John Churchill, Duke of Marlborough. It had a reputation for unusual bravery, but also one for bad luck, several times suffering heavy losses and surrender through no fault of its own.[19] In 1741, the 24th lost eight hundred of its one thousand men in a battle in Spain, and a century later the regiment was nearly wiped out in India when it charged the Sikh's Krupp-made artillery with nothing but bayonets. The Zulu War was not to change their luck. Yet, when 820 rank-and-file soldiers of the 24th's first battalion (1/24th) landed in Cape Town in 1874, the men must have felt happy enough. Cape Town had long housed a British garrison to protect the sea route to India. While the city was anything but lovely to the eye, it had everything that the long-service veterans of the 1/24th could hope for. There were many bars that sold cheap gin—"square face" it was called after its square bottle—and cheaper peach brandy called "cape smoke," which cost only nine pence a bottle and tasted like raisins in wood alcohol. There was gambling of all sorts, and there were prostitutes, hundreds of them—exactly six hundred, if one could believe police records.[20] They were available in every shade from black to white, but the whiter they were, the more they cost.

The men of the 24th lost no time in getting down to their drinking and brawling. The city jail soon overflowed with redcoats or "Tommies," as they were sometimes called even then. The cat-o'-nine-tails was in regular use as well. The temptations of the flesh and the lure of the Kimberly diamond fields to the north were too much for some of the men. Eight deserted almost immediately, followed by eighteen more in 1875 and nineteen in 1876. In 1877, when the Gaika and Gcakela tribes rose against the British in what came to be known as the Ninth Frontier or "Kaffir" War, the 1st Battalion of the 24th marched off to do most of the fighting (after a few months they were joined by the 24th's 2d Battalion, made up largely of young recruits). For eleven months the 24th marched, bivouacked, and marched again. Sometimes they skirmished and, with the help of their African allies, the Fingoes, occasionally fought deadly battles. In one large battle the steady, well-aimed fire from their modern Martini-Henry rifles stopped a courageous charge by thousands of African warriors. When the fighting ended, perhaps five hundred Africans had died, some within 30 yards of the British line.[21] One of those killed was a woman who had led the charge. An African chief who had fought with the British cut off her head and kept it in a sack; he happily showed it to any British officer who would look.[22] It was an unequal war. In eleven months of campaigning, not one man of the 24th was killed in battle, although twenty-one men died of disease. Only one soldier deserted while the regiment was in action.

By the end of the Ninth Frontier War in 1878 the men of the 24th were generally considered to be the best troops in South Africa. They were well-disciplined, good shots, and steady in the face of the enemy. They were tough men who ran every day before breakfast, marched all day, ate whatever was available, and learned to ignore heat, cold, insects, and most of the worst African diseases. Their uniforms were faded, torn, and patched, often with hide rather than cloth. Their once white sun helmets were brown with grime (some men dyed their helmets brown with tea as a kind of camouflage). They were veterans, and they were confident. They wore a regimental badge on the green collar of their tunics with a motto taken from the Order of the Garter: *"Honi soit, qui mal y pense"* (shamed be anyone who thinks evil of it). They didn't know how to pronounce the French words, but they knew the idea. They were not men to be taken lightly.

In December 1878, both battalions of the 24th Regiment joined the other British troops that were assembling for the planned invasion of Zululand. Although sometimes they had to make do with putrid beef, they had few complaints about the food. The canned beef from Chicago was very good, and often there was fresh meat and vegetables. Lime juice was added to their diet, and so was quinine, but they usually took too little to prevent malaria. They drilled, ran, marched, did rifle practice, tried to cope with the weather, and waited for the bugle call that signalled the "grog" ration. It was summer in South Africa, and by noon it could be 120 degrees Fahrenheit in the shade, but much of Natal and Zululand lay at elevations above 4,000 feet, where water froze at night. The long drought that had plagued Zululand and Natal broke late in December with tremendous thunder storms. The lightning displays were terrifying, even to officers experienced with South African rainy seasons. It rained so hard that canvas tents offered no protection, and cooking fires couldn't be started. Everyone was soaked to the skin. Sometimes hailstones weighing 3 ounces fell, and the men huddled under cover. A private wrote home that he had seen a hen killed by the hail in one such storm.[23] An officer who was commanding a supply column saw a more remarkable sight. He took shelter under an oxcart when a hailstorm struck, and when the storm ended and he crawled out, six of the oxen had been killed.[24]

The infantry was joined by batteries of the Royal Artillery. Each battery had six 7-pound muzzle-loading cannon and two rocket tubes tended by 130 men who wore blue uniforms, not red. The artillerymen were newly arrived and were coming down with fever; four had died recently and nine others were very ill. Many of their horses were weak too. Grazing was poor, and several horses were showing symptoms of a deadly horse disease that was endemic in Natal. Even so, the artillery was a formidable force. Their Hale's rockets were mostly meant to flame and sizzle, terrifying unsophisticated opponents, but their cannon could fire explosive shells or canister (huge shotgun shells) more than 3,000 yards. Even a solid shot could do terrible damage to masses of men, and the shrapnel from a single explosive shell could kill a score of men. At close range cannister was devastating. Still, there were few cannon available. The main weapon was the rifle. The mounted men carried carbines, but every British infantryman was armed with a Martini-Henry rifle. It looked like a Winchester, so familiar to Americans in the West at this same time, but it was not a repeating rifle. Brass cartridges were fed into the breech one at a time and ejected by a lever underneath the stock. It fired a 480-grain, .45 caliber bullet, powered by 83 grains of black powder. The rifle kicked phenomenally and overheated easily, but it was very accurate up to 900 yards, and its soft lead bullets expanded on impact, inflicting large and usually fatal wounds. At 100 yards, one of its bullets could pass through three men and kill a fourth if they were standing in a row. Each man also carried a 21½-inch triangular bayonet. Made in Germany, some of those bayonets bent when used, and several British newspapers blamed the British defeat at Isandlwana on defective bayonets. As we shall see, a few bayonets did bend, but most of them were sound, and the Zulus feared them as weapons. There were no hand grenades, but later in the war American-designed machine guns—''Gatling guns''—were used with varying success, until they jammed, which was often. Officers were armed with regulation Wilkinson swords, first issued in 1822, as well as various kinds of .45 caliber revolvers.

Although the British had superior weapons, they were usually greatly outnumbered in their colonial wars. Native troops helped to equalize the odds, so British Colonial armies recruited native allies whenever possible, usually paying them more than they paid their own soldiers. At the start of the Zulu war, the British could field only slightly more than five thousand white Imperial troops against what they thought might be 40,000 Zulus. Native allies not only evened the odds a little, they could serve as mounted scouts (the only British cavalry in Natal at the start of the War were a few infantrymen who were more or less able to ride a horse) and could be invaluable, as the British found out in their most recent ''Kaffir'' war, by marching well ahead of the white soldiers and forcing the enemy to reveal their positions. So the British recruited several native cavalry units. The best was Colonel A. W. Durnford's Frontier Light Horse. These two hundred or so Africans rode well, and each man was armed with a modern Martini-Henry carbine, which he knew how to use. There was another well-equipped cavalry unit of African Christians, the Edendale Troop. Those men prayed every morning before breakfast, then fought very well. There were also some three hundred young Zulus who had suffered a grievance at the hands of an older regiment and fled to Natal with their commander, Mvubi. They were eager to settle scores with their former countrymen, even if they had to fight for the "red soldiers" to do so. There were also some older Zulus who had fled Zululand when Cetshwayo defeated their leader, Prince Mbulazi, in 1858. They had lived in Natal for twenty-one years and were not quite so keen on fighting. The Zulus were armed only with their traditional spears and clubs.

In addition to the Zulus, there were seven thousand or so other Africans divided into three battalions of what was called the Natal Native Contingent. A few of them had modern rifles but virtually no ammunition, and a few more had old muskets, which they usually forgot to load in the heat of the battle. They were also terrible shots, and their white officers and NCOs were as worried about being killed by them as they were by the Zulus. The Zulus who fought with the British wore their feathers and furs. They were large, impressive men who marched with discipline and were clearly ready for a fight. The British were impressed by them, but they thought the other native soldiers were ridiculous. They wore ragged and filthy European castoff clothes and hats. When it was hot, they wore only their hats (one man was photographed wearing a battered top hat and nothing else) and a red cloth tied around their heads so that they could be distinguished from the hostile Zulus. No one actually counted heads, but in all, there were probably nine thousand African allies in the British forces at the start of the war. As one of their British officers who spoke Zulu said of them after Isandlwana, "they were a cheery lot, great fun, but useless as fighters."[25]

That is not entirely true. Many of the Natal Africans did join the British only to get a daily beef ration, and others went along as spectators to the awaited clash between the British and the Zulus. Most of them were terrified of the Zulus, especially at night. But some Africans in the Natal Native Contingent fought well, and with better leadership they might have fought better. All of their officers and NCOs were white. Some of the officers, like Durnford, still held the Queen's Commission, and others had previously done so before resigning to move to South Africa. A few were gentlemen with little military experience, but some were battle-toughened veterans of wars throughout the Empire. The NCOs made the toughest redcoats look like choir boys. They were runaways and adventurers from every European country, and many were only a step ahead of the law in South Africa. They were tough, brawling drunkards who were never far from the civilian sutlers who followed the army with gin wagons. As one of their officers put it, "They were mostly men of from 35 to 50 years of age, big, burly powerful men who could work like horses when they were on the job and who could drink like the Sahara Desert when they were not."[26] Some would fight well, but others would run; few knew anything about soldiering, and when it came to leading African troops they were hopeless.

As the men of the 24th and the other British regiments waited for orders to "have a slap" at the Zulus, there was little for them to do. Except for their daily tot of rum, no alcohol was available to them, and some men were caught trying to steal gin from the quartermaster's stores. They were flogged. A little later, when other British troops defeated the Zulus at a place called Gingindhlovu, the men happily referred to it as "Gin, gin I love you." A few ate unripe native fruit and came down with diarrhea, but most men simply sat around (they often wore red wool nightcaps with a tassel on the end, which may have kept their heads warm but made them look absurd) smoking their inevitable short-stemmed pipes, playing cards, and writing letters home. Most of them used no punctuation at all, but a war correspondent who was with them at the time called letter-writing their principal recreation.[27] The poverty of their backgrounds was poignantly emphasized by the concern they expressed that their families might not be able to afford a postage stamp to write them in return.

A few of the men wrote about their fears. Corporal Brown, a veteran of the 24th's 2d Battalion, wrote to his wife that fighting the Zulus would not be as easy as fighting the Kaffirs had been. He concluded on this somber note: "I am very sorry to have to tell you that there will be many a poor wife lose her husband and many a father and mother lose their son. I am afraid, but I hope and trust to the Almighty that I shall not be one of them for my own darling's sake."[28] But most of the men, like Owen Ellis, a veteran private of the 1st Battalion, were cocksure: "We are about to capture all the cattle belonging to the Zulus and also burn their kraals; and if they dare to face us with the intention of fighting, well, woe be to them."[29] Another wrote "we're looking forward to have a slap at the niggers."

The men of the 24th, like the men in the other British regiments that would soon come to blows with Zulu armies, would fight well. Whatever their backgrounds once were, they were now a disciplined, brave fighting force. Wellington's words about his army early in the century might still apply: "They are the scum of the earth and it is really wonderful that we should have made of them the fine fellows they are. With such an army we can go anywhere and do anything." Many British officers who commanded troops in the Zulu War would have agreed, not only about the men's fighting abilities but about their social origins as well. What their officers thought and did were the most important things in these soldiers' lives. Soldiers and NCOs in nineteenth-century European armies had virtually no power to act independently. Everything they did, from training drills to fixing bayonets before charging, they did on their officers' orders. British soldiers were trained to obey without question. They obeyed so blindly that foreign observers were often critical of them. So were their own senior generals, like Lord Kitchener, who wrote that the British soldier was "usually too dependent on his officers and lacked individuality."[30]

Their officers were criticized too, and it cannot be denied that some British officers were capable of astonishing stupidity.[31] Recall the quip that British soldiers were "lions led by donkeys." To take one example from many, General Lord Raglan, who commanded the British army that was allied with the French army in the war against the Russians in the Crimea, never got it into his head that if his men were to fight during the Russian winter they would need warm clothing. Perhaps that is not so surprising, because Lord Raglan always referred to the Russians as "the French." All British soldiers criticized their officers at times and feared them, but they followed them and wanted to be led by true gentlemen.[32] With rare exceptions, like Field Marshal Robertson, almost all British officers were gentlemen, and their caste of warrior officers was a world apart.

John Baynes, himself a British colonel, imagined what most officers of the pre–World War I British army would accept as their ideal. In reading what he wrote, try to keep in mind that he was absolutely serious:

> The ideal officer is a tall man, about six foot, and lean. He has one of those thin, aristocratic faces with a faintly Roman nose which epitomize the well-bred Englishman. His eyes are blue, and very penetrating in their stare. Always immaculately turned out in uniform or civilian clothes he has a large wardrobe of expensive but unostentatious clothes, all of which come from the best tailors in London. His legs are very thin, enabling him to wear the straightest and narrowest boots imaginable. These, like his shoes, are made by the best makers, and are kept supple and highly polished under all conditions.

> . . . In manner he is dignified, and always carries himself erectly. Calmness in times of stress and danger is one of his main attributes. He is also very brave physically. . . .[33]

Baynes added that the ideal officer excelled at sports, although he did not take winning seriously, was an excellent hunter and fisherman, and a superior horseman. He was devoted to his regiment, knew "all about wine," and was a "sound judge of port," although he drank in moderation. The ideal officer had an "impeccable" background, coming from a "good family" and being educated at a well-known public school. Baynes's description might sound like a Gilbert and Sullivan parody, but it was not. In all likelihood most British officers of the nineteenth century would have seen this smug self-portrait as a reasonable ideal too. The officer he imagined was a bit too strait-laced, perhaps, and not everyone could be 6 feet tall and blue-eyed, but that *was* the ideal.

The gulf between officers and private soldiers was so vast that it is often difficult for Americans to comprehend. This was an age when men were born unequal and remained unequal. Officers were as different from their soldiers as were squires of the manor from their servants and farm laborers. The distinction should not be surprising. Officers and men in the ranks came from totally different worlds of experience. British officers, almost without exception, were the sons of the landed gentry, the clergy, politicians, and civil servants, or the sons of other officers, usually colonels and generals. They were gentlemen. Some were aristocrats. Among the officers who fought against the Zulus were barons and viscounts, and the sons of barons and viscounts. Almost all went to good public schools. Like Baynes's ideal officer, most of the officers in the Zulu war went to Harrow, Eton, Wellington, Winchester, Cheltenham, Charterhouse, or Rugby. Even though their brothers often attended Oxford or Cambridge, very few of the men who became officers went to a university. Some tried but failed to qualify. Others went to a military college, Sandhurst or Woolwich. Most simply headed for the army, but not until they had been shaped by their experiences in public school.

In 1870, there were only seven "great" public boarding schools. They taught boys to endure "sickness, vice, brutality, cold, starvation and privation," hardening them and creating strong peer bonds.[34] The schools were run by Oxford- or Cambridge-educated clergymen, who imparted what came to be known as "muscular Christianity" to their young charges. Religion, the classics, and a smattering of history were topics for gentlemen; practical knowledge, including science, was not taught. Manly games were central, critical thinking was not. A commission set up to examine the public school curriculum was reluctant to consider new subjects: "It is not easy to win steady attention from a high-spirited English lad . . . who like his elders, thinks somewhat slowly, and does not express himself readily, and to whom mental effort is troublesome."[35] Public schools were, as T. H. Huxley said, designed to teach "gentlemanly habits, strong class feeling, and eminent proficiency in cricket."[36] They also taught their boys to rule people from the lower classes.

Despite the anti-intellectualism of Victorian public schools, a fair number of these public school officers developed their own intellectual interests, usually in naturalism, and a few became recognized as men of knowledge later in life. It is fair to say that most, however, were not bookworms (Lord Wolseley, for example, could not spell very well). They were men of action who rode, hunted, and gambled (something Baynes neglected to mention). Most were, in fact, proficient at several "manly" sports, including boxing. As a young man, Lord Grenfell (another who served in Anglo-Zulu War) went so far as to spar with the best British professional heavyweight boxers. Their military training included some instruction in tactics, but it concentrated on horsemanship, swordsmanship, and gymnastics. Most of them were not obsessed with physical fitness, but they were active, vigorous men. Officers were usually larger than the men in the ranks and healthier. Most officers towered above their men, and as late as 1900 their life expectancy (war aside) was age sixty; in the same year, men from the lowest classes had a life expectancy of only thirty.[37] Until 1870, officers purchased their commissions, ensuring the continuity of wealthy men in the military caste, but after that time, thanks to army reforms, "purchase" was abolished, and new officers had to pass an examination to qualify. That eliminated some (it almost eliminated Winston Churchill, who twice failed before passing just well enough to qualify for the cavalry but not high enough for the more demanding infantry), but since, with rare exceptions, only the sons of gentlemen were interested in a military career, it did nothing to alter the class composition of the British officer corps.

Gentlemen were accustomed to leisure, and even very young junior officers usually had much leisure time available to indulge their private interests, usually hunting. They spent much of their spare time killing animals and sometimes, by accident, themselves. They were all tended by soldier servants, even on campaign, and they lived well. They were acutely conscious of "class" and did everything they could to reaffirm their superiority. Unlike people from the lesser classes, whom they thought capable of every meanness, in principle they never lied or cheated with money. In reality, some officers were conveniently forgetful about their debts, and a few were outright criminals. For example, during the Anglo-Zulu War, a major in charge of procuring supplies for the army conspired with local contractors to rake off large profits for himself. He was found out and dismissed from the army. A captain who embezzled soldiers' pay went to jail.[38] Officers not only felt superior to all darker-skinned people—they were called "niggers" or "wogs"—they felt superior to other Europeans and, of course, to Americans. Jews were scorned. There were very few Jewish officers, and none ever rose to the rank of general. It is a certainty that no British officer could imagine a Zulu as his equal. Officers' journals during the Zulu war were often harshly racist about all Africans, including the Zulus. Even the most sympathetic officers were patronizing toward Zulus as human beings—they might be brave, but they were indecisive, superstitious, childlike, dirty, smelly, and well, black![39]

Officers' accents were very different from those of their soldiers, and they usually avoided swearing, unlike their soldiers, who rarely *failed* to swear. Many officers used expressions like "By Jove" even in the heat of battle, and in the "better" regiments they affected the kind of lisp that caused "regiment" to be pronounced, "wegiment." When angry, however, even very senior officers swore mightily and inventively, and the men were greatly partial to an officer who was talented at swearing. They even liked officers like Major Wilsone Black of the 24th, who swore in Gaelic. That most men couldn't understand the words wasn't important. It was the intent that seemed to matter, and, after all, officers couldn't always understand their men's accents either.

As we have seen, the Zulus were not sexually repressed, but a good many British officers were. Sex was simply not very much on the minds of many of them. A remarkable number of prominent British officers led virtually sex-free lives. Colonel Baynes has summarized their feelings with exceptional candor: "Even when fully mature they blotted out thoughts of sex as though they were something evil. A high proportion never married, and many of them felt that it was almost virtuous not to do so." Baynes pointed out that this attitude was an asset to an officer, because

> . . . it made him contented with his lot as a bachelor. He felt that in living as a single man in a semi-monastic community he was fulfilling the highest purpose of life. The temptations of sex, of lust and "filth,"

were removed. He could meet girls occasionally, admire them and possibly flirt with them a little, but he could avoid the messy, animal business of having intercourse with them.[40]

The army believed that younger officers should not marry, as the distractions of a wife and children would deflect them from their paramount goal, the pursuit of glory in war. However, Baynes overstates their celibacy. Sex was permitted to officers, even with native concubines if it was done discreetly, and some officers were remarkably lusty men who ruined their careers by their overzealous pursuit of women who happened to be the wives of prominent men or fellow officers. Some preferred boys. Colonel Hector Macdonald, the hero of the British victory over the Dervish army outside Omdurman in 1885, was later threatened with a court-martial on charges of having homosexual relations with schoolboys in Ceylon. He shot himself. Not all sexual relationships ended tragically. So many officers had romantic escapades in Natal during the Anglo-Zulu war that Sir Garnet Wolseley (who replaced General Chelmsford at the end of the war) quipped that when they returned home they sang about the *wives* they left behind them. The town of Ladysmith in Natal stands as a reminder that some British officers could be romantic by any standard. Ladysmith was named after the wife of Sir Henry Smith, former governor of Cape Colony. When Smith was a young officer serving with Wellington's army in Spain he had fallen in love with a thirteen-year-old Spanish girl named Juana and had married her. He later wrote that her expression "inspired me with a maddening love which from that period to this (now thirty-three years) has never abated under the most trying circumstances."[41]

But in general Baynes was correct. Many officers, including some who fought the Zulus and later rose to high rank, married late in life and displayed little interest in their wives—or in sex, for that matter. Neither Kitchener nor General Gordon (who once wrote that he found war "indescribably exciting") was ever known to have had a sexual experience with a woman. Both generals were visibly and notoriously fond of being around pretty young men, but there is no direct evidence that either man actually had homosexual experiences. They, and many others, apparently did without sex. They much preferred war. Frere's phrase, "celibate manslaying gladiators," characterized British officers far better than it did the Zulus.

If many officers were not visibly interested in sex, there was nothing hidden about their eagerness to achieve glory by performing heroic acts that would lead to medals, honors, and promotion. Baynes did not mention their almost single-minded pursuit of glory, yet glory was the driving passion of their lives. And not only *their* lives. Their mothers, sisters, aunts, and wives, if any, were usually behind them in encouraging glorious heroism. Mortally wounded officers were known to dictate letters to their mothers as they lay dying, telling them how pleased they knew their mothers would be that their mortal wounds were received in honorable combat. In February 1879, when Captain W. E. Montague of the 94th regiment received orders to sail for South Africa after the defeat at Isandlwana, he was overjoyed and rushed home to tell his wife: ''Nelly gave a slight shiver . . . that was only for a second,—little more. Then she gave a faint smile, and laid both hands on my shoulders, saying as she kissed me, 'I'm so glad, Ned, because I know you are glad.' And after that she burst out crying.''[42]

Bravery was essential, and most officers probably agreed with Lord Wolseley, who believed that all English gentlemen were born brave.[43] Officers felt the eyes of other gentlemen-officers on them at all times. They stood disdainfully as enemy fire whistled by, and often they recklessly exposed themselves to death. If an officer was seen ducking his head as a bullet or shell whistled by, he was likely to be scolded and shamed by a senior officer's curt rebuke: ''Don't bob!'' Most did not ''bob'' or flinch. They sought out danger, including hand-to-hand combat, and although some years later it was regarded as beneath an officer's dignity to kill or even to carry a weapon, even senior officers at the time of the Zulu War carried weapons and used them freely and well. In fact, most officers were remarkably violent men. For example, every officer carried a sword, and some used them viciously in hand-to-hand combat. Percy Barrow, a boyish-looking red-haired major of the 19th Hussars, commanded a detachment of mounted infantry during the Anglo-Zulu War. He used his sword to kill four Zulus in one battle. He wrote that he regretted not having more men behind him so that he could have ''cut hundreds of them to pieces.''[44] Many officers exulted in killing and enjoyed nothing more than close combat. Lieutenant Carrington of the 24th wrote about a battle in 1878 in which he ''potted'' (shot) several Africans at point-blank range. He was annoyed that he did not have a ''bayonet or something to skewer more of the enemy.''[45] There was an undeniable zest for battle in many of those men. Officers were expected to display conspicuous gallantry. As we shall see later, some officers in the Zulu War were not brave; in fact, there were some cowards, but most of them were brave men who enjoyed the experience of combat.

They were all commissioned officers of the Queen, but like private soldiers, their primary loyalty was to their regiment (in those regiments that had two battalions, an officer's loyalty was to his battalion). Most officers, like most men in the ranks, joined a regiment as very young men and remained in it throughout their military careers. Regiments were often referred to as families; in fact, it was common for sons to follow their fathers, and even grandfathers, into the same regiment. A few regiments were so selective that no man without high social rank could hope to be accepted. At the time of the Zulu war, most British infantry regiments had two battalions of about eight hundred men each. The regiment was commanded by its "colonel," who might be a very senior officer with the rank of lieutenant general in the army. When serving in "his" regiment, however, he was its "colonel." Each battalion of infantry was commanded by a lieutenant colonel, and beneath him there might be one or two majors, four or five captains, and perhaps seven lieutenants, often called subalterns. At the time of the Zulu war, an infantry regiment with two battalions might have as many as sixty or sixty-five officers (cavalry regiments were only half as large).

For the officers, their regiment was their life and their identity. Part family, part men's club, part private army, each regiment had its own distinctive uniform, badges, mottos, nicknames, songs, customs, toasts, mascots, and traditions of all kinds. Regiments cherished their regimental silver, trophies of war, drums, and, most of all, their battle honors emblazoned on their two large silk flags called "colours"; one flag represented the Queen, the other, the regiment. To lose either of those flags to the enemy was a disgrace too terrible to imagine; officers and private soldiers often gave their lives to prevent that ultimate disgrace (two officers died trying to save "the Queen's colours" at Isandlwana).

Unless a regiment was actually on a military campaign, its officers had few duties. Except for the colonel, his adjutant, and a few others on special duty, officers could easily discharge their duties in an hour or so in the morning, and they were free to enjoy themselves much of the time. On board troop ships bringing reinforcements to Natal, officers drank champagne in the ship's lounge, while the soldiers were crowded below decks. As noted earlier, very few read for pleasure (it was said that an officer "put his books away" when he joined his regiment). Their first love was hunting and shooting, and many were devoted to other sports, especially polo and cricket. Many officers boxed, and this was a time when officers could box against men in the ranks. Officers usually won. Some also used their fists freely in brawls with civilians while in Natal.[46] They usually won those fights, too. Most of them were dedicated to gambling—on almost anything from cards to personal bets. Few who remained in the army gambled as heavily and lost as regularly as Colonel Durnford who died amid controversy at Isandlwana. An officer's honor required that he pay his gambling debts promptly, although he could and often did neglect to pay merchants' bills for years!

In most respects, the life of a regiment centered on its mess, which was almost always a highly formal affair. After drinks (whisky, sherry, or brandy, never beer or gin, which were the private soldiers' beverages), they sat down to eat at a table headed by their colonel. Food was served in several courses, and wine flowed freely. Whether the colonel was dotty, witty, or a martinet, he proposed a toast. Field Marshal Horace Smith-Dorrien, who as a young officer miraculously survived Isandlwana, had a toast (always the same) for every day of the week. On Wednesdays, it was, "our swords"; on Saturdays, "to sweethearts and wives . . . may they never meet." Other officers might propose toasts of their own, and Baynes's ideal notwithstanding, it was an unusual regiment that drank sparingly in 1879. Some regiments had officers who drank wine copiously at breakfast. Even when regiments were in the field, they carried linen tablecloths, fine china, crystal, and silver, along with fine wines, champagne, whisky, comfortable chairs, and sometimes even carpets. Needless to say, they dressed for dinner unless they were on campaign. There was a prohibition against anything resembling serious conversation in the mess. Officers spoke of sport, horses, or the weather. They would not discuss women or politics until after dinner, when they drank still more, smoked cigars, played billiards or cards, and sometimes hurled themselves at one another in adolescent wrestling bouts. If, as sometimes happened, an officer were hurt in one of those scuffles, he could not complain.[47]

There can be no doubt that the regimental life of Zulu warriors helped to train and motivate them for war, and when a Zulu regiment was drinking, boasting, dancing, remembering past battles, and hoping for new ones, it became warlike enough for anyone's taste, but Zulu regiments were not assembled most of the time. Zulu men, especially older ones, spent most of their lives attending to mundane matters, especially their families and their herds. A British regiment was different. It was assembled *all* the time, and its officers were obsessed with war. In many regiments officers drank toasts for a chance to fight; in others they actually offered prayers in the mess for war to break out. When they finally experienced war, they usually enjoyed it. General Sir Ian Hamilton wrote: "War put me very nearly out of my mind with delight."[48] General Wolseley, who as a young officer "longed to hear the whistle of a bullet fired in earnest," recalled a charge in which he was badly wounded: "What a supremely delightful moment it was!" Captain the Honorable Julian Grenfell wrote this to his mother "I *adore* war. It is like a big picnic. I have never been so well or so happy."[49] It wasn't just camping out that they liked, it was fighting, and they certainly were not shy about expressing their feelings. Wolseley wrote the following in a letter to, of all people, his elderly aunt: "Man-shooting is the finest sport of all; there is a certain amount of infatuation about it that the more you kill the more you wish to kill."[50] Even "Old Blood and Guts," General George Patton, might have thought Wolseley was a bit too frank, at least in a letter to a delicate old lady. Unlike Patton, Wolseley did not have his wrist slapped for his bloodlust. By the time of the Zulu War, he was the most prominent general in the British army. Wolseley was desperate to lead the British forces against the Zulus, but by the time he actually arrived in Natal and was able to take command, the war was virtually over. Some officers wept when they arrived in Natal too late to fight against the Zulus. Others were simply depressed because they had arrived too late for what they referred to as the "fun."

It would be misleading to suggest that all British officers were enthusiastic about war and compared it to a picnic. Some served well and fought bravely without expressing any pleasure in the acts of combat. Julian Grenfell's older brother Francis, who served in South Africa in the Ninth Kaffir War as well as the Zulu War, and who later became a field marshal, was no fire-eater. He was a distinguished officer, a boxer, and a brave man, but his great love in life was painting. There were others like him who served in the Anglo-Zulu War.

Almost all officers sought after medals and promotions as tangible rewards for their service. Most of those who survived the Anglo-Zulu War were later knighted and rose to high rank. At least ten became generals, and four rose to the rank of field marshal. Many were decorated for exceptional bravery, and many others could have been. For example, Colonel Sir (later Field Marshal) Henry Evelyn Wood, one of Chelmsford's senior commanders, had been awarded a VC (Victoria Cross, Britain's highest award for bravery) before he was twenty years old. He was perhaps the most successful of the British commanders in the Zulu War, and he always exhibited such great personal courage that he deserved several more VCs, but the medal could be awarded only once. Wood was not pleased. His commander of native horsemen was the utterly fearless Colonel (later General Sir) Redvers Buller. Buller did win a VC in the Zulu War, and like Wood he earned it a dozen times over. But others who deserved recognition were overlooked. By modern standards, their quest for promotion and medals may seem petty, even unworthy, but that is not how the search for glory was seen in those days. Colonel Arthur Harness of the Royal Artillery served under Chelmsford in the South African campaign of 1878. Like most British officers in that unglamorous war, he saw little chance to advance his career, as he complained in a letter to his family: "There is nothing to be gained in the way of glory or anything else in this vile country." Harness's chance came. He was one of a very few senior officers who served throughout the entire Zulu War. He won the respect of his fellow officers and, after the war, was decorated by Queen Victoria at Windsor Castle.

Officers throughout the Empire clamored for a chance to achieve their own glory in Zululand. They pleaded and plotted for a posting to Chelmsford's army as what were called "special service" officers—officers who performed various staff duties. Only a few were accepted at first. One of the "lucky" ones was a tall, twenty-year-old lieutenant with the 95th Regiment named Horace Smith-Dorrien. Lord Chelmsford was formerly the colonel of the 95th, and one of his staff officers, Lord Grenfell, had been at Harrow with Smith-Dorrien. Connections helped. Smith-Dorrien joined Chelmsford's army as an officer in charge of transport in time for the start of the war. Other officers who were turned down at the start of the war eventually made it to Natal. Before the war was over, a roster of Chelmsford's officers looked like a "Who's Who" of the British army. Other British officers volunteered to command native troops, joining many former British officers who had emigrated to South Africa. A listing of some of the officers who served with special distinction would include the names Durnford, Barrow, Barton, D'Arcy, Shepstone, Erskine, Vereker, Raw, Lonsdale, and Hamilton-Browne.

Officers serving with the regiments that were already in South Africa were also eager for war and glory. A photograph was taken of the officers of the 2d Battalion of the 24th Regiment just before the war. Thirty-one officers are shown, the full complement for a battalion. One, probably Lieutenant Colonel Henry Degacher, had a gray beard, and eleven others—the more senior officers—wore thick black beards. But there were younger officers sitting in front, and six of them were clean-shaven. One man towered over the rest. He had an immense drooping moustache, and he looked as though he couldn't wait for the killing to start.[51] A photograph of the officers of the 1st Battalion taken at the same time would have shown men who looked very much the same. But there was to be a difference. Only a few officers in the 2d Battalion would be killed, but most of those in the 1st Battalion would die at Isandlwana.

Although the invasion of Zululand, which would afford many officers a chance for glory, was not supposed to start until Frere's ultimatum expired on January 11, Colonel Wood sent armed patrols into Zululand on January 6, and his entire force marched on January 10. The "right" column invaded near the coast on the twelfth under the command of Colonel Pearson. Chelmsford ordered his forces of the central column across the frigid Buffalo river on January 11. The British troops were ferried over the river in ponts, but the African troops had to ford the river as best they could. Locking arms to avoid being swept away in the fast current, they charged across the 100-yard wide, neck-deep river. They formed human chains both above and below the crossing point, splashing their arms to frighten away crocodiles. The rest of the African troops crossed the river buzzing like bees, perhaps to make certain that the crocodiles were intimidated. The water was so cold that the men's teeth chattered loudly, and even the stoical Zulus sucked in their breath audibly as they crossed. The current was so fast that several African soldiers drowned. The British were not sure how many. Wagons were lost, too, and there was great distress among the headquarter's staff when a wagon loaded with champagne was swept away. Chelmsford's officers did not campaign without their comforts, including champagne, port, and whisky. There was no oath of temperance on this march.

Many British officers approached the campaign as little more than an elaborate hunting expedition. Colonel Degacher managed to get his well-bred pointer across the river without any difficulty.[52] Degacher hoped to have time to shoot some birds in Zululand. While British soldiers fretted about the price of a stamp, their officers loaded their expensive shotguns into wagons and handed their dogs over to their servants. Most officers found it necessary to carry with them an astonishing array of expensive goods: several pairs of handmade leather or porpoise-skin boots, hats, scarves, writing tables, folding chairs, and canvas bath-tubs; silver hairbrushes, mirrors, and brandy flasks; watercolors and sketch pads; silk handkerchiefs; leather-bound diaries; jars and tins of delicacies; liquors of all sorts; and several changes of clothing, including mess jackets and fancy white dress shirts.

One of the first officers to cross the river was thirty-two-year-old Major George Hamilton-Browne, who was the "commandant" of a large native force. Like so many British officers, including Wolseley and later T. E. Lawrence and Field Marshal Viscount Montgomery, he was an Anglo-Irishman. Although Hamilton-Browne came from a military family (his father was a general and his brother a regular officer) he was never commissioned as a regular officer, because he had fought several duels while still a teenager, and army regulations forbade dueling.

He was only 5′7″ but was stocky, strong, and very tough. He was known as "Maori" Browne, because he had fought with his customary zest as a teenager in the Maori wars and spoke Maori. He had also fought in Australia, South Africa, and America against the Sioux the year before Custer's fight at the Little Big Horn.[53] He would yield to no man when it came to love of war, but he was an experienced campaigner and he knew how to wait. Like so many officers, Hamilton-Browne had a pet dog, but he left the dog in the care of his Hottentot servant. As soon as he dried himself in the hot sun on the Zulu side of river, he took four spears from his native troops, balanced a shield on top of them, and lay down in the shade waiting for the war to start.

# Chapter 4

# "They Were Like Lions": Isandlwana

Chief Sihayo was a wealthy and powerful man, a personal favorite of King Cetshwayo, but he had been suffering a run of bad luck. It could hardly have pleased the corpulent old chief when two of his young wives fled to Natal after their infidelity had been discovered. Then it must certainly have been unpleasant for him to learn that the British were making a terrible fuss about his sons' entry into Natal to capture the women and return them to Zululand. Sihayo had always been a remarkably jovial man with many friends among the British, with whom he traded in Natal. Unique among Cetshwayo's chiefs, he sometimes wore Western clothes. He was not warlike, but now, in an ironic twist of history, the British were demanding that his sons be turned over to them for trial. Worst of all, perhaps, Sihayo's territory, including his personal homestead, was near the border, directly in the path of General Chelmsford's invading central column. His home was to be the scene of the war's first battle.[1] It would be a deadly little comedy.

As Hamilton-Browne watched the British camp grow on the Zulu side of the Buffalo River, he was horrified to realize that despite standing orders that every camp must be laagered, this huge, sprawling collection of men, animals, and supplies was not fortified in any way. He need not have worried, because there were no Zulu regiments nearby. The men of the district who had not reported to King Cetshwayo for mobilization were hiding in caves with their wives, their children, and as much food and stock as they could protect. Chelmsford's troops were stalled by the muddy, marshy Bashee Valley ahead of them, so while engineers, aided by African and British soldiers, tried to make the route passable for wagons, the general decided to make good use of the time on his hands by punishing the luckless Chief Sihayo. He ordered none other than "Maori" Browne to lead the attack with his 1,300 native troops, supported by four companies of the 24th. Hamilton-Browne was ordered to capture the chief's cattle but on no account to kill any women or children. Perhaps Sihayo's luck wasn't all bad: At least he was not at home when the British attacked. He and his oldest son, Mehlokazulu, were with the king at Ulundi. Sihayo's cattle were defended by his younger sons, including Nkubikazulu, who was wanted by the British for killing Sihayo's wives, and a few hundred armed men from his district.

As Hamilton-Browne's corps of Natal natives moved cautiously through the thick brush of a rocky gorge toward Sihayo's cattle kraal, a Zulu voice challenged them, demanding to know by whose orders they came. One of "Maori" Browne's white colonial officers, Captain Duncombe, roared back in fluent Zulu, "By the orders of the Great White Queen!" The battle appears to have been scripted by Lewis Carroll, but the Zulus were not amused. They responded by opening fire with an assortment of rifles, and the British forces returned their fire. To add to the improbability of this opening clash of the war, a British cannon far to the rear fired a single shell that exploded on a rocky crag above Sihayo's kraal. The shell exploded near a Zulu war doctor who was engaged in a ritual to protect Sihayo's property. The man was cut cleanly in two. The British had fired at random, but the Zulus were convinced that the shell was aimed at the war doctor and were decidedly impressed.[2]

As soon as the firing began, Hamilton-Browne's native troops, who had been singing war songs and brandishing their spears, headed smartly for the rear. They were intercepted and herded back toward the fighting by several hundred men of the 24th, who had their bayonets fixed. Only the three hundred Zulu allies showed any zest for combat. They, along with some of the white officers and NCOs, had a brief but bloody hand-to-hand encounter with Sihayo's men. Zulu stabbed Zulu with spears, shouting something that sounded to Maori Browne like "gussie" as they speared an opponent. One of Hamilton-Browne's Zulus fell at the feet of a British officer named Harford. The man had an enormous spear wound in his back that almost cut him in half. The wounded Zulu was in terrible agony, and Harford thought briefly about shooting the man to put him out of his misery but decided against it.

In many ways, Harford was perfect for this first, so innocent, battle. At the time of the battle, Lieutenant Henry Charles Harford was twenty-seven years old. He was at least as interested in insects and birds as he was in battles or military honors, and yet he was always a reliable officer who sometimes performed acts of exceptional bravery. As much as any of the British officers, he was a paradox. He was born in England to a family of the landed gentry. When Charles was twelve years old, his father retired from the 12th Lancers as a captain to move to Natal, where he became, at least for a while, a successful tobacco farmer. Charlie, as the boy was known to his teenage friends, grew up in the outdoors, riding, camping, hunting, and developing his interests as a naturalist. He learned to speak Zulu by playing with Zulu children and with the sons of Natal whites who also spoke Zulu. He seems to have been blissfully happy as a boy, yet in 1870, at the age of eighteen, he inexplicably left Natal for England to pursue a career as a soldier. He was granted a commission in a good regiment, the 99th. He may have joined the army to please his father, but he was anything but an indifferent officer. In fact, he quickly became the regiment's adjutant. When war with the Zulus became imminent, he resigned from his regiment to seek duty in Natal. His fluent Zulu got him a position as a staff officer in the Natal Native Contingent with the temporary rank of captain.

The fight at Sihayo's kraal was Harford's first experience of combat. The battle began as little more than long-range sniping, but as Zulu rifle fire grew heavier, Harford gave his commander, Maori Browne, a scare when he dropped to his hands and knees. Hamilton-Browne tells the story:

> Well we were in rather a hot corner and he [Harford] was standing to my right rear when I heard an exclamation, and turning round saw him lying on the ground having dropped his sword and revolver. "Good God, Harford," I said, "you are hit!" "No, sir," he replied, "not hit but I have caught such a beauty." And there the lunatic, in his first action, and under heavy fire, his qualms of nervousness all forgotten, had captured some infernal microbe or other, and was blowing its wings out, as unconscious of the bullets striking the rocks all round him as if he had been in his garden at home. He was just expatiating on his victory and reeling off Latin names—they might have been Hebrew for I knew or cared—when I stopped him, and told him to get as quick as he could to the right flanking company and hurry them up. He looked at me with sorrow, put his prize into a tin box and was off like a shot.[3]

At that point, Hamilton-Browne couldn't have been blamed for writing Harford off as hopeless, but as the Zulu fire increased, Harford developed a lively interest in the battle. First, when he observed a Zulu sniper taking dead aim at Colonel Glyn, the aging, diminutive commanding officer of the 24th, he shouted and hustled the colonel out of harm's way. As he did so, a bullet just missed his own head. He was not at all alarmed. Instead, he was amused by his good "luck," as he put it in his journal. Apparently he had no concern that his luck might run out, for a few minutes later he launched a one-man attack on a group of Zulu riflemen who were firing on the British from a cave halfway up a steep cliff. Rifle fire by soldiers of the 24th had failed to dislodge the Zulus, so Harford ordered a white colonial corporal to follow him and clambered up the cliff to deal with the problem. To appreciate what Harford was about to do, you must understand that it was hardly his problem alone. The Zulus in the cave had been exchanging fire with elements of the 24th Regiment for some time, and there were hundreds of British soldiers in the immediate vicinity, not to mention dozens of officers, any one of whom could have taken it upon himself to silence the Zulu snipers or could have ordered someone else to do so.

For whatever reason, Harford took the war into his own hands, and as soldiers and officers alike watched (Lord Chelmsford and Major Clery, Glyn's adjutant, later told Harford that they'd been watching him and offered congratulations), he began to climb up the rocky slope. Harford's luck was remarkable. As he climbed over a boulder, a Zulu shoved his rifle right into Harford's face and pulled the trigger. The gun misfired, and the Zulu scrambled away. At point-blank range, Harford, who was a hopeless marksman, emptied his revolver at the man, managing to inflict one minor wound with his six shots. As Harford tried to reload, his revolver jammed and he threw the gun away. He turned to borrow a revolver from the corporal he thought was right behind him only to discover that the man had lagged far behind. Disgusted, Harford went back, only to hear the corporal shout at the top of his voice, "Captain Harford is killed!" Assuring the man that he was alive and cursing him soundly in the bargain, Harford grabbed the corporal's revolver and once more climbed back up toward the cave. First he shouted in Zulu for the snipers to surrender. Startled to hear his own language, one Zulu did so, but the others declined Harford's offer, so Harford marched into the cave, "although I must say I had some slight misgivings."[4] Somehow, Harford captured four armed Zulus and took them back down for safekeeping. A few days later, he performed a similarly suicidal feat, crawling into a rocky cleft to kill two Zulu snipers who were firing down on British troops and to capture another. Once again, there were hundreds of men who could have taken action, but the only man who did was Charlie Harford, the beetle-collector who couldn't shoot straight.

The firing at Sihayo's kraal began to taper off, but, before the action ended, a Zulu managed to throw a stone that struck the Scottish Major (later, Major General Sir) Wilsone Black in the testicles. Black fell to his knees in pain, swearing so loudly and ferociously in Gaelic that several British officers who witnessed the "wound" howled with laughter. It was a fitting end to this frolicsome fracas. Twelve Zulu bodies were found, and some others may have been carried away by their comrades. Two Zulus on the British side had been killed, and eighteen members of Hamilton-Browne's native battalion had been wounded, including a white lieutenant and two white NCOs. (One of them was a Swiss corporal named Schiess, from whom we'll hear again.) The British burned Sihayo's homestead and took about five hundred head of cattle. They were delighted to discover that among the Zulu dead was Sihayo's son Nkubikazulu, named in the British complaint that Frere used to justify the invasion.

The British officers were enormously pleased with themselves. They were mildly annoyed that the Natal native troops had proved so unreliable, but not much had been expected of them anyway. All in all, it had been a splendid little fight. They'd taught Sihayo a lesson, and the vaunted Zulu warriors had been no more formidable than the laughable "kaffirs." The British had been overconfident beforehand. Now they were supremely sure of themselves.[5] Chelmsford was so pleased that he ordered two wounded Zulu prisoners released as soon as they were well enough so that the Zulu people would see how the British made war.

## VICTORY HILL

The next battle was fought on a much larger scale, but it did nothing to lessen British confidence. Early on the morning of January 22 there was another battle at a place near the coast that the Zulus called Ombane, which meant Victory Hill. The army that Cetshwayo sent to meet the British there was led by Umatyiya, a man of sixty or so, and several local chiefs, principally Gogide. The Zulu army numbered about six thousand men, but they were *not* Cetshwayo's finest. Two of the five Zulu regiments were almost as old as their leader; they contained men who were fifty-five years old. Another seven hundred or so men came from the Tonga, a coastal people who were neither Zulu nor warlike. The three remaining regiments were filled with warriors who were 35–40 years old. Still, the Zulus outnumbered the British more than 2 to 1, and they were waiting in their classical formation. Once the British blundered into the chest, the horns would surround them.

The British force consisted of almost five thousand men, including two battalions of Imperial infantry. The British commander was Colonel Charles Knight Pearson, a good fifteen years junior to his Zulu adversary, but an experienced soldier who had served with the 3d Regiment, the famous "Buffs" (so named because of the buff-colored cuffs, shoulder flaps, and collars on their scarlet tunics), since entering the army. He was now colonel of the regiment. Early in the morning of January 22, half of Pearson's force was having breakfast in an area of very thick brush some 20 miles inside Zululand. The remainder of Pearson's force was trailing behind him by nearly a day's march, but he had 2,400 men, including colonial cavalry; a Naval brigade of two hundred men; a Royal Artillery battery with cannon, rockets, and a Gatling gun; the inevitable Natal Native Contingent; and, most important, five companies of "Buffs."

Pearson's column, slowed by fifty heavily loaded wagons, was spread out over miles of trail. Worried that the almost impenetrably thick brush might conceal Zulus, Pearson sent a detachment of native cavalry ahead. The cavalry blundered into the Zulu left horn, which abruptly left its position of ambush and began a precipitous attack. The rest of the Zulus followed. Pearson reacted quickly. His cannon, Gatling gun, and nearly a thousand rifles caught the Zulus while they were still maneuvering in columns. Many were killed. Even so, the left wing deployed rapidly and in perfect formation. But the right wing became entangled in brush so thick that the Zulus could barely make their way through it. All the while, the British were firing furiously. The fight lasted an hour and a half.

It is not a battle that history has celebrated. The Zulus charged before the British were close enough to be enveloped, the older regiments did not charge at all, and the younger regiments did not always charge with reckless abandon. British fire stopped the Zulus' charge cold; their lines bent and then stopped. Even so, the Zulus were obviously not the pushovers many of the British soldiers had expected. The British rifles fired many thousands of rounds, their cannon fired sixty-five shrapnel shells, and their Gatling gun, which fired seven hundred rounds per minute, blazed away. Still, the Zulus held their positions around the British and returned fire for ninety minutes. The British tried to drive them back by firing 24-pound rockets, which roared and blazed through the air before they exploded with a very loud bang. Those rockets had demoralized Africans in earlier colonial wars, but as a British artillery officer commented with surprise, the Zulus showed the "utmost contempt for them."[6] Ninety minutes is a very long time to stand up to intense fire, but the Zulus stood until the British charged them with fixed bayonets. Men of the Buffs and the Naval Brigade charged, with the "Jack Tars" well ahead of the soldiers. A Zulu prisoner said that those "ferocious men in their white pants" (the sailors wore white duck trousers) broke the Zulus' will with their utterly fearless attack.[7] The Zulus retreated.

The British displayed arrogant self-confidence and courage. The Buffs and the sailors fought with discipline, and so high was their morale that they were eager to fight the Zulus hand to hand. The African allies of the Natal Native Contingent ran away, as usual, leaving five of their white officers to the Zulus, who, according to a British sergeant, stabbed them "cruelly . . . in twenty or thirty places."[8] Even though the Zulus were clearly not at their best in this battle, the British were surprised and impressed. Sergeant J. W. Burnett of the 99th, who had nothing but scorn for the Natal "kaffirs" who left their white officers to die, had this to say about the Zulus: "I never thought niggers would make such a stand. They came on with an utter disregard of danger."[9] Lieutenant Courtenay, a cavalryman of the 20th Hussars who was attached to a colonial mounted unit, was impressed too. He pursued the retreating Zulus and took some of them prisoner: "They were fine-looking intelligent fellows, and talked and laughed with the men when they gave them food." Courtenay didn't think much of Zulu marksmenship—neither did anyone else—but he admired their fighting qualities: "They move very fast, and charge in large bodies with the greatest determination and courage."[10] Other Zulus thought that the warriors who fought at Victory Hill were anything but impressive. As Meklokazulu, Sihayo's son, who was an officer with the Zulu left horn at Islandlwana, said, "We do not know how it is the Coast Zulus did not fight better. We looked down on them, and complained that they fought so badly."[11]

The Zulus fought much more bravely than Mehlokazulu thought. Zulus who fought in the battle told the border agent Eustace Fannin that they were greatly impressed by the discipline of the British troops and by their appallingly destructive fire.[12] A warrior who had fought in the front ranks said, "The whites shot us down in numbers, in some places our dead and wounded covered the ground, we lost heavily."[13] A forty-year-old induna from the same *uMhapho* regiment told his story years later:

> "We were told to advance and, grasping our [weapons], we went forward packed close together like a lot of bees . . . we were still far away from them when the white men began to throw their bullets at us, but we could not shoot at them because our rifles would not shoot so far. . . . As we advanced we had our rifles under our arms

> and had our assegais in our right hands ready to throw them, but they were not much good for we never got near enough to use them. We never got nearer than 50 paces to the English, and although we tried to climb over our fallen brothers we could not get very far ahead because the white men were firing heavily. . . . The battle was so fierce that we had to wipe the blood and brains of the killed and wounded from our heads, faces, arms, legs and shields after the fighting."[14]

The Zulus were surprised that the British did not pursue them farther. Retreat to the Zulus meant defeat and wholesale slaughter. No one counted all the Zulu bodies. With the thick cover of brush, many could be not seen, but a British sergeant counted 390 Zulu bodies. A number of guns were recovered. They were obsolete muzzle-loaders. British losses were ten killed and sixteen wounded, all by long-distance rifle fire. Impressed by the Zulus but still very pleased with themselves, Pearson's men marched deeper into Zululand. Only a few hours later, other British troops would learn more about Zulu warriors, including how they reacted when their enemy retreated.

## ISANDLWANA

On January 17, after three days of ritual protection at the king's kraal, Cetshwayo's regiments were ready, and he told his commanders what he wanted. The venerable warrior Tshingwayo, who was no less than seventy years old but still physically fit, would command the main force of about 20,000 men. Tshingwayo was told to march slowly so as not to tire his men and to attack Chelmsford's column, but he was not to attack a fortified position. He was also instructed not to invade Natal. Before attacking the invading British troops, he was to attempt to negotiate a peaceful settlement. The king's strategy continued to be entirely defensive. In addition to the force he sent to defend against Colonel Pearson's advance nearer the coast, Cetshwayo asked local chiefs to use their men to screen Colonel Wood's western column until more men could be spared to deal with them. Wood's forces easily scattered those local troops. Despite the threat of the British invasion, when the Zulu regiments left the king's kraal, a sizable proportion of the Zulu army had not yet reported for duty.

While the Zulu army was moving slowly toward Isandlwana, Chelmsford was considering his options. He had no fear of a Zulu attack; he longed for one. When he had commanded the British forces against the "kaffirs" in 1877–78, he had seen at first hand how volleys of British rifle fire could destroy a native attack no matter how bravely it was pressed home. He even ordered his artillery not to open fire until the Zulus were within 600 yards in order not to "scare them away."[15] Unlike Cetshwayo's, Chelmsford's strategy was offensive. He would be delighted if the Zulus were to attack, as virtually everyone told him they would, but he did not believe the Zulus would dare to attack, so he actively looked for the Zulu forces, planning to attack *them*. Chelmsford had personally scouted ahead of his troops, and it was he who chose the campsite at Isandlwana. On January 20, he ordered his column to march through the mud of the Bashee Valley and camp at Isandlwana. Isandlwana was the tongue-twisting Zulu name for a massive rocky butte that the British troops of the 24th Regiment thought looked like the Sphinx badge they wore on the green uniform collars of their scarlet tunics. Isandlwana, the sphinx, was only 7 miles as the crow flies inside Zululand.

As Commandant "Maori" Browne led his Natal Native Contingent toward Isandlwana, he was almost ambushed by at least 1,500 Zulus, who were hidden in a deep gully. These men were the retainers of a local chief named Matshana. Hamilton-Browne's own Zulu troops spotted the ambush in time to give warning, and Hamilton-Browne's men reached the camp at Isandlwana without a fight. Soon large canvas tents were set up for the British troops, and the men settled down. The African soldiers camped separately. The camp slowly consolidated as wagons rolled in, along with herds of cattle to be slaughtered for beef. As the British officers examined the camp, which spread over three-quarters of mile, most of them liked it because it was on a slight elevation overlooking a great plain. If the Zulus were to attack—as few expected—they could be seen for at least fifteen to twenty minutes before they could come to grips with the British army. By then, everyone believed, British firepower would have slaughtered them. Their commander, General Lord Chelmsford, did not order the camp fortified. He did not have experienced wagon drivers, and it could have taken all night to unhitch the two hundred teams of oxen and mules and to manhandle the one-ton, 18-foot-long wagons into a huge circular barrier. Lord Chelmsford meant to keep moving, and by the time a laager, as the Boers called it, had been formed, it would have been time to break camp, hitch up the wagons, and move on to the next campsite. Or so he later said. He had been warned that it was foolhardy not to laager every camp, and his adjutant, Colonel Bellairs, had issued a general order to all officers to do so. But Chelmsford chose not to laager. Chelms-

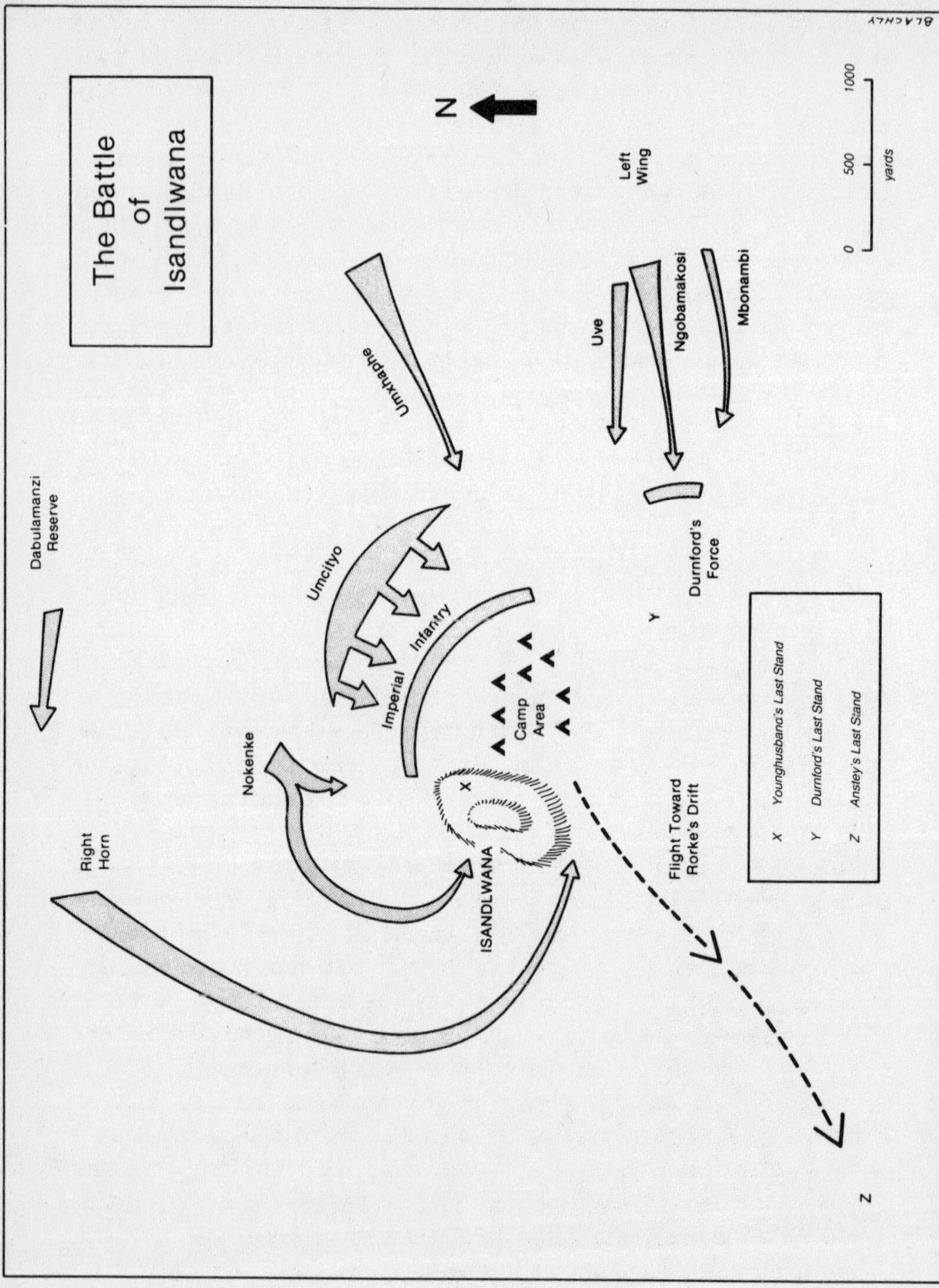
The Battle of Isandlwana
N
0
500
1000
yards
Dabulamanzi Reserve
Umxhaphe
Left Wing
Uve
Ngobamakosi
Mbonambi
Umcityo
Imperial Infantry
Durnford's Force
Camp Area
Nokenke
Right Horn
ISANDLWANA
Flight Toward Rorke's Drift
X Younghusband's Last Stand
Y Durnford's Last Stand
Z Anstey's Last Stand
BLACHLY

ford had not laagered his previous camps in Zululand, and when an officer asked him if he wanted to laager the camp at Isandlwana, Chelmsford dismissed him, saying, "It would take a week."[16]

Chelmsford's army was so large that laagering every night the way smaller Boer "commandos" or American pioneers did would have been difficult. In the camp that first night were 1,300 white soldiers and 2,500 Africans. There were also several hundred wagon drivers, not to mention 1,507 oxen, 49 horses, and 67 mules. In campaigns like this, generals had to move fast and take risks. The ground at Isandlwana was too hard and rocky to allow the digging of trenches, and there were no thorn bushes available for a fence. It was enough, most of Chelmsford's officers felt, to surround the camp with pickets and send bands of horsemen off to scout distant hills. If the Zulus were foolish enough to attack, the Imperial infantry would have plenty of time to form themselves into squares, and no men—least of all black "savages"—could stand against the concentrated fire-power of their rifles.[17]

Many of the colonial volunteer officers had been upset when General Chelmsford failed to laager his previous camps, but then at least there had been no sign of Zulu warriors. Now, in addition to Matshana's 1,500 men, scouts reported seeing many small groups of armed Zulus to the north and east of Isandlwana, and some of the spies that Chelmsford had sent to Ulundi had returned with the news that the main Zulu army had left Ulundi on January 19 with orders to attack Chelmsford's column. Chelmsford was unconcerned, but his colonial officers were alarmed. Thirty-one-year-old Captain Rubert de la Tour Lonsdale was in command of the Natal Native Contingent attached to Chelmsford's column. A former officer in the Black Watch Regiment who had fought in West Africa and in the Ninth Frontier War, Lonsdale was horrified that once again nothing was done to fortify the camp. According to Hamilton-Browne, Lonsdale said to him: " 'My God, Maori, what do you think of this camp?' I replied, 'Someone is mad.' The Colonial officers were loud and long in complaint. Duncombe, the translator, said, 'Do the staff think we are going to meet an army of school-girls? Why in the name of all that is holy do we not laager?' "[18] Another officer, F. L. Phillips of the Natal Mounted Police, felt so strongly about entrenching the camp against a Zulu attack that he complained to Colonel Crealock, Chelmsford's military secretary. Chelmsford sent back a scathing reply: "Tell the police officer my troops will do all the attacking."[19]

Dinner for the British officers that night was a merry affair, with much drinking, joking, and storytelling. Zulu scouts had watched the British forces march to Isandlwana. It would have been difficult not to see them and hear them with their drums, bugles, and random shooting. A few hours before Chelmsford's men left the camp, an audacious Zulu military leader named Zibhebdu walked and crawled unseen through the entire British camp. He heard men laughing in their tents, although he could not understand what they said. But it was obvious that the camp was not fortified.

When morning came on January 21, all was well. The pickets around the camp had passed a peaceful night, and the many mounted men sent out to search for the Zulu army had reported nothing terribly alarming. Later in the day some of these horsemen reported contact with small numbers of Zulus, and Lord Chelmsford sent the Natal Native Contingent, including Lonsdale, Hamilton-Browne, and Harford, 10 miles out of camp to the southeast. When they made contact with Zulus they were not ordered back to the camp but were told to remain where they were, even though they had no food or blankets. They spent a cold, sleepless, and panicky night of January 21 waiting to be overwhelmed by Zulus. Several Zulus who were taken captive during the day had said that the Zulu army was approaching from the northeast, not the southeast, but before dawn on the morning of January 22 Chelmsford assembled half the men in his command and marched off to the southeast to support Lonsdale and his native troops. If Chelmsford had not been so overconfident, he would have recalled those men to the camp. Instead, he marched off to join them. The senior officer left in camp, the 5′5″ Brevet Lieutenant-Colonel Henry B. Pulleine, was a jovial man and a formidable whist player, but he had never commanded troops in combat. Chelmsford was obviously not concerned about Pulleine. He marched away without even leaving Pulleine any orders. Major Clery, one of the staff officers who left camp with Chelmsford, hastily scribbled a note directing Pulleine to defend the camp and another ordering Colonel Durnford to bring his forces from Natal to the camp and to "support" Chelmsford.

As Chelmsford was marching out of camp, the Zulu army was asleep in a valley about 6 miles to the north. They had scouted the camp for two days, but they were not preparing to attack on the twenty-second. On that day, the moon was "dead" and war was not propitious. Instead they planned to send peace delegates to talk to the British. On the next day, January 23, there would be a new moon, and if necessary the Zulu army would attack, physically refreshed and ritually prepared. As daybreak came on the twenty-second, the Zulu army was beginning to stir, waiting for the herds of cattle and sheep that were being rounded up to feed its more than 20,000 men. The men had slept on mats carried for them by their udibi boys. The area around Isandlwana was 4,000 feet in elevation, and even summer nights were very cold, with a dew so heavy that it was like mist. Most of the men had found some food at kraals along their march, but they were hungry this morning, and many young men were sent out to find cattle and drive them to the army for slaughter. Cold and hungry, the sun not high enough to warm them, the Zulu army waited, and its leaders tried to choose peace delegates.[20]

British patrols had seen several parties of Zulu scouts on the previous day, and Zulu fires had burned on the hills around Isandlwana the night before. This morning, as Chelmsford marched away from camp, more mounted patrols led by white colonial officers resumed their vigil. A patrol led by Lieutenant Charles Raw pursued some Zulus who were driving a herd of cattle to the north. The cattle disappeared into a ravine, and the patrol peered cautiously down into a deep, steep-sided valley. A hundred feet below, in total silence, as far as the eye could see, sat Zulu warriors. The patrol fired a single volley and rodc back pell-mell to warn the camp. Almost in unison, more than 20,000 Zulus climbed out of the ravine and began trotting toward the British camp almost 6 miles away. All thoughts of peace gone, their officers trotted with them, trying to sort out their regiments, making certain that the two horns took the correct angle of attack and that the men of the chest did not attack before horns were ready. Regiments of very young men with their black shields ran alongside regiments that had men in their fifties, their shields almost all white. Their recent boasts and challenges to older regiments drove the younger men on, and their officers tried to slow them. The older regiments moved more slowly. They were ready to fight, but as several men of these older regiments admitted after the battle, unlike the young warriors they did not expect to defeat the British.

At mid-morning, while the British troops in the camp waited expecting another false alarm, reinforcements arrived from Natal in the form of Colonel Durnford's Natal Native Horse. Lieutenant Colonel Anthony W. Durnford was another Anglo-Irish soldier from a military family. He had defied Army tradition by marrying while he was a young lieutenant, but his wife scandalously began to take lovers (perhaps because Durnford was a compulsive gambler who neglected her). Because Army officers were not permitted to divorce, Durnford's wife was sent home to England while he went to South Africa. There he had an unrequited, but passionate nonetheless, love affair with Fanny Colenso, the daughter of the Bishop of Natal. He had served in South Africa for seven years, losing the use of his left arm to a spear thrust. He was a kind and considerate commander, and his African troops were fiercely loyal to him. Durnford was intelligent and as brave in battle as any man, but he was rash, always charging off in search of action, and he craved independent command to the point of insubordination. Chelmsford had already sent him one harsh rebuke on that score. Durnford's men were 250 cavalry and three hundred infantry. One hundred of the horsemen were Basutos, and the rest were from the Ngwane tribe. They were disciplined and experienced soldiers, each armed with a modern rifle. Durnford outranked the camp commander, Lieutenant Colonel Pulleine, and when he arrived at about 10:30 he took command of the camp.[21]

The arrival of Chelmsford's orders had interrupted Durnford's morning meal, so still wearing his mess jacket, he joined Pulleine in his tent and was served breakfast. Durnford's orders were to support Chelmsford, who was 10 miles or so away to the east, but Pulleine's orders were to defend the camp. The two officers discussed the situation, trying to reconcile conflicting reports about the Zulus' movements. After about an hour, at 11:30, a report was received that the Zulus were moving away from camp toward Chelmsford. Thus far Durnford had done nothing rash, and his decision now to move out of camp to support Chelmsford's flank was entirely reasonable. His orders were to support Chelmsford. Durnford marched his more than five hundred men several miles to the northeast of the camp to engage what later turned out to be the leading elements of the Zulu army's left horn. Before leaving, Durnford asked Pulleine for some men of the 24th to support him. Only when the Pulleine's brash adjutant, Lieutenant Teignmouth Melvill, reminded both senior officers that Pulleine's orders were to defend the camp, did Durnford agree to leave the British infantry behind, but he told Pulleine to support him if he got into trouble. The redcoated infantry snatched breakfast while waiting for the Zulu forces to appear.

When the chest of the Zulu army was seen later in the morning, Pulleine did not order the British infantry to take up a tight defensive position around the camp. He sent them *toward* the Zulus, to take up an extended semicircular line more than a mile north of the camp to support Durnford's men, who were firing effectively on the extreme right. There was a gap of several hundred yards between the British infantry and Durnford's men on their right flank. What is more, the British left flank was completely undefended, and there was no organized reserve behind them. The tents and wagons of the camp had been left undefended. There were perhaps two hundred men, half of them white, still in camp, but they were not organized into fighting units. Some were not even armed. Somehow, everyone in command seemed to have forgotten everything they had ever been told about Zulu tactics. Almost

A half century before the battle of Isandlwana, a Zulu king, Shaka, had created a highly disciplined military force that used new weapons and tactics to build an empire the size of the state of Georgia. Warriors like the two above, pictured just before the war in 1879, killed 52 British officers and 806 red-coated soldiers: one of the most shocking defeats in British military history. *(Killie Campbell Africana Library, Durban)*

The Zulu king, Cetshwayo, had done nothing to bring the war about and had, in fact, done everything in his power to avoid it. In his words, he felt like a man trying to "ward off a falling tree." *(National Army Museum)*

The British plan to destroy the Zulu Empire was devised by Sir Bartle Frere (upper left, *National Portrait Gallery, London*). When the British suffered disastrous defeat in the war's first great battle, Frere blamed Colonel Anthony Durnford (upper right).

Below: The British were commanded by General Lord Chelmsford, pictured with his staff just before the British invasion in January 1879. Seated to his left is Lieutenant-Colonel John North Crealock; standing at Chelmsford's left shoulder is Lieutenant A. Berkeley Milne. Chelmsford and his troops were supremely confident. *(Killie Campbell Africana Library)*

General Chelmsford was so overconfident, his primary concern was that the Zulus would run away before the massed fire of his rifles and cannon could destroy them. But he was also worried about the difficulties of transporting his ammunition and supplies through roadless Zululand by heavily loaded wagons across rivers and ravines. *(Local History Museum, Durban)*

After delays caused by the terrain and heavy rain, General Chelmsford's column camped under a rocky butte called Isandlwana. Despite warnings from all sides that he should encircle the camp with his heavy wagons, Chelmsford dismissed the idea as impractical. *(National Army Museum, London)*

The scene after the battle at Isandlwana shocked Chelmsford's men when they returned after the fighting. More than 850 white men lay dead on their backs, their stomachs slit open by razor-sharp spears. Tents and wagons had been burned; the battlefield was strewn with everything a British army carried into battle—whiskey bottles, armchairs, writing desks, canned meat, money, photographs, letters, and cricket pads. *(National Army Museum)*

Fifty survivors of the battle at Rorke's Drift are pictured here along with their officer, Lieutenant Gonville Bromhead and his dog, Pip. These men were the survivors from the 24th Regiment where their comrades died at Isandlwana. *(Local History Museum, Durban)*

The day after the battle at Isandlwana, a Zulu force of 4,000 men led by Prince Dabulamanzi, pictured here before the battle (*Local History Museum, Durban*) attacked a British supply depot at Rorke's Drift.

Lieutenant Teignmouth Melvill (left, *National Army Museum*) rode away from the doomed British army at Isandlwana in a desperate attempt to save the British battle flag. When Melvill was unhorsed, Lieutenant Neville Coghill (middle, *Local History Museum, Durban*) rode back to help him. Both men were killed. In the war's next battle at Myer's Drift, the British were defeated again. Taken by surprise, the British commander and most of his men were killed. Sergeant Anthony Booth (right), pictured after the battle, won the Victoria Cross (Britain's highest award for Valour) for rallying the survivors. *(National Army Museum)*

Thanks to the leadership of officers like Colonel Evelyn Wood (top left, *National Army Museum*), whose men won the important battle of Kambula, and the fighting spirit of men like Commandant "Maori" Hamilton-Browne (right, *Werner Laurie*), along with better tactics and superior weapons, the British eventually dominated the fighting.

At Rorke's Drift, the Zulus hurled themselves at the British position for ten hours; they left 1,000 of their dead on the battlefield, many of them piled on top of one another. Eleven British officers and men were awarded the Victoria Cross, more than were awarded in any single battle before or since. *(The Defense of Rorke's Drift,* by W. H. Dugan, *The South Wales Borderers and Monmouthshire Regimental Museum)*

In later battles, the British fortified their camps and fought shoulder-to-shoulder as pictured (above) at the battle of Gingindhlovu. After this battle, like others, the British pursued the retreating Zulus, killing everyone, including the wounded, without quarter. The Zulu prisoners shown after the battle (below) were among the very few taken throughout the war. *(Local History Museum, Durban)*

The war's final battle (above) was fought at Ulundi, where the British, shown in their huge square formation, their cavalry within the square, inflicted terrible losses on the Zulus. After the battle, the Zulu army dispersed and King Cetshwayo was captured. King Cetshwayo (below), shown in captivity in Cape Town, eventually convinced the British to allow him to return to Zululand, which was by then in the grip of a civil war. He died in 1884, probably poisoned by a rival. A few months later Sir Bartle Frere died.

everyone, that is. Lieutenant Melvill was one of the few officers aware of the danger of the British position; he wanted the British infantry to fight "shoulder to shoulder," but his concern was not enough to persuade Pulleine to pull back his men.

Melvill was worried, but the veteran soldiers of the 24th were not. They were in high spirits. They had destroyed the attacks of "kaffirs" a year earlier without the loss of a single man, and only ten days earlier they had enjoyed "potting" some Zulus at Sihayo's kraal. Now they saw a chance to pot a great many more. Although they had to leave their breakfasts behind, they were joking as they took up their positions. Five hours after Chelmsford and his troops left the camp under the sphinx, a rider gave Chelmsford a vague message from Pulleine to the effect that the camp was under attack but the Zulus were "withdrawing." Curious, but not overly concerned, Chelmsford asked a Navy officer serving as an aide to take his powerful telescope, climb a tree, and have a look at the camp. The aide, Lieutenant Berkeley Milne (who became an important admiral in World War I), said that everything appeared to be in order. When Chelmsford's military secretary, Lieutenant Colonel Crealock, was told about the message, he said in his usual flippant manner what Chelmsford himself must have thought: "How very amusing! Actually attacking our camp—most amusing!"[22] Chelmsford's troops marched on.

The British infantry watched the Zulus approach, a dark mass against the distant green hills. One of the transport officers in the camp was a twenty-year-old lieutenant named Horace Smith-Dorrien. As a general, he played a central role in the early stages of World War I. He wrote that "the Zulus were seen coming over the hills in thousands. They were in most perfect order, and seemed to be in about twenty rows of skirmishers one behind the other."[23] Other British transport officers joined Smith-Dorrien in watching the Zulu advance. Instead of shouting war cries as the British expected them to do, the Zulus made what the British characterized as a "buzzing sound"; it was more a hiss (*zhi, zhi, zhi*) than a buzz, and it was meant to convey menace and triumph. The Zulus surprised the British again when, instead of increasing the pace of their advance, they slowed and opened a heavy rifle fire against the British troops. As Smith-Dorrien put it. "The Zulus nearly all had firearms of some kind and lots of ammunition."[24]

Although the British troops were surprised by the volume of Zulu rifle fire, they were not alarmed. The Zulu fire was high, and the British veterans quickly returned it. Lying down or kneeling, some behind rocks, at their officers' orders they sent volley after volley into the massed

Zulu ranks. Several British transport officers who survived the battle, having no specific duties once the fighting started, were up with the infantry at that point and remarked on the men's light spirits. The infantrymen were having a grand time, laughing and making jokes about their shooting. And not without reason, because the Zulu lines were staggered by the British fire. The two British cannon did little damage; they were firing high, and the Zulus easily ducked under the projectiles shouting *umoja*—wind. But even without counting the large Natal contingent, some of whom were also up on the line firing at the Zulus, there were at least 1,300 well-aimed rifles firing volleys into their ranks. A few hours earlier, the Zulu warriors who opposed Pearson's men had been shattered by similar fire power, and so were these Zulus, who, unlike the men who fought against Pearson, were the best the Zulu army had to offer. Zulu survivors recalled men "tumbling" over upon one another, driven backward by the impact of the heavy .45 caliber British bullets. The Zulus lay down to escape the bullets, crawled forward, then rose to rush ahead and take fearful casualties again. Zulu bodies began to pile up like "peppercorns," as one observer put it. Some regiments of the Zulu chest even began to withdraw. At least one large body of Zulus retreated over a ridge to safety.

British fire power had so completely stopped the chest of the Zulu attack that British officers ordered their men to cease fire. The soldiers laughed again, congratulating each other on their shooting. They had "potted" more Zulus than they could count. Zulu bodies lay in black lumps all across the grassy slope in front of the British line. The lull lasted ten to fifteen minutes. The camp was calm. In addition to the native soldiers held more or less as a reserve and the assorted wagon drivers, cooks, bandsmen, orderlies, doctors, and quartermasters, there were substantial numbers of redcoats from the 2d Battalion of the 24th and Royal Artillerymen. Some of those men were loading wagons that Chelmsford had ordered sent to him, and others were opening ammunition boxes. A few officers were in camp as well: Melvill, Cochrane, Coghill, Smith-Dorrien, and Gardner, among others. Except for Melvill, they did not seem unduly concerned about the progress of the battle.[25] Neither was Pulleine. He had ample time during the lull to recall his scattered troops and form them into a tight square with his ammunition and his wounded in the center, but despite Melvill's warnings he did nothing. It is possible that the Zulu officers allowed the chest to slow its attack to allow time for the horns to encircle the British. If so, after ten or fifteen minutes, they had waited long enough. An officer of one regiment leaped to his feet and shouted insults at his men, reminding them of their boasts before the battle. "Why are you lying down? What was it you said to the umCityo [their rival regiment]? There are the umCityo going into the tents."[26] That officer, named Mkhosana, deliberately exposed himself to British fire and was quickly shot dead, but his men rose and charged, and at the same time the horns burst into the undefended camp area.

Despite the shouted commands of its tall, aristocratic-looking leader, Sigwelewele, the left horn had been pinned down by the fire of Durnford's men, who held a strong position. Although the British infantry companies were apparently adequately resupplied with ammunition, when Durnford's Africans ran low, the quartermaster denied them a resupply on the grounds that the ammunition belonged solely to the 24th.[27] Down to their last rounds, Durnford's men slowed their fire and then wavered. Now, as Hamilton-Browne watched through his binoculars from a hill a few miles to the east, he saw the Zulus drive a herd of cattle ahead of them and break through Durnford's men in a rising cloud of dust and smoke. Durnford's men were pushed aside and, at the same time, the Zulu right horn spilled down a slope into the tent area, stabbing everyone they met, orderlies, wagon drivers, grooms, surgeons, and hundreds of Natal native troops, who fled in panic down what came to be known as "fugitives' road" to the south. When officers of the infantry companies saw the disaster in their rear, they ordered buglers to sound retreat. The redcoats withdrew, firing as they went. As soon as the redcoats began retreating, the Zulus of the chest rose with a cry of "usutu," and for the first time they charged recklessly, sprinting forward toward the camp. Some British soldiers were shot down or stabbed, but others formed up into small squares and held their ground. For unexplained reasons, some of the British infantry appear to have left their bayonets in their tents, and others had no time to fix bayonets, but two large groups of infantrymen formed squares and fixed their bayonets.

More and more Zulus swarmed into the dust-covered British camp. Horses, mules, and oxen struggled to get free as the Zulus charged. Their regiments intermingled, men with a single red feather in their headdress fought next to others with white or blue feathers, or older men with polished headrings. A warrior from the left horn recalled those terrible moments a few years after the battle. As he charged the camp he saw some mounted white men trying to escape:

> After that there was so much smoke that I could not see whether the white men had got through or not. The tumult and the firing was wonderful, every warrior shouted "Usutu!" as he killed anyone, and

> the sun got very dark like night [there was a partial eclipse of the sun]. The English fought long and hard; there were so many of our people in front of me that I did not get into the thick of the fight until the end.[28]

The British may have thought that the sudden darkness caused by the two-thirds eclipse was the end of the world. For most of them, it was. Strangely, the Zulus were not disturbed by the sudden darkness. With all the smoke and dust, some may not even have noticed.

Despite the confusion, the Zulus were finally able to fight as they had hoped to, with their short-handled stabbing spears. On the British side, some individuals in the camp area fought desperately, but many had no guns and most were no match for Zulu spears. Most of the men of the 24th did not break and run, and neither did a hard core of Durnford's men, but the other native soldiers ran for their lives, and so did British officers and men who were in the tent area when the Zulu horns began to close. Men who did not have horses had little hope. Some men tried to hide in tents, and others sat down with their hands over their eyes, but most of them ran or walked, firing when they could and one by one falling to Zulu spears or bullets. As the Zulus charged into the retreating six British infantry companies, a few of those men ran too, dying far away, singly or in small groups. No one got farther than 2 miles from the camp. There a group of redcoats with Lieutenant Edgar Anstey formed up and fought until they were killed. Think of it. *Only* 2 miles! Two miles of terror, exhaustion, and death, and then no men on foot were left alive. In photographs, Anstey was a handsome blond man who looked remarkably like General Custer whose last stand at the Little Big Horn has been so celebrated. Anstey's last stand has gone unnoticed.[29]

Many men who were able to find horses also tried to escape. Lieutenant Wallie Erskine of the Natal Native Contingent was wounded by a spear as he rode away. He pulled it out of his thigh and rode on, but when a Zulu jumped in front of his horse and shot at him Erskine was indignant: "Who the hell do you think you're firing at?" he shouted in Zulu. The warrior stared at the Zulu-speaking white man in amazement. Erskine remembered seeing a British infantryman in a red coat running for his life. A Zulu yelled at him, "Where are you going, white man?" and speared him in the back. As the man feebly attempted to pull the spear out, the Zulu rushed up, pulled the spear out and stabbed again, shouting "usutu!" Erskine remembered that the Zulu was left-handed.[30]

Four British transport officers—Smith-Dorrien, Essex, Cochrane, and Gardner—along with an artillery officer, Curling, managed to find their horses and shoot their way out through the Zulus. Later, Lieutenant W. F. B. Cochrane commented in a report on the bravery of the Zulus as they fought hand to hand. To Cochrane the Zulus seemed "perfectly fearless."[31] The ground near the camp was so rocky and cut up by gullies that horses could move only at a trot; Zulus ran alongside trying to stab the escaping men or pull them off their mounts. The British shot them at point-blank range. Along with the five Imperial officers, several colonial officers and NCOs escaped, and so did a handful of men from the 24th mounted infantry and bandsmen. Wounded men without horses pleaded with the mounted men for help. Curling saw Smith-Dorrien dismount to put a tourniquet on a wounded soldier's arm. Major Smith of the Royal Artillery rode up shouting at Smith-Dorrien that the Zulus were right behind. Smith and the private soldier were speared to death, but somehow Smith-Dorrien escaped. Standish Vereker, the third son of Lord Gort, was serving as a colonial officer with the Natal Native Contingent. He managed to find a horse and was riding out of camp when a native soldier in his regiment indicated that the horse belonged to him. Vereker dismounted and gave the man the horse. Trooper Charles Sparks of the Natal Mounted Police was riding out of camp next to a 6′6″ saddler named Pearce. Zulus were all around them yelling "kill the white men," when Pearce said "my oath" and turned his horse back toward the camp saying that he had to retrieve his regulation bit before his sergeant major saw him and gave him a "choking off." Pearce disappeared in the smoke and dust. Both he and his sergeant major were killed.

Most of the fleeing white men, including the Imperial officers, did not stop to help others. Lieutenant Curling remembered the pleas of the wounded as he passed them by. So did an unarmed interpreter, J. A. Brickhill, who could not find a weapon but did locate a horse. He saw the mounting panic:

> A simultaneous forward movement was now made by all the Zulus, and many of our mounted men who had ridden in for ammunition were closely followed in by them. Troops of all descriptions were now streaming through the various camps towards Rorke's Drift nek. Going down to the 1/24th camp, I saw Mr. Dubois, who asked me in Zulu how it looked. I replied, "Ugly." He said, "Yes; the enemy has scattered us this day." Above the 1/24th camp, I met my poor tent companion, Quartermaster Pullen, who shouted to the running soldiers, "Come on, men, rally here, follow me. Don't be running away like a parcel of women. Let's try and turn their flank." Men were running away everywhere. I could see no officers. I saw one of the field pieces brought to the corner of the camp. The men jumped

> off and took to their heels. Simultaneously with this, the only body of soldiers yet visible rose from firing their last shot and joined me in the general flight. Panic was everywhere and no officer to guide, no shelter to fall back upon.

Brickhill found a horse and joined the flight:

> Our stampede was composed of mules, with and without pack saddles, oxen and horses in all stages of equipment, and flying men, all strangely intermingled, man and beast, all apparently impressed with the danger which surrounded us. One riderless horse that came up alongside of me I caught and handed to a poor soldier who was struggling along on foot. But he had scarcely mounted before he was knocked off by a Zulu bullet. How one's heart soon steels itself against pity at such times! I came up with poor Band Sergeant Gamble, tottering and tumbling about amongst the stones. "For God's sake, give me a lift," he said. I replied, "My dear fellow, it's a case of life and death with me." Closing my eyes, I put spurs to my horse and bounded ahead and that was the last I saw of him. The next I came up with, also a soldier, said, "Well, I'm pumped. I'm done. The Zulus can just come and stab me, if they like," and quietly sat down on a stone to await his death.[32]

While the desperate individual struggles in the camp area and along the escape routes continued, at least three large groups of British soldiers formed into squares and held the Zulus off. Another group formed around Colonel Durnford. Despite the chaos, many of his African soldiers and white officers somehow found a way to rally to him. Instead of trying to escape on foot, Vereker fought his way back to Durnford on foot. Despite the fact that Durnford was wearing his mess waistcoat, he was as heroic in fact as Custer was in legend. Tall and commanding, Durnford was everywhere, encouraging his men as their square grew smaller, clearing jammed carbines with his one good hand, and roaring out his commands to fire in volleys.[33] Durnford's men stood together firing at his command until their ammunition was exhausted. Zulus remembered his voice screaming "fire." At the end, Durnford's men fought with hunting knives. A Zulu described it: "[T]hen they formed a line, shoulder to shoulder, and back to back, and fought with their knives."[34] They died together, Vereker close to Durnford.

As long as the other large groups of British infantrymen still had ammunition, the Zulus did not charge them. Later, when the ammunition failed, they closed in, and the British fought them with pistols, bayonets, and even pocket knives. A warrior named Kumbeka from the umCityo regiment recalled his part in the combat:

> At Isandlwana I myself only killed one man. Dum! Dum! went his revolver as he was firing from right to left, and I came beside him and stuck my assegai under his right arm, pushing it through his body until it came out between his ribs on the left side. As soon as he fell I pulled the assegai out and slit his stomach so I knew he should not shoot any more of my people.[35]

Zulus remembered a tall corporal who killed four Zulus with his bayonet before it became lodged in a fifth man, and he was killed. One Zulu described the fighting like this: "Some Zulus threw assegais at them, others shot at them; but they did not get close—they avoided the bayonet; for any man who sent up to stab a soldier was fixed through the throat or stomach, and at once fell. Occasionally when a soldier was engaged with a Zulu in front with an assegai, another Zulu killed him from behind."[36] A different Zulu said, "They were hard to kill; not one tried to escape."[37] After the war, a Zulu warrior recalled how amazed he was when some of the British soldiers actually began fighting with their fists.[38]

The soldiers of the 24th learned that war against the Zulus was not a lark. There were probably no jokes at the end. All of the officers and men of the 24th whom Chelmsford left in camp died. But they did not die easily. Even after their ammunition was gone, the Zulus were in no hurry to see who among them could boast of stabbing a "red soldier." No Zulu warrior said that any man among them saved the last bullet for himself. They fired their last bullets against the Zulus, and then they fought with whatever they had until they were killed. Captain Reginald Younghusband was one of the last to die. When his men's ammunition was gone, Younghusband was seen shaking hands with his men before he led them in a suicide charge into the waiting Zulus. A Zulu from the right horn remembered the sun flashing off Younghusband's sword. The Zulus did not face him hand to hand. Eventually he was shot from a distance. Sixty men of C Company died with him. Some of the Zulus said that the last men to die were two officers from the 2d Battalion, because both men fought until they were killed by thrown spears, and both men, the Zulus remembered, wore monocles. Others remembered a tall officer who fought savagely from the bed of a wagon, killing many Zulus before he died. Some remembered a soldier who climbed up to a cave on the sphinx and fought until he was finally killed at dusk. Except for those diehards, the fighting was over around 2:00 P.M. Zulus shouted news of the British defeat from hilltop to hilltop. A British border agent in Natal heard the news only a few hours after the battle, and Africans in Cape Town knew it by the following day.[39]

# Chapter 5

# "All We Saw Was Blood": Rorke's Drift

After Chelmsford's aide had reassured him that all was well in the camp, he ordered his column on to the east toward the new camp he planned to make, but because some of the supplies he had asked for from Isandlwana had not yet arrived, and perhaps because he was a little worried, he took a small escort and rode back toward the camp. About the same time, two Africans of the Natal Native Contingent who had been left in camp reported to Hamilton-Browne carrying haversacks filled with rations and two bottles of whisky. They handed Hamilton-Browne a jovial note from two young officers of the 24th explaining that they had found Hamilton-Browne's dinner going to waste, so they had eaten it. In return they were sending the whisky. One of those light-spirited officers was Edgar Anstey.

Hamilton-Browne ordered the rations distributed before he rode forward to look at the camp. He came to a rise and was horrified to see that the camp was surrounded by Zulus. He hurriedly sent a message to Chelmsford. About the time that Lieutenant Anstey was fighting his last stand, someone on Chelmsford's staff received the message from Hamilton-Browne saying that the camp was surrounded and that everyone would be killed if Chelmsford did not rush back with all his force. If Chelmsford got the message, he did not believe it, partly, no doubt, because the idea was preposterous, and partly, perhaps, because Hamilton-Browne was not a regular officer. Another of Chelmsford's aides, Major Gossett, agreed, dismissing Hamilton-Browne's report as "bosh."

Soon afterward, however, another officer arrived, and Chelmsford was convinced. Captain Rupert Lonsdale had ridden back to camp in the early afternoon hoping to speed up the delivery of rations for his men of the Natal Native Contingent. Lonsdale, still bothered by a concussion he'd suffered a few days earlier in a fall from his horse, and exhausted by several days of fever, sleepless nights, and hard riding, was dozing in the saddle while his horse, "Dot," took him back to Isandlwana. Barely conscious, Lansdale rode into camp, annoyed by what in his confusion he took to be importunate natives. Puzzled by what seemed to an extraordinary lack of propriety in camp, he looked about and discovered that everyone wearing a red coat and a white sun helmet was *black,* and they all carried bloody spears. Some, in fact, were stabbing those spears into white bodies, and a few were beginning to take notice of Lonsdale. He was still not well, and his horse was as exhausted as he was, but somehow Lonsdale persuaded the horse to run, or at least trot, out of camp, and they made it unhurt, although it took Lonsdale two hours to cover the five miles to Lord Chelmsford. When he arrived, there was no longer any doubt in Chelmsford's mind that the camp had been attacked and that serious fighting had taken place. Although Chelmsford reasoned that the majority of the garrison must have withdrawn to a better position, his forces were obviously needed, and he quickly ordered his whole command to march back to Isandlwana. His tired infantry marched back to Isandlwana at double time.

They arrived at 6:30, just before the African dark fell with its usual equatorial suddenness. Three companies of redcoats fixed bayonets, cheered, and charged, driving off some Zulu stragglers before the rest of Chelmsford's force drew up. Colonial Lieutenant John Maxwell charged into camp with the men of the 24th, leaving his own Natal Native Contingent trailing behind. Maxwell found "about 8 or 10" drunken Zulus asleep in some wagons. He called to some men of the 24th who unhesitatingly, as Maxwell put it, "put the bayonet through them."[1] It was pitch dark by then, the moon obscured by clouds. It was too dark to search for survivors, so there was nothing more the troops could do. They had been up since 1:30 that morning and had marched about 35 miles in 100 degree heat carrying more than 40 pounds per man. Most of them flopped down to sleep on ground that they would later learn was the site of some of the heaviest fighting earlier that day. It was a very cold night, and despite their exhaustion most of the men could not sleep, although a few pushed aside stiff and cold bodies and lay on what they thought was rain-slick ground. A wounded mule screamed for hours until someone located it and put it out of its misery, and somewhere outside of camp a drunken Zulu sang loudly. Dozens of men took pot shots at the sound of his voice, but he sang all night.

After midnight the clouds blew away, and in the thin light of the new moon the men began to see the extent of the carnage. Chelmsford could no longer deny that a disaster had taken place. His first comment was, "My god, I left one thousand men in camp." Chelmsford did not try to sleep. Instead he kept busy inspecting his sentries. Maxwell was awakened after a few hours' sleep by the general and a staff officer, Major Lord Grenfell. He was asked to show the anxious officers the location of his sentries. Although Maxwell was not the duty officer and did not know where the sentries were placed, he tried to do as he was ordered. Despite the darkness, he found all but the last sentry before falling head first into a deep gulley. Maxwell tried to break his fall with his hands, which landed in the disemboweled stomach of a British soldier. Maxwell was not hurt and, beyond commenting that "my hands and wrists were a nice mess," did not seem terribly upset.[2] Even though there was no water for Maxwell to wash his hands, he handed out hardtack to his men that night without qualms.

Chelmsford tried to hurry his troops away before dawn came so that they would not be able to see clearly what lay at their feet. He did not succeed. The men arose to find their uniforms caked with blood, entrails, and brains. Some had slept in pools of blood. Others had lain only a foot away from a dead comrade. Colonel Degacher had slept with his arms close to his body in fear that if he reached out, his hand might touch the body of his younger brother, who had been left in the camp. In the hills, jackals howled, waiting for the British to leave. Despite the cold, the smell was already oppressive. As one British soldier later wrote, it smelled like a sweet potato that had been cooked just when it was beginning to go bad—sweet, cloying, sickening.

The first British officer who returned to the scene of carnage and wrote about it was Hamilton-Browne:

> Just before daybreak orders were given to fall in and as soon as I got my men into their places I galloped across the camp to my tent to try and save some papers, medals, etc. My God, in the grey dawn, it was a sight! In their mad rush into the camp, the Zulus had killed everything. Horses had been stabbed at their picket lines. Splendid spans of oxen were lying dead in their yokes, mules lay dead in their harness and even dogs were lying stabbed among the tents. Ripped open sacks of rice, flour, meal and sugar lay everywhere. They had even in their savage rage thrust their assagais into tins of bully beef, butter and jam. Among all this debris singly and in heaps, or rather in groups of two or three, lay the ripped and mutilated bodies of the gallant 24th showing how, when their formation was broken, they had stood it out, and fought back to back or in groups until they had

> been run over and destroyed. That they had fought to the last gasp could be seen by the number of dead Zulus who lay everywhere in amongst them, the bayonet wounds on their bodies telling of the fierce, though short combat that had taken place after the right horn of the Zulus had swept round the hill. I had just time to get to the door of my tent, inside of which I saw my old setter dog, dead, with an assagai thrust through her. My two spare horses were also lying killed at their picket rope, with my Totty (Hottentot) groom dead between them. . . . I saw the bodies of two of my officers lying dead with heaps of empty cartridge shells by their sides. Both had been splendid shots and I bet they had done plenty of execution before they went under. As I reined up I glanced out to the left and left front of the camp, and saw heaps and heaps of Zulu dead. Where the volleys of the 24th had checked them, they lay in lines, and the donga I had ridden over on the morning of the 21st was chock-full of them. Surely the 24th had died game, but bitter as I felt, a thrill of admiration passed through me when I thought of the splendid courage of the savages who could advance to the charge suffering the awful punishment they were getting.[3]

With the fighting over, the Zulus finished their work of stripping the corpses and putting on their tunics (unless the uniforms were too bloody) before throwing them on their backs and disemboweling them. Dressed in British uniforms, they looted the camp, spearing whatever they did not take with them. Even small cans of sardines were speared. One thing that was not stabbed was a pair of cricket leg pads. Which officer carried them into battle is unknown.[4] The Zulus carried on, looting, disemboweling, and stabbing until they were exhausted. One warrior said that if Chelmsford's troops had returned to the camp before it fell, the Zulus would have been too tired to continue the fight. He was an older man and may have exaggerated the fatigue of younger warriors, but he could not have exaggerated their thirst. They drank everything they could find in camp, including all the alcohol and some chemicals from the hospital tent, which killed several of them. Tired, drunk, but victorious, they then saw to their own dead and wounded. Some were covered with their shields and left on the battlefield. Others were tossed into wagons and carried away to be dumped into grain pits or piled in huts. A greater problem was the wounded. There were thousands of them, many with terrible wounds. Friends and relatives helped most of those suffering men to nearby kraals.

The Zulus now realized that the British were a new kind of enemy. They fought "like lions," and even Zulus could not face the massed fire of their rifles and live. A thousand or more Zulus had been killed on the battlefield, and thousands had been wounded, many of them so terribly that when British officers saw them several years after the war they could not understand how they could have survived.[5] The British did not realize that most of them did not survive. Perhaps the British had learned a lesson, too. Lieutenant Melvill, who died trying to save his regiment's colors, had tried to warn his senior officers about the Zulus the day before the battle. He had said the Zulus would "charge home" and that the British should be in a laager or standing shoulder to shoulder.[6] Some of them did stand shoulder to shoulder, but by then they were too few and the Zulus were too many. After the battle several Zulu indunas said that the British gave them the battle by dispersing their forces.

Only a few hours after the fighting ended at Isandlwana, more Zulus and Britons would learn those same lessons. Late that afternoon, a force of Zulus would attack a small British garrison at Rorke's Drift, where Chelmsford's army had crossed the Buffalo River into Zululand.

## RORKE'S DRIFT

As Chelmsford marched his tired, worried men back toward Rorke's Drift, he feared the worst. Heavy firing had been heard during the night, and flames could be seen, but the fight at Rorke's Drift was not another disaster, it was a remarkable victory for the British. A single company of men from the 24th plus a few other British soldiers and civilians held off close to four thousand Zulus. More men were awarded the Victoria Cross in that battle than in any other battle before or since. For both reasons—victory and heroism against the odds—the fight at Rorke's Drift has remained Britain's best-known and most popular Victorian battle.[7] The decision to award eleven Victoria Crosses for the battle was transparently political—Britain needed heroes badly just then—but no one could deny the heroism that the embattled white men showed. Many more than eleven of them fought with remarkable courage. When the battle is seen in perspective, however, Zulu courage was even more remarkable. Unlike Isandlwana, where most Zulus were less than reckless with their lives, at Rorke's Drift most Zulus displayed utter disregard for their safety. They charged into the muzzles of British guns, and then they did it again and again, for almost ten hours. In this most remarkable example of human courage, the single most remarkable fact is that most of the Zulus who fought so savagely were middle-aged men who should have been enjoying the Zulu equivalent of a rocking chair, pipe, and slippers.

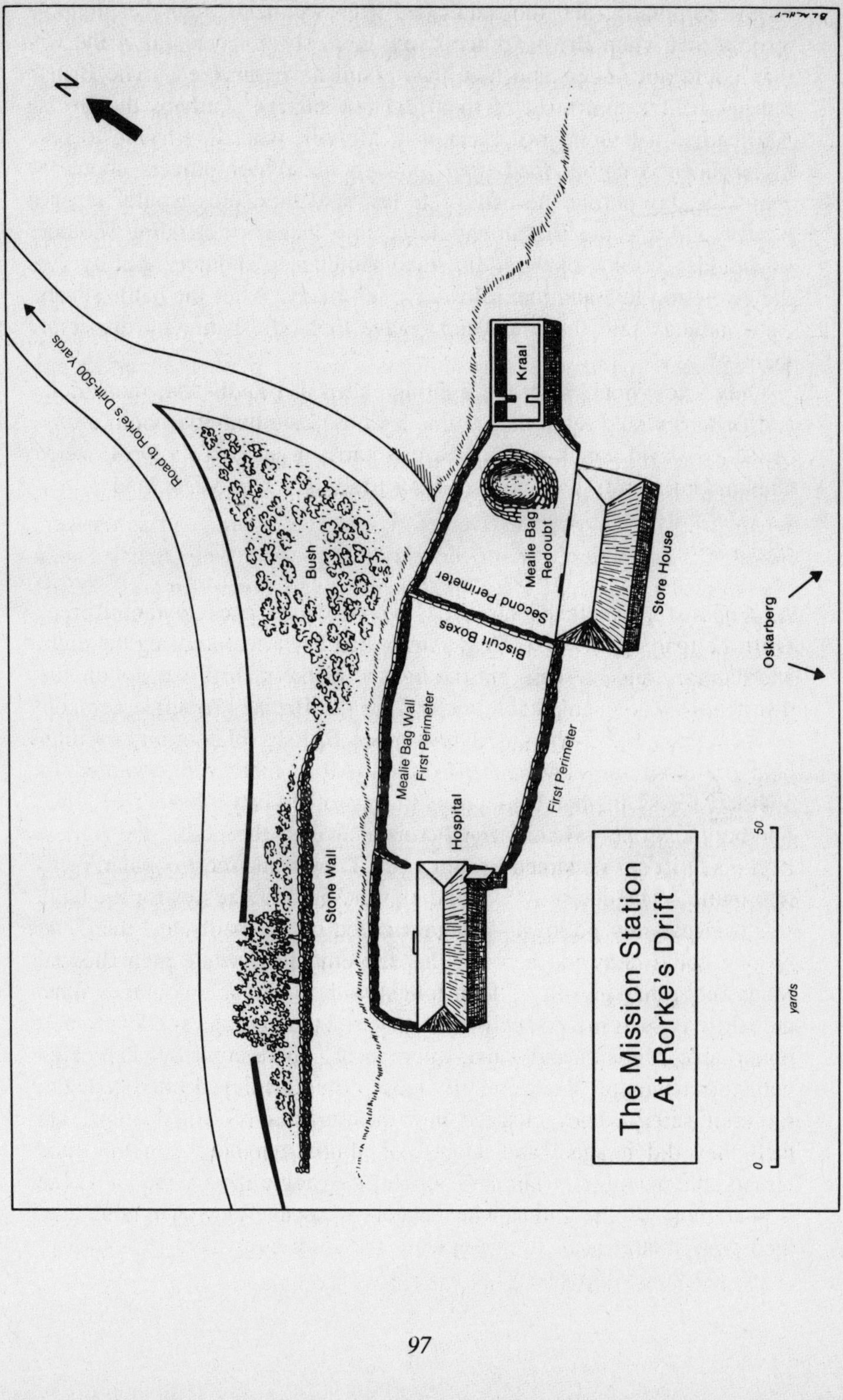
N
Road to Rorke's Drift-500 Yards
Bush
Kraal
Mealie Bag
Redoubt
Store House
Second Perimeter
Biscuit Boxes
Oskarberg
Mealie Bag Wall
First Perimeter
Hospital
First Perimeter
Stone Wall
The Mission Station
At Rorke's Drift
0
50
yards

The Zulu reserve at Isandlwana, their "loins," was composed of three overage regiments—not exactly senior citizens just along as spectators, but hardly warriors in their prime either. One of those regiments, the *Dlondlo,* couldn't resist becoming part of the right horn and as a result took some casualties as they swept into the rear of the camp at Isandlwana. Most of those men stayed near the battlefield to tend to their wounded and to loot the camp, but some of them joined the two regiments that were trotting south toward Rorke's Drift. Those other regiments were the Thulwana and the Dloko. The Dloko, perhaps two thousand men in all, were between forty-one and forty-four years old. They were junior to the Thulwana, King Cetshwayo's own regiment, the regiment that he had served in as a young man. Although some members of the Thulwana had fought a bloody brawl with a younger regiment, the Ngobamakosi, only a year before, the Thulwana had last fought a major battle in 1858, when it defeated the men of Cetshwayo's brother. Although some younger men had been added to this regiment, the majority of its warriors were forty-five years old, and some were closer to fifty. The Zulus in those two regiments were married men who wore the headring. They had lived in relative ease for some years. Many were paunchy and graying, their prime years as fighting men well behind them. To put the age of those men in perspective, consider that Colonel Evelyn Wood, who commanded the left column in the British invasion, was forty-one years old, and General Chelmsford was fifty-one. General Sir Garnet Wolseley, who would later replace Chelmsford as the British commander, was only forty-six. Try to imagine a British or American combat infantry regiment in which all the men in the ranks were forty-five or older.

If the men in the ranks of those two senior regiments were willing to trot along in the rear of the battle as a reserve, and we can't be sure that they were, their commander was spoiling for a fight and war honors. In his passion for the glory that only battle could bring, he was no different from most Zulu commanders (or British officers, for that matter), but in his case it was imperative that he win a victory. He was Prince Dabulamanzi, "the divider of water." A handsome man, strongly muscled, with the huge, powerful legs of the royal family, he had a reputation for cruelty. There is a photograph of him, sitting on a horse scowling down at John Dunn, and his commanding presence is striking.[8] He looked as if he could lead men, but Dabulamanzi still had a great deal to prove. He was King Cetshwayo's kid brother, only thirty-five years old, and here he was commanding a corps of three senior regiments, including the king's own Thulwana. Zulu commanders were supposed to be older men with war honors, but Dabulamanzi was younger than his men by a decade and had little experience in battle. He was determined to have his battle, and as the fighting at Isandlwana ended, he ordered his old regiments toward Rorke's Drift. About three thousand warriors began trotting slowly south toward Natal. Dabulamanzi led them riding a white horse.

Although Dabulamanzi was interviewed extensively after the war (the British did not like him and said that most Zulus didn't either)[9] it is still not clear what his plans were, except that he was looking for trouble. He found his chance when he encountered a leader of a younger regiment near the Buffalo River, which divided Zululand and Natal. This regiment, the Dluyenge, had been part of the Zulu right horn at Isandlwana but had been too far back to see any real fighting. Instead, it veered south, trying to cut off the escape of the men who were fleeing toward Natal. Now in the late afternoon, many of those warriors were already across the Buffalo inside Natal, where they were burning farmhouses as they meandered west toward Rorke's Drift. This regiment, composed of unmarried men in their early twenties, quickly challenged Dabulamanzi to order his graybeards to join them in attacking Rorke's Drift. Challenges like that could not easily be ignored even by a cautious commander, and Dabulamanzi was anything but cautious. He jumped at the chance for a fight and ordered his men to link arms and cross the still flooded Buffalo River into Natal.

Because King Cetshwayo had ordered his commanders not to cross over the river into Natal, Dabulamanzi had just made one mistake. He was about to make another by attacking a fortified position, and to compound this error, he did not even send scouts ahead as Zulu commanders routinely did. He simply ordered all three regiments to attack, and off they went. They were wet and cold from crossing the river, tired from a long march, and hungry. Few, if any, had slept the night before, and most had not eaten for twenty-four hours. Prince Dabulamanzi made one concession to Zulu tradition by stopping his men just short of Rorke's Drift. Out of sight of the British position, the three regiments squatted down and took snuff. Zulus loved snuff and often prepared for battle by stopping to inhale the strong powdered tobacco, which each man carried in a tube that fitted through a hole in his earlobe.[10]

The unmarried men of the Dluyenge regiment ("the men from the Leopard's den") carried black shields with white spots; they wore vests of cowtails over their chests and backs. Men of the Dloko ("the mambas") had red shields spotted with white and wore otter-skin bands around their heads. The older men of the Thulwana (named after a famous

Basuto chief) carried white shields and wore green monkey-skin ear flaps; they also wore a single white ostrich plume held by an otter-skin band in their headdress. A white shield was target enough for a rifleman; wearing a white plume in addition was almost suicidal. In a few minutes, almost four thousand Zulus would rise to attack a fortified position they had never seen. They would attack as bravely as men ever have.

Four hundred yards south of the drift where Chelmsford's troops crossed the Buffalo River into Zululand, a Swedish missionary named Otto Witt had established a mission station on a site originally developed as a farm by an Irish settler named Jim Rorke.[11] In addition to a large brick and stone house with a thatched roof, there was a well-built stone chapel and a stone-walled kraal. Only 200 yards away, a 680-foot-high hill, which Witt named the Oscarberg after the Swedish king, loomed over the little station. It was a plain but pleasant little place, with a 3-acre orchard and some gardens. Chelmsford paid Reverend Witt to use his mission, and Witt's house quickly became a hospital, his chapel a storehouse. Chelmsford garrisoned the station with B Company of the 2d Battalion of the 24th. That was the company he could most easily do without on campaign, not because its private soldiers were any worse than the rest of the men in the battalion, but because its officer, Lieutenant Gonville Bromhead, was so hard of hearing that he could not be counted on to hear orders during a battle.[12] He could not chat with his men either, making him an unpopular officer. He was also lazy. His commanding officer, no great bundle of energy himself, wrote a confidential report declaring Bromhead "hopeless."

In addition to B Company's eighty-four men, there were a dozen or so able-bodied soldiers from other units; an army chaplain, Reverend Smith; James Langley Dalton, a former sergeant major who was now a commissary officer; and his civilian assistant. There were thirty-six men in hospital, including three who had been wounded in the fight at Sihayo's kraal. They were tended by Surgeon Major Reynolds and three assistants. Finally there was a three-man Royal Engineers detachment in charge of supervising the ferrying of supplies over the river: a private and a sergeant commanded by Lieutenant John R. M. Chard. In all, there were 137 British soldiers in the station. There were also substantial numbers of African soldiers from the Natal Native Contingent. British estimates of their numbers varied, as they always did where African troops were concerned, but there were probably between two hundred and three hundred of them. The British agreed that these men would be useless in a fight and that their officer, one Captain Stephenson, and their white NCOs were not much better.

About 2:30 in the afternoon, while Dabulamanzi's men were still some miles away, some officers of the Natal Native Contingent who had escaped from Isandlwana rode up to the drift, where they told Chard about the British defeat.[13] Chard hurried back from the river to talk to Bromhead. Chard was four years senior in rank to Bromhead, so now that there were some decisions to be made, he took command. His first decision was to evacuate the mission station and run for the nearest British garrison at Helpmakaar, where there were two more companies of the 24th. Dalton, who was a party to their conversation (one wonders how much of it Bromhead actually heard), pointed out that they would have no chance fighting in the open, and encumbered by the thirty-six wounded men from the hospital, they couldn't hope to outrun the Zulus. Dalton insisted that their only hope was to stay and fortify the mission as much as possible. Chard finally agreed, and so, more polite historical accounts record, did Bromhead. It was not the first time that a British sergeant major had to set his officers straight.

In reality, as the private soldiers who survived the battle agreed, it was Dalton who organized the defense, not Chard or Bromhead, and of all the brave men who were soon to fight there, he was said by them to have been the bravest.[14] Dalton held the rank of Commissary, a quasi-military title that was almost, but not quite, equivalent to being an officer. He had previously served as sergeant major of the 85th King's Light Infantry. At his height and age—he stood 6′2½″ and was fifty years old, with a closely cropped gray beard—he would have fitted in well with the men of the Thulwana. The mission station was packed with thousands of 200-pound bags of corn and 100-pound wooden boxes of biscuits—"hardtack," Americans called it (the Zulus captured many boxes of the stuff at Isandlwana but found it too hard to eat).[15] There were also slightly smaller boxes of excellent Australian and American canned beef. Dalton and Chard set the men to work building a wall around the station, linking the stone buildings and two parked wagons into a continuous parapet. The Natal native troops, for once, were invaluable.

By 4:30, as the Zulus were taking snuff less than a mile away, the defenses were finished. The two British officers and their men were ready to fight. Rarely have two such unprepossessing officers achieved such a prominent place in history. Bromhead, as we noted, was very nearly deaf. Despite his descent from a prominent scholarly ancestor who established the Gonville and Caius College at Cambridge University, he was considered by his fellow officers to be rather less than bright. Major Clery said that he was "a capital fellow at everything except soldiering'' and that he suffered from ''unconquerable indolence.''[16] He came from a long line of soldiers. His grandfather died a lieutenant general and a baronet, and his father was an officer too, although he had an unremarkable career, and one of Gonville's brothers had served with Wolseley in the Ashanti war and was one of the general's favorites.[17] Favorites aside, Wolseley was no more impressed by Bromhead than he was by Chard. After awarding the Victoria Cross to both officers, Wolseley wrote: ''I have now given away these decorations to both the officers who took part in the defense of Rorke's [sic] Drift, and two duller, more stupid, more uninteresting even or less like Gentlemen it has not been my luck to meet for a long time.''[18] Later General Sir Henry Ponsonby discussed the battle that these two thirty-three-year-old lieutenants, Chard and Bromhead, had led at Rorke's Drift with two senior officers, Colonel Evelyn Wood and Colonel Redvers Buller. Ponsonby wrote a letter to his wife saying, among other things, that Wood found Chard to be a ''dull, heavy man who seemed scarcely even able to do his regular work.'' Wood was quoted as adding that Bromhead was ''brave but hopelessly stupid. [Wood and Buller] could understand Chard and Bromehead [sic] bravely resisting to the death—but that they should have actively ordered any defence was impossible. They both believe this was done by a Commissary named Dalton.''[19] Captain Walter Parke Jones, who later served with Chard, was delighted when Chard was sent back to England. He wrote that Chard was amiable, but that as an officer he was ''hopelessly slow and slack.''[20] Presumably the prospect of a Zulu attack helped to concentrate his mind at Rorke's Drift. Those two physically homely, overweight officers, neither of whom looked like a Victorian hero, served many years after the battle at Rorke's Drift, and neither achieved any distinction. Indeed, neither was promoted again, although Bromhead served until 1891 and Chard until 1897. But fate found them at Rorke's Drift, and they became Victorian heroes. To generations of Britons they were the ''young'' officers who defeated the Zulu ''hordes.''

The defensive wall was built in great haste. Despite Dalton's best efforts, it was hardly perfect. For one thing, the water wagon had somehow been left outside the walls and had to be retrieved at bayonet point during the night. Still, the position would be a tough nut to crack. The wall around the 400-yard perimeter was high enough to shield the defenders and heavy enough not to be pushed over. The hospital had been loopholed, and all the patients able to shoot, plus six soldiers of B Company, were waiting for targets. There was a huge supply of ammunition, and it was liberally handed out.[21] The men fixed bayonets and waited. About 5:00 P.M., a lookout with a telescope saw the Zulus advancing. As soon as the alarm was given, all the African troops, along with their white NCOs and Captain Stephenson, bolted. Someone—the garrison was understandably forgetful about just who it was—shot one of the NCOs in the back as he ran away. The 400-yard perimeter was obviously too much for the remaining troops to hold, so they frenziedly built an interior wall that cut the perimeter they would have to defend by two-thirds. The new wall, 6 to 8 feet high, was finished just before the Zulus arrived.

Still on his white horse, Dabulamanzi ordered his regiments into position. Next to him was an enormously fat officer, also on a white horse. Before Dabulamanzi signaled the attack, he sent a dozen or so of his best marksmen up the slopes of the Oscarberg hill, where they could fire down into the British position. The Zulu regiments moved quietly, not singing or shouting. They didn't fire either; they simply advanced, very slowly, very calmly, and then they charged, the young men of the Dluyenge in the lead, the older regiments following. Having done no scouting, the Zulus knew nothing about the British defenses. Their first charge ran directly into the strongest point of the defense line. At close range, the Martini-Henrys' heavy bullets lifted the Zulus into the air before knocking them on their backs. Confused and unable to find a weak spot in the defenses, hundreds of Zulus swirled around the perimeter walls. Fire from the hospital loopholes killed them by the dozens. One of the first to fall was Vumangwana, the fat officer on a white horse. He was at least fifty years old, and officers of his rank were expected to lead from the rear, but he could not resist joining the attack.

The Zulus recoiled from the British guns, taking cover wherever they could find it. A few minutes later they charged again, fighting their way into the hospital and vaulting over the parapets. They were shot and bayoneted or stabbed with spears that had been thrown over the wall. Some Zulus grabbed British rifles, trying to pull the weapons away, but they were shot or bayoneted, many by James Dalton, who was up and down the line shooting some Zulus and bayoneting others. When he couldn't be everywhere at once, he roared orders to the men, "Here, pot that fellow!" Still, the Zulus were too many and too determined. Despite British bayonet charges, some of which were led by Bromhead, the Zulus drove the British back from their perimeter wall into the smaller interior enclosure. In the hospital, white and black men fought with indescribable ferocity, bayonet against spear. The British slowly dragged their wounded away, leaving a few behind but rescuing the majority. Partly by firing the hospital's thatched roof, the Zulus finally drove the British out of the loopholed hospital.

The huge blaze fueled by the hospital's thatch roof was the Zulus' undoing. It helped to drive the British out of the building, but it burned so fiercely that it illuminated the entire area. Private Henry Hook, a twenty-eight-year-old veteran soldier who won a Victoria Cross for his many acts of reckless bravery in the hospital, called it "a splendid light to fight by. I believe it was this light that saved us. We could see them coming, and they could not take us by surprise from any point."[22] Despite the light, the Zulus charged again, and the British shot them down again. British heroism was commonplace. Several of the British soldiers had been killed or wounded by rifle fire from the Oscarberg heights, where the Zulu marksmen kept up a continuous fire. When a soldier was hit by a heavy .577 caliber bullet fired from a modern Snider carbine, he suffered a smashing wound that usually killed him instantly, but some of these Zulus were firing homemade bullets from old-fashioned muzzle-loaders. Men hit by those bullets were often able to crawl or limp around, handing ammunition to others who were still able to shoot. Dalton was shot through the shoulder and turned pale, but he continued to direct the fight. Men routinely endured terrible wounds and Surgeon Reynolds's equally terrible surgery, without a whimper. (British surgeons had chloroform but, in the belief that pain was a stimulant to recovery, seldom used it.) Reynolds extracted thirty-six pieces of shattered bone from the back of a soldier shot in the shoulder blade before sewing the man up, all without anesthetic. At the wall, the men kept firing and stabbing. No one among them was more remarkable than Corporal Friederich Schiess. He limped out of the hospital, the spear wound in his foot from Sihayo's fight now infected, and took his place at the wall. He was promptly shot in the other foot. Somehow he stayed in the fight until the end, repeatedly exposing himself by standing on the parapet to bayonet Zulus. He won a Victoria Cross also. There was even comic relief provided by the red-bearded Reverend George Smith, who tirelessly carried ammunition to the men at the walls. The British soldiers, needless to say, did not stop their usual outpouring of obscenities just because the Reverend paid them a visit. After the fight they laughed about his persistent refrain: "Don't swear men, don't swear, but shoot them boys, shoot them!"[23]

If the Zulus found anything to laugh about, it has not been recorded. After each charge, they fell back into the darkness, away from the relentless British fire. Private Henry Hook described what it was like from the British side of the wall: "They could not get at us, and so they went away and had ten or fifteen minutes of a war-dance. This roused them up again, and their excitement was so intense that the ground fairly seemed to shake. Then, when they were goaded to the highest pitch, they would hurl themselves at us again."[24] Even "goaded to the highest pitch," it took astonishing courage to charge the British position. The wall was a solid line of muzzle flashes, and to get near it the Zulus had to charge over a well-lighted flat, open area already littered with spears, shields, and bodies. Bodies were everywhere (two British soldiers who escaped the burning hospital by hiding in the brush outside the mission were repeatedly stepped on by Zulus, who paid them no attention at all), and close to the wall dead Zulus lay in human "heaps," as the British called them. Zulus who lived long enough to reach the wall tried to use those mounds to vault over the 8-foot-high wall, only to be shot or bayoneted. They tried to grab British rifles or bayonets and pull the soldiers down to them in deadly games of tug-of-war. Sometimes the British grabbed their spears and stabbed back. They shouted things like, "Another one bit the dust!"[25] It is difficult to imagine this sort of "Western movie" bravado, but that is how they spoke. Of course, they had to shout to be heard. The sound of so many rifles in one enclosed space must have been almost deafening, and the savage sounds that men made as they stabbed at one another cannot be described.

It is impossible to imagine, really, what it was like for the Zulus. Shouting "uSutu," they ran toward muzzle flashes, through clouds of black powder and smoke from the burning thatch, stepping on dead friends and running through pools of blood. They hurled themselves at the 7- or 8-foot-high wall of 200-pound bags with such force that in several places they pushed it back and almost toppled it over. One attack like this would have been an awe-inspiring display of courage, but at Rorke's Drift there were dozens of attacks. From five in the afternoon until sometime after 2:00 A.M., the Zulus charged, old and young warriors together. Later, a warrior said that "all we saw was blood." It may have been meant as a metaphor, but it was close to a literal description.

When the firing ended, the British defenders were exhausted, their hands and faces black from gunpowder. The firing had been so constant that as their notoriously hard-kicking rifles became hot and fouled, men were forced to alternate shoulders and finally, toward morning, to fire their rifles at arms' length. The men's shoulders were so badly bruised and swollen that even veteran officers who saw them the next day were shocked. Bayonets were bent, and men's hands were blistered by their overheated rifles. Several men had broken the stocks of their rifles while using them as clubs. Most men had minor wounds of some sort. Fifteen lay dead, two others were dying, and ten more were seriously wounded. Almost all had been hit by bullets. The wall had been too great a barrier for stabbing spears to be effective, and the Zulus had carried no throwing spears in this battle.

These Welsh, Irish, and English soldiers had done as well as any men could, but when day broke and they saw the Zulus assembled just out of rifle range, many among them, including the indomitable and now wounded James Dalton, thought they were finished.

We'll never know if the British could have withstood another charge. After the Zulus took snuff again, they formed a column and trotted slowly away to the northeast. In one of the war's most bizarre moments, they soon found themselves marching parallel to Chelmsford's troops, who were marching southwest. The two columns passed within 100 yards of each other, but neither army fired at the other. A Zulu-speaker with Chelmsford shouted a question, and a voice from the Zulu ranks said that they were men of the Thulwana. Lieutenant Charlie Harford was amazed by the encounter and expected the Zulus to attack at any moment, but except for one man the Zulus kept their distance. As the two armies remained motionless staring at each other, one young Zulu sprang in front of a mass of squatting warriors exhorting them to attack. Suddenly he dashed down a hillside toward the British troops brandishing his spear. When he came to within 30 yards of the British, he was shot. The other Zulus only watched his charge; they had not even risen from their squatting position.[26] The Zulus later explained that they were too exhausted for another fight just then. The British, who were exhausted too, and very short of ammunition, were relieved to see the Zulus continue their march away from Rorke's Drift.

When Chelmsford's men reached the mission station they found a scene of utter devastation. Charlie Harford recalled that it looked as if a hurricane had struck. Everyone who wrote about the scene that morning was staggered by the litter of Zulu bodies. Around the perimeter alone were 370 bodies. Many others were found in the brush and near the river where the Zulus crossed into Zululand. As the British counted bodies, they saved a few wounded Zulus, but most of the wounded were killed. Sometimes a wounded man tried to resist. One wounded Zulu grabbed Henry Hook's leg and tried to take his rifle. He was killed, too. The Africans of the Natal Native Contingent did not believe in saving wounded enemies, and they were out in force. Sergeant George Smith of B Company wrote that more than eight hundred Zulu bodies had been counted.[27] Many others must have died later of their wounds. Dead Zulus were still being found in caves around Rorke's Drift six weeks later.[28]

"Maori" Browne was no stranger to battle, but he was as impressed by the carnage as everyone else: "The dead Zulus lay in piles, in some places as high as the top of the parapet. Some were killed by bullets and the wounds, at that short range, were ghastly but very many were killed by the bayonet."[29] He was struck by how many of the Zulus, bayoneted in the midsection, lay dead on their knees and elbows, "with their knees drawn up to their chins." Hamilton-Browne wrote that he had never seen anything like it on a battlefield before. This last comment by Hamilton-Browne suggests what the savagery of the fighting was like: "One huge fellow who must have been, in life, quite 7 feet high lay on his back with his heels on top of the parapet and his head nearly touching the ground, the rest of his body supported by a heap of his dead comrades."[30]

Later in the day, when the brass cartridge cases inside the wall were counted, it was estimated that the British had fired more than 20,000 rounds at the Zulus. The ground was completely covered by the torn paper packets in which the cartridges had been wrapped. How the Zulus repeatedly found the courage to charge to their deaths is still a mystery. How middle-aged men had the physical stamina to do so is another unanswerable question. Whatever the explanation, the attack on Rorke's Drift was the Zulus' own "Charge of the Light Brigade"—repeated over and over again. The incredible bravery of these men had gone for nothing. They had failed, they had left the battleground without victory, and so without honor or booty. As the survivors of the Thulwana regiment passed by kraals near Isandlwana looking for food, women cruelly ridiculed them: "You! You're no men! You're just women, seeing that you ran away for no reason at all, like the wind!"[31] The tired old warriors marched on. They had lost, that was all that mattered. They would fight again in later battles but they would never fight again as they had at Rorke's Drift.

Captain John Maxwell was as horrified as the others by the carnage, but he was most startled by the sight of a head-ringed Zulu hanging from a butcher's scaffold. British reports of the battle make no mention of that man, but Maxwell was told that he had been hanged as a spy. We do not know what the Zulu warriors thought about that dead man whose body dangled before their eyes throughout the battle.

# Chapter 6

# "Zulu Pluck": The Second Round of Battles

After the battles of January, the two sides drew back from each other. Chelmsford fortified Rorke's Drift and Helpmekaar; Pearson halted his column and put his men inside an elaborate fortress at a place called Eshowe; and Wood laagered his forces in northwest Zululand. Lord Chelmsford sent for reinforcements. Instead of the three battalions he requested, the British Government sent him six battalions of infantry, two regiments of cavalry, and three batteries of artillery. In all, 10,500 men and 1,800 horses embarked for South Africa and war with the Zulus. Queen Victoria wrote to General Chelmsford and to Lady Frere (oddly, not to Sir Bartle), to express her confidence in their leadership. Prime Minister Disraeli did not share her enthusiasm: He thought Chelmsford was incompetent and confused, and Frere self-righteous and opinionated.

The white population of Natal was panic-stricken. Government officials expected a Zulu invasion, and the people frantically fortified their towns. Some families fled for the coast to seek passage to England, but most prepared to defend themselves. Houses were loopholed, streets barricaded, and outlying farms evacuated.

The people of Natal could have rested easily. For one thing, despite the great Zulu victory at Isandlwana, the African residents of Natal showed no signs of hostility toward the white colonists. And the Zulu armies did not invade Natal. Their king had ordered them not to. Instead, they limped away to nearby kraals to tend their wounded and to be cleansed after their killing. So few of the wounded survived that the Zulus believed the British bullets had been poisoned. It is impossible to know with any certainty how many Zulus finally died, but the traditional estimates are far too low.[1] Zulu warriors themselves were appalled by their losses. They usually said that there were too many to be counted. Among the dead were two sons of old Commander Tshingwayo. Cetshwayo, too, was horrified by the price paid for victory. After the war he told his captors that more Zulus died at Isandlwana than in any other battle.[2] Cetshwayo said that five hundred men were killed in the umCityo regiment alone, and he probably overlooked some lesser-known men who died later of their wounds.[3] The king added such comments as "a spear has been thrust into the belly of the Nation" and "there are not enough tears to mourn for the dead." At least five thousand Zulus must have died from wounds received in the three battles fought on January 22.

For the Zulus, death meant more than tragic loss of life. It also meant pollution, which endangered the living. On the day of a man's death no one in the kraal of the deceased could eat or drink, not even water. The cattle could not be milked, and no one could work in the fields or even talk. If the deceased was the kraal's head man, there could be no work for a month, and no sex. Death put everyone in danger. The living had to take protective medicines and observe food taboos. Even cattle had to receive protective medicines and be prayed over. It is not clear how carefully those practices were observed in the kraals close to Isandlwana and Rorke's Drift, which were turned into hospitals for wounded men, but we know that as outlying kraals learned of the deaths of their sons and fathers, the Zulu Kingdom was paralyzed by grief and mourning. Make no mistake, Zulu grief was not just a theatrical display demanded by custom. People truly grieved for their lost loved ones. Men's tears mingled with those of women. The Dutch trader Cornelius Vijn was in a Zulu homestead after the battle at Isandlwana. The headman of the kraal had been killed in the battle, and Vijn remembered the women's grief: "[I]n the night they wailed so as to cut through the heart of anyone. And this wailing went on, night and day, for a fortnight; the effect of it was very depressing; I wished I could not hear it."[4] Except for Vijn, there are few direct reports of those dreadful times, but one from a slightly earlier battle came from John Dunn, who found an old man sitting by the corpse of his son "quite stupified with grief," saying "he was my only one." A young woman who saw the bodies of her two brothers screamed and died, falling next to them.[5]

The British soldiers were mourning their own dead and vowing revenge. In Britain, almost a thousand households wept for their loved ones. The wives of the dead private soldiers of the 24th boarded a ship for home. They were poor and utterly forlorn, with little hope of help from the army, which scarcely recognized their existence. The hard-hearted

Hamilton-Browne was touched by their misery. He was disgusted by the religious platitudes that their fellow British "do-gooders" offered them, but he was impressed when an American, an apparent ex-Confederate colonel, gave the women his money in addition to his prayers. It may come as no surprise that throughout the Anglo-Zulu War, the British were sublimely oblivious to Zulu grief and mourning for their dead. Nowhere in their voluminous books, diaries, letters, and reports is there any indication that they realized a dead Zulu warrior was a son or a brother or a father, or all three. They admired Zulu courage—"pluck" was the term they used most—but seemed to think of them as men who lived only to die, bravely, of course, by British bullets, shells, or bayonets. Zulus were splendid fighters but not real people, more like dangerous black game that made the hunt especially exhilarating.

So many Zulus had been killed and so many were still dying of their wounds that it would be ten days before even a small minority of the king's army assembled at the royal kraal at Ulundi to report their deeds and receive the war honors they had earned. Finally, the men heard their king's praises, and after they recounted their deeds they were rewarded for their bravery. It was decided that men who were the second or third to stab a British soldier would be allowed to boast of their prowess and wear willow-weed necklaces to proclaim their heroism, along with those who stabbed first. Mpatshana, who fought with the elite Ngobamakosi regiment of the left horn (the regiment that wore a single red feather), explained that this was allowed because "they had been fighting such formidable opponents who were like lions. . . . This custom was observed in regard to Isandlwana because it was recognized that fighting against such a foe and killing some of them was of the same high grade as lion-hunting."[6]

Cetshwayo honored his men as called for by Zulu tradition, but he was annoyed that they had kept much of the booty from Isandlwana for themselves. He was also angry that his men had not brought him a British officer as a prisoner as he had ordered (Cetshwayo wanted to interrogate an officer about the reasons for the British invasion). Most of all, he was appalled by the Zulu losses. The horror of the aftermath of the fighting was captured in the simple account of a young Zulu boy who visited the battlefield at Isandlwana a few days after the battle:

> We went to see the dead people at Isandlwana. We saw a single warrior dead, staring in our direction, with his war shield in his hand. We ran away. We came back again. We saw countless things dead. Dead was the horse, dead too, the mule, dead was the dog, dead was the monkey, dead were the wagons, dead were the tents, dead were the boxes, dead was everything, even to the very metals.[7]

The Zulus now knew the terrible power of British rifles, and they knew that the "red soldiers" would stand and fight bravely. They also knew that when the British fought behind barricades they could not be beaten. Cetshwayo and his generals realized that their chances of victory against British tactics and firepower were slim, but younger warriors continued to hope for what they considered a fair fight. Vijn said that the general attitude of the younger warriors was defiant: "Why could not the Whites fight with us in the open? . . . They are constantly making holes to shoot through."[8] Cetshwayo's young warriors may not have lost their fighting spirit, but Cetshwayo was still hoping for peace.[9] It would be six weeks before he sent his regiments to war again. It would also be six weeks before his warriors had recovered from the battles of January 22.

While the Zulus healed their wounds, and some boasted of their exploits, the British had little boasting of their own to do, but they did not hesitate to criticize one another in every way available. They convened a military board of inquiry to investigate the causes of their disastrous defeat at Isandlwana. The board was a solemn mockery of inquiry. It heard some testimony but reached no conclusions worth mentioning. Lord Chelmsford himself delivered some astonishingly self-serving and ungracious pronouncements. First, he declared that the men of the 24th whom he had left in camp "lost their presence of mind" and "retired hastily." Next he announced that he had ordered Durnford to take command of the camp. There had been no such order, and Chelmsford knew it. Finally he declared that Durnford had had ample time to laager the camp and should have done so. Recall that he had said earlier that it would take a week to do so. He also did not acknowledge the fact that he had left no orders for Pulleine and was visibly relieved when Major Clery told him that Clery himself had left orders for Pulleine to defend the camp. The world was left with the idea that both Durnford and Pulleine, now dead, had been incompetent, and their men, the dead men of the 24th, had panicked. They deserved better from their commander. Since Chelmsford was blameless by his own account, someone else must have blundered. True enough, Durnford's move out of camp made the defeat more likely, but Durnford had orders to support Chelmsford, whose flank was threatened. No matter, Chelmsford and Frere needed a scapegoat, and Durnford—dead Durnford—was the obvious choice. Chelmsford's benefactor, Sir Bartle Frere, cabled London that Isandlwana was "poor Durnford's disaster," and that was how it would usually be referred to.[10] Frere must have known that he was lying.[11] It was not the first time.

Durnford was by no means the only one criticized. Chard and Bromhead, as we have already seen, were dismissed as fools, and Curling, who suffered a nervous breakdown, was scorned. So was Colonel John Russell, whose scouting was seen as leaving Chelmsford blind. In truth, Russell had not done well, but many others not under Russell's command had scouted too, including, we must add, Chelmsford himself. They hadn't found the main Zulu army either. But now even his friends, such as Major Clery, concluded that Russell "lacked flint," "was always 'below the occasion' in a crisis," and had been unnerved by Isandlwana.[12] Others were subjected to as much scorn, especially in a spate of letters that British officers somehow felt compelled to write to General Sir Archibald Alison, who served as a sort of informal head of British military intelligence.[13]

No one suffered more in those letters than Captain Alan Gardner, about whom Major Clery wrote with a venomous pen: "I must tell you about another of our heroes out here—a man named Gardner in the 14th Hussars. His case has caused a good deal of ire." Explaining that Gardner (who was on special service with Chelmsford's staff) rode out of camp with Chelmsford (and Clery), and that Chelmsford had sent Gardner back to camp with a message for Pulleine, Clery added that Gardner took command of some troops in the camp but left them while they were still fighting (as survivors were alleged to have said) to gallop out of camp toward safety in the Natal town of Dundee. Gardner apparently sang his own praises too loudly and unconvincingly when called before the court of inquiry. Clery added that those who saw Gardner's less than heroic action "have made up a song about it which they used to sing in chorus at the mess at Helpmekaar, and this ditty wound up at every verse as follows: 'I very much fear/That the Zulus are near/So, hang it I'm off to Dundee.' This has now got into the newspapers, who had already found out about it, and were rather hard on him."[14] Apparently, Gardner tried to cover his less than stalwart actions with claims of heroism that properly belonged to other men. When rumors began that Gardner would receive a medal or a promotion, his fellow officers were furious and suggested that what he really deserved was a court-martial, shooting, and "other unpleasant things."[15] The British could be every bit as hard on cowards—real or fancied—as the Zulus.

While the Zulus tried to heal their wounds and tend their fields and herds, Chelmsford waited for reinforcements. His surviving officers and men fortified the Rorke's Drift mission station and their supply post at Helpmekaar. There was food—"bully" beef and hardtack—and plenty of ammunition, but little else. They had lost almost everything else at Isandlwana, and so they lived without tents, blankets, or extra clothing.

An Englishman, Joseph Swan, had invented the incandescent light a year earlier, but Chelmsford's men did not even have candles. For officers the losses at Isandlwana were a financial blow. Eight officers compared notes and calculated that their losses totaled £13,500. For officers and men alike, the losses meant physical discomfort. It poured rain every night, soaking men to the skin and turning the churned-up ground into lakes of water and mud. Most men slept lying in the mud. Some just shivered all night, too cold to sleep.

Wise after the fact, the British now expected a Zulu attack at any moment, so the men were not allowed to leave their fortified camps even to defecate. In a few days, there was a plague of flies so numerous and voracious that fires of hay had to be kept burning around the horses to prevent them from being driven mad. Men carried torches, which they used to burn flies by the thousands.[16] In a short time more than half of the British troops were ill with dysentery or typhoid. Those who were not too sick craved alcohol. Soldiers stole it, and those who were caught were flogged. Officers drank the little liquor they had left in the privacy of their tents (a few senior officers did have tents), being reduced to rationing a few bottles of bad gin. On one memorable occasion, Charlie Harford (a teetotaler) used Wilsone Black's and Hamilton-Browne's last bottle of gin to preserve some beetles. When the swearing—in English and Gaelic—finally ended, Harford, who was very popular, was forgiven. But, as Hamilton-Browne wrote, "I do not think the dear fellow ever quite understood what an awful sin he had committed or realized what a wicked waste of liquor he had perpetrated."[17]

Aside from such alarms as the time an officer mistook the sound of frogs for Zulus and called the camp to arms (he was sent back to England), there was little action. British officers at Helpmakaar helped to while away the time by making a pet out of a juvenile baboon. The baboon had the run of the fort. When a new officer arrived, the baboon approached him in greeting. The officer drew his revolver and shot the baboon dead. Not knowing that he had just killed the camp pet, he boasted about his "trophy." It was quickly arranged for the officer to be transferred. He was more than happy to get away.[18]

Slowly Zulus began to return to their homesteads in the Nquthu district across from the British camps. Some of them were seen sending up smoke signals. Zulu scouts became bolder, sometimes sniping across the Buffalo River at British water parties. One was wearing a clean white dress shirt like the dozen shirts Harford had lost at Isandlwana. Another was seen sitting in a folding armchair. On one occasion two Zulus were seen performing a ritual on a ridge across the river; the fire they were tending was blowing smoke toward the British, who interpreted the action as a magical attempt to drive them away. Hamilton-Browne and Duncombe crossed the river and shot the two Zulus. One was a woman.

Spirits rose briefly one morning fourteen days after Isandlwana, when Colonel Degacher's pointer was found sitting outside the gate to the British laager waiting to come in. He was badly cut by spears but had survived, and somehow he had found his master. (Bromhead's spaniel, Pip, who had survived the fighting at Rorke's Drift was still with his master). Not all the hunting dogs that the British officers took to Isandlwana returned to their masters. British officers riding on patrol were attacked by packs of well-bred British dogs. Officers tried to reclaim their dogs, but they had become so vicious they had to be shot. Although British troops continued to stay behind the walls of their camps, some of the colonial officers began to lead raids into Zululand. A typical raid was described by Hamilton-Browne. Under the cover of night, several dozen mounted men would surround a Zulu kraal, then wait for the earliest light so that they could see their targets. The thatched houses were then set on fire, and, as the occupants fled, the British opened fire. It was said that these targets were ''military kraals,'' not ordinary homesteads, but even military kraals sometimes contained women and children. The war had taken a nasty turn.

In England, the Government and the public grew impatient with Chelmsford. They wanted news of a victory and were dismayed when the next battle reported in the newspapers was anything but a victory. It was another disaster, pure and simple. At a place called Myer's Drift in the far northwest of Zululand, sixty-two British regulars died, along with fifteen of their African allies, two wagon drivers, and a civilian surgeon. The battle was a tragic example of what could happen when a British commander refused to learn even the rudimentary lessons of war against the Zulus. To make matters even worse, the only other British officer in the same battle was brought before a court-martial on charges of cowardice in the face of the enemy. That was not quite the news the British public and the British Government were waiting for.

The British maintained a force of five companies of the 80th Regiment at a place called Luneberg in the Transvaal, just across the border from the extreme northwest corner of Zululand. Luneberg was garrisoned by the British, partly to restrain the Zulus, but mostly to restrain the neighboring Boers and a nearby kingdom, the Swazi. The British troops at Luneberg had to be supplied from the town of Derby in the north by wagons that cut across a part of Zulu territory. In the second week of March, a supply convoy to Luneberg ran into heavy rain and flooded rivers. Because the convoy was late, the commander at Luneberg, Major Richard Tucker, sent Captain David Barry Moriarty with H Company of the 80th to bring the convoy in safely.

Moriarty, a genial Anglo-Irish officer who, despite his white hair, was only forty-two years old, worked hard to get the supply wagons over the flooded Intombwe River at Myer's Drift, but the river became impassable before he managed to get all the wagons across. Disgusted, he camped seventy men and most of the wagons on the far side of the river, leaving a few wagons and thirty men under Lieutenant Henry Harward on the other side. Moriarty laagered the camp on his side of the river and went to sleep. On March 11, Major Tucker rode the 5 miles from Luneberg to see for himself what had happened to his supplies. He found a camp that was laagered in name only. There were wide gaps between the wagons, and near the river there was no wagon barrier at all. Tucker told Moriarty that his defenses simply would not do! Moriarty listened, but after Tucker left, he did nothing. He expected the river to subside enough the next day for him to cross the rest of the wagons, and it would have been too much bother to move the wagons that he had more or less in laager, so he went to sleep, literally. His sole precaution was to post two sentries just outside of the wagons. At 4:00 the following morning, March 12, Harward on the opposite bank thought he heard something and ordered his men to stand to. Moriarty woke up but ignored the commotion and soon went back to sleep.

While Moriarty slept, one thousand or more Zulus under the leadership of Mbilini, a lean and perpetually scowling Swazi prince who had sworn loyalty to Cetshwayo, were moving into position only a few yards away from Moriarty's sleepy sentries. Mbilini commanded local Zulus, not men of the royal regiments, but they were as well-armed as royal troops and would be more than good enough for the task at hand. The rugged territories along the western and northern boundaries of Zululand were controlled by several powerful chiefs, who usually observed only nominal allegiance to Cetshwayo. Each chief controlled his own army, sometimes as large as several thousand men, who were not members of the royal army. One such chief, who controlled a large Zulu population in the Nkandla forest, took no part in the war. A few went to the other extreme by sending men to join the royal army on a particular campaign against the British. But most fought only if British troops approached their territory. The territory of Mbilini was near Myer's Drift. When Mbilini's scouts reported to him that the "red soldiers" were at Myer's Drift with undefended wagons filled with booty, he attacked, and the battle was even easier than he expected it to be. Shortly after 5:00 A.M., the Zulus charged between the loosely laagered wagons and speared most of the British soldiers before they could get out of their tents. Moriarty fired a few shots with his revolver before he was speared. A Dutch wagon driver named Sussens, who escaped, reported that he yelled, "Fire away men, I am done." Later accounts have added words about "death and glory," but whatever Captain Moriarty managed to say while he fell with a spear in his back was of little help to his men. They were either already dead or trying to swim across the river.

Zulus dived into the water after them, and black men and white fought hand to hand for their lives in the swollen river. Most of those contests were won by Zulus, who had been swimming like otters since childhood, but one British soldier managed to escape by more or less swimming under water until he reached the opposite bank. Exhausted and half-drowned—the man later said that he did not know how to swim—he somehow found himself lying on a grassy bank looking up at a Zulu with a spear. The two men struggled, and somehow the half-drowned British soldier managed to kill the Zulu with his own spear.[19]

A few more of Moriarty's soldiers managed to get to the other side of the river, where a defense had been formed by Lieutenant Harward and a color sergeant named Anthony Booth. While the fighting was still furious, Harward found a horse and rode off toward Luneberg, leaving his men to their own devices. Harward banged on Major Tucker's door at 6:30 A.M. According to Tucker, he "gasped out, 'The camp is in the hands of the enemy; they are all slaughtered, and I have galloped in for my life'."[20] The stalwart Harward then fainted! Tucker rushed to Myer's Drift with 150 mounted men and found Sergeant Booth still holding out along with forty other survivors, including Sussens, who was stark naked but unhurt. Booth was awarded a Victoria Cross for his heroism. Harward was court-martialed. Tucker buried the seventy-nine disembowelled men of Moriarty's command. He found the bodies of thirty Zulus, most of whom had been killed by Booth's men. The Zulus had made off with 250 head of cattle, eighty Martini-Henry rifles, and 90,000 rounds of ammunition. It could not have been a pleasant ride back to Luneberg.

Cetshwayo and his counselors faced an impossible dilemma. They had not wanted war, and they were hoping to find a peaceful settlement, but after Isandlwana the British were more implacable than ever. The king and his Great Council could not tolerate the presence of British troops in Zululand forever. Pearson's column was inside an impregnable fort at Eshowe near the coast, and Wood was in a fortified position in the west. It was bad enough that the British were in Zululand, but to make matters worse both commanders continued to send patrols out to steal Zulu cattle and burn their kraals. Still Cetshwayo restrained his royal regiments until mid-March, when events combined to force his hand. First it was obvious to Zulu scouts that General Chelmsford was assembling a large force across the Zulu border at Tugela Drift to relieve Pearson's beleaguered garrison at Eshowe. The British at Eshowe were amused when the Zulus surrounding the fort shouted, ''Come out of your holes you little red soldiers,'' but the growing death toll from disease and reduced rations was no laughing matter. Chelmsford's relief column was due to march for Fort Pearson at Eshowe on March 13. All day March 11 and 12, lookouts at the fort saw large numbers of Zulus streaming south to oppose Chelmsford. On the fourteenth, a day after the relief expedition had been canceled, men at the fort saw the Zulu army marching back past Eshowe. The size of the army was estimated at from 20,000 to 35,000 men. If the higher estimate is accurate, it was the largest army that King Cetshwayo would mobilize during the war. Chelmsford was unaware that such an enormous Zulu force was waiting to confront him. He had postponed his relief march because his transport was not yet ready. This time, a lack of transport had saved Chelmsford.

At the same time, Colonel Evelyn Wood's mounted troops under the command of Lieutenant Colonel Redvers Buller were raiding more and more aggressively. In addition, Wood had just persuaded Cetshwayo's half-brother, Hamu, to abandon the king and come over to the British with all his cattle and people. Now Cetshwayo was forced to act. He again gathered his regiments, which had dispersed after their futile march to stop Chelmsford. After the men had been purified and protected at the royal kraal, Cetshwayo personally gave them their orders. According to a warrior from the Thulwana, he assigned each regiment its place in the chest, loins, or horns of the army, and he instructed his officers carefully.[21] The army was to march against Wood's forces, but it was *not* to attack if Wood was in a fortified position; it was to sweep past him toward the Transvaal, forcing the British to fight it in the open field. Cetshwayo gave command to his prime minister, Mnyamana, with the aged Tshingwayo second in command. This force was composed of the same regiments that had fought at Isandlwana. There were about the same number of men as at Isandlwana—perhaps 22,000—but they now had the more than one thousand Martini-Henry rifles that they had captured, and more ammunition than they could carry. The royal army trotted out of Ulundi toward the west on March 26.

That same day, Wood issued orders to attack the stronghold of a troublesome Zulu chief of the Qulusi people on a nearby rocky plateau known as Hlobane. Chelmsford had asked Wood to make the attack in an effort to draw Zulu strength away from Pearson's surrounded men. Chelmsford was planning to attempt his march to Pearson's relief in a week, and he hoped to divert Zulu regiments away from his route of march. Wood agreed, even though his spies had already warned him that the king's army would leave Ulundi to attack *him,* not Chelmsford, on March 26 or 27. Wood also knew that Hlobane would be a tough assignment. He wrote to Chelmsford that he would attack, but added, "I am not very sanguine of success."[22] No wonder. Hlobane was a natural fortress, and there were probably four thousand Qulusi Zulus on its 3-mile-long flat top.

Wood had a powerful force, including two battalions of imperial infantry—from the veteran 13th and 90th—and a battery of Royal Artillery, 110 men with six guns. Wood also had mounted men, and he ordered two columns of horsemen to converge on Hlobane. Lieutenant Colonel Buller led one column of almost seven hundred white colonial horsemen up the eastern end of the plateau, while Lieutenant Colonel Russell, the man without "flint," took a force of 640 horsemen to the western end. Wood followed, leading "Wood's irregulars," 270 or so friendly Zulus, who trotted as fast as Wood and his officers rode. The path up the plateau was narrow and rocky, with a precipitous 1,000-foot drop for the careless. To achieve surprise, Buller led his men up the path at night, but as torrential rains suddenly fell, men (including an Austrian Baron) and horses slipped to their deaths, and other men became lost. By the time the men reached the top it was dawn, and the Zulus were waiting for them. To make matters worse, Russell's force went to the wrong place, so it did not create the intended diversion, and Wood's men couldn't find the right path up the escarpment.

The battle quickly became a nightmarish hand-to-hand struggle on top of the plateau, where Buller's men were being shot down. Wood's men were under fire too. Wood saw a Zulu aiming at him and calmly said to Llewellyn Lloyd standing next to him that the man was aiming belt high. The bullet passed through Wood's sleeve and killed Lloyd. A few minutes later a Zulu shot and killed Wood's horse. In an effort to clear away the Zulu riflemen, Wood ordered a white colonial officer, Colonel Frederick Weatherly, to lead his men in a charge. Weatherly refused three times, so Wood's aide and closest friend, Captain Ronald G. E. Campbell of the Coldstream Guards, yelling "damned cowards" at Weatherley and his men, charged the Zulus himself and was killed.

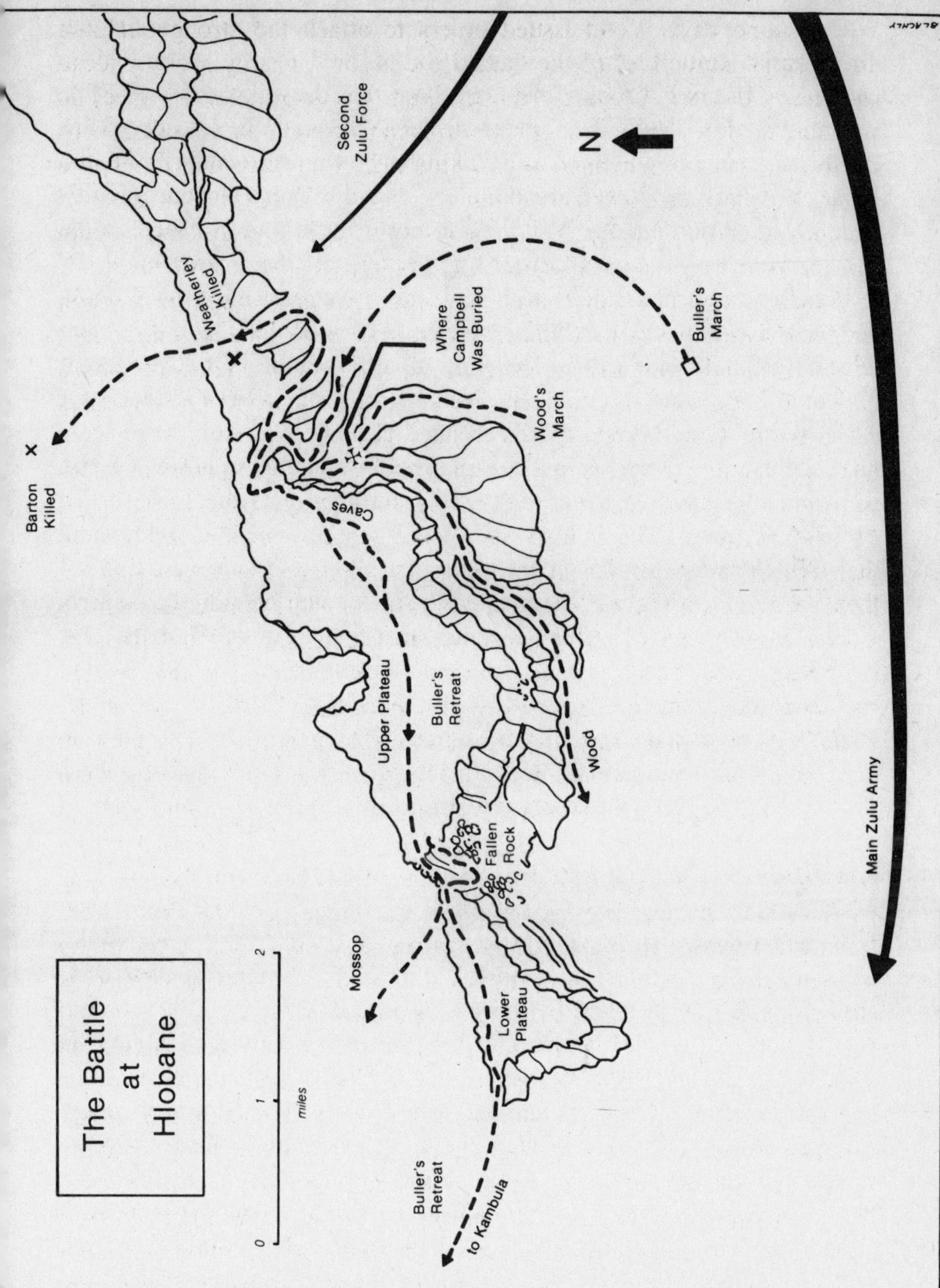
The Battle at Hlobane
Second Zulu Force
N
Weatherley Killed
Where Campbell Was Buried
Buller's March
Wood's March
Barton Killed
Caves
Upper Plateau
Buller's Retreat
Wood
Main Zulu Army
Fallen Rock
Mossop
Lower Plateau
Buller's Retreat
to Kambula
0
1
2
miles

Wood had been very fond of Lloyd and had truly loved the gentle, kindly, aristocratic Campbell, second son of the Earl of Cawdor. Wood insisted on burying the men then and there, but the only available Bible was in Wood's saddle bag under his dead horse. Wood ordered his bugler, a man known only as Walkinshaw (who according to Wood "was entirely unconcerned about bullets") to climb up a slope to Wood's dead horse. Wood added, "While I do not want you to get shot for the saddle, you are to take all risks for the sake of the prayer book."[23] Walkinshaw returned safely with the saddle bag and the prayer book, and Wood conducted the burial service, even though the Zulus were almost within a spear's throw when he finally rode off. One wonders if he would have done the same for Walkinshaw had he been killed.

As Wood looked down the sheer-sided cliff, he was stunned to see a huge Zulu army racing across the plain below in five columns, which were already very close to cutting the British forces off from their fortified camp at Kambula. The Zulus were a terrifying but splendid sight, more than 20,000 men, black against the green plain, the sun sparkling off their spears, each regiment's distinctive shields and headdresses clearly visible as splashes of color. For the British on top of Hlobane, the sight was more terrifying than splendid. A seventeen-year-old colonial cavalry trooper named George Mossop had been separated from Colonel Buller, so he asked a passing horseman where Buller was. The man pointed toward the sound of heavy firing, then began to ride off toward the huge Zulu army. Mossop warned him that there were thousands of Zulus in the direction he was taking. The man shrugged and, with an undeniably clear insight into the situation, said "There's niggers everywhere, kid."

Orders were given for everyone to disengage and ride for Kambula, but some were caught up in hand-to-hand combat, some lost their way, and others fell over the cliff. Many were killed, some by Zulu women, who fought alongside the men in this savage encounter.[24] One man somehow became wedged between rocks halfway down the cliff; Zulus later said that he sniped at them for several days. The teen-age trooper George Mossop lived to write about his experiences on Hlobane. Ghastly as Mossop's experiences were, some men had even worse times. As Mossop rode back trying to find his way to the path down the mountain, he discovered that he was surrounded by Zulus. He had no idea what to do, but his horse, Warrior, made the decision for him by charging straight at one of the Zulus. The man ducked away from the horse's charge, and Mossop escaped. When Mossop reached the top of the route down the steep mountain, he saw a disorganized mob of white men shooting at Zulus, who shot and stabbed at them as they tried to escape. He met a friend, whom he asked if he thought there was any chance of getting away. " 'Not a hope!' the man said just before he blew his own brains out."[25] His account continues:

> A lot of his brains and other soft stuff splashed on my neck. It was the last straw! I gave one yell, let go the bridle of my pony, and bounded down into the pass. My feet landed fairly on the smooth rump of a dead horse, slid from under me, and I shot down, coming to rest on my back upon a dead Zulu. On I scrambled, down over dead horses, men, and rocks, until I reached the jam of horsemen. Madly, blindly, recklessly, I fought—my only thought to get away from all these horrors.[26]

Buller, who was everywhere, it seemed, grabbed the terrified boy, cuffed his ear, and sent him back for his horse. Realizing that he had no chance of escape without a horse and suddenly remorseful for leaving Warrior to Zulu spears, Mossop somehow climbed back up the slippery path, past white men and Zulus, and found Warrior, who whinnied with joy to see him. Before Mossop could mount the horse, Zulus were on him, stabbing him in the arm. Leading Warrior by his bridle, Mossop jumped over the cliff, preferring whatever lay below to Zulu spears. Incredibly he survived, although he landed on a rock, and a dead horse landed on him; more amazing still, Warrior was standing there patiently when Mossop finally got to his feet. Mossop led Warrior down the slope and managed to reach the plain below. Mossop was weak from his fall and loss of blood, and Warrior was unsteady, obviously more badly hurt by his fall than Mossop at first realized. Still the horse struggled on, with Mossop holding on, almost unconscious. Both horse and rider were so far gone that they blundered into a circle of Zulus, but Warrior again saved them by sprinting away at the last moment. Soon Mossop was so overcome by thirst that he had to dismount for water. When he saw many Zulus running toward him, he tried to mount but was too weak to manage it, so he stared blankly at the warriors coming on and almost passed out before the sight of their spears reminded him of the pain in his arm, and he finally dragged himself into the saddle. Despite his injuries and the fact that the broken saddle frame had rubbed Warrior's back bloody, the horse carried Mossop back to Kambula, where man and horse collapsed.

When Mossop came to the next morning, he ran to see Warrior. The horse was still lying down, apparently dead.

> I lifted his head on my knee. He knew me at once, and gave a pitiful whinny, shuddered twice, and died. I laid his head down, and, taking one of his small silken ears in my hand, caressed it gently, with such

> a big lump in my throat that, had I not jumped up and run away, I would have blubbered right there in front of the horse-guard. Only a little Basuto pony, but he had a great heart and—he loved me.[27]

As the most advanced portions of the Zulu columns spread out across the plain below Hlobane, they unexpectedly found the area filled with fleeing white horsemen. Most of the horsemen were able to outride the Zulus and, like Mossop, rode back to Kambula as best they could, thankful to have gotten away with their lives. But some small groups of men, usually led by British Imperial officers, fought rearguard actions to allow others to escape. Buller still held the head of the pass, and he was joined by Lieutenant Edward Browne, whom Lieutenant Colonel Russell sent to help Buller just before riding off with most of his men. The Boer leader, Piet Uys, was there too. He was killed when he tried to save his son from Zulu spears. So was Colonel Weatherley, who had certainly not distinguished himself in the battle up to then but, when he was well clear of danger, realized that his fourteen-year-old son was in danger. Weatherley rode back into the Zulus and died next to his boy.

Several British officers stopped to pick up men who had lost their horses. Some rode back several times in desperate displays of gallantry, fighting Zulus with pistols and swords as they tried to save horseless men. No one expected quarter from the Zulus, and several officers were overtaken and speared as they rode double. Although he was wounded and so was his horse, Captain Robert Barton, like Captain Campbell a special service officer from the Coldstream Guards, led his troop of eighty or so men to safety before he saw that one of his officers was on foot. Although his horse was weak, he pulled the man, Lieutenant Poole, up behind him, and they slowly trotted toward safety. A Zulu chief named Tshitshili, seeing that the horse was on its last legs, trotted along with several other Zulus behind the British officers for 7 miles until the horse collapsed. Poole was killed first, and Barton was surrounded. Because Cetshwayo had again ordered his men to capture a few British officers for him to interrogate at Ulundi, Tshitshili approached Barton, put down his rifle and spear, and motioned for Barton to surrender. Barton did not understand. He raised his pistol, but it misfired three times, and another Zulu shot Barton. Because it would not do to have another man claim first spear, Tshitshili then dashed up and speared Barton. Fourteen months later Tshitshili unerringly led Wood to the spot where Poole and Barton had died. Tshitshili amazed Wood by recalling that Barton had a few small pockmarks on his face. Wood insisted that Barton had no pockmarks and took out a photo of Barton to prove his point. Tshitshili was right.[28]

It was dark before all the mounted men returned to their camp at Kambula. Buller was the last one in. He had shown the reckless courage that everyone else now took for granted from him, saving dozens of men in utter disregard of his own life. Redvers Buller was a large, powerful, tireless man of forty who was constantly in the saddle; he could be ferocious, but he was fair, and men would follow him anywhere. Now, after this calamitous defeat, he was finally cold, wet, hungry and exhausted. But as soon as he heard that some of his men might still be out on foot, he rode all alone into the darkness leading extra horses. He returned with seven men he'd found 8 miles away.

Wood and Buller were often characterized as "bloodthirsty" men, and they certainly were capable of savage acts in the heat of combat. Both had been troublesome as boys. Buller had been expelled from Harrow, although he later went to Eton. Wood ran away from school when he was flogged unjustly, and he won a Victoria's Cross before he was twenty. Yet both officers had tender feelings for their men. This had been a bad battle, a defeat with no gain. Ninety-four white men were dead, including fifteen officers; more than a hundred of Wood's Zulu allies had died too. There were only seven wounded. Hundreds of horses had been lost as well. Wood and Buller were exhausted and grieving, but there was more bad news to come. Lieutenant Edward Browne, whom Wood recommended for a Victoria Cross for his heroism in helping Buller and others form a rear guard, reported to Wood that neither he nor any of his men would ever again serve under Lieutenant Colonel Russell. Everyone knew that Russell had certainly not done well, but now Browne was saying that in addition to Russell's incompetence as a commander, he had no stomach for battle. At a critical point in the retreat down Hlobane, when Russell's mounted men could have supported the fleeing men, he had ordered his men to ride back to Kambula.[29]

To have a coward under his command was too much for Wood, but Lieutenant Colonel John Cecil Russell was no ordinary officer. Russell came from a socially prominent Scottish family. He was educated at Oxford (Buller and Wood had gone to the best public schools, but neither had a university education), served in an elite cavalry regiment, was close to Sir Garnet Wolseley, and had served as an aide to the Prince of Wales. He was "well connected," to say the least. Still, as we have seen, this was not the first time that he had done badly. His scouting before Isandlwana was criticized as sloppy, and after that battle he had fallen into a torpor, showing no interest in his command of cavalry, as even his friends admitted. Russell had to be gotten rid of, but Wood was ever sensitive to social rank. There was no court-martial. Instead, Wood sent Russell to Natal to supervise the cavalry remount depot in the capital city. Despite the disgrace and continuing rumors, after the war Russell rose to command of the 12th Lancers and ended his career as an equerry to King Edward VII. British officers detested cowards, but men of high social rank could be forgiven much.

During the night of March 29, Wood had much more than Russell on his mind. The Zulus were sure to attack on the following day. While Wood sleeplessly paced his defenses, the Zulu leader, Mnyamana, called his commanders to a conference. He repeated Cetshwayo's orders to feint at the British camp while menacing the supply lines, hoping to bring the white men out in the open to fight. He intended to begin his advance about midday after a laggard force of four thousand Qulusi joined his royal troops. The Ngobamakosi regiment—the men of the red feather—who had led the Zulu left horn at Isandlwana, would now spearhead the army's right horn. Its young officers protested Cetshwayo's plan, insisting that the army should attack the British camp. Nothing was settled, but Mnyamana was worried about the impetuous and insubordinate men of his right horn. That night, the Zulu army slept on the plains near Hlobane, 10 miles from Kambula. The Zulus were tired. They had run from Ulundi in two days, covering more than 50 miles. Most of them had run additional miles, and had fought battles, as they had chased the British horsemen fleeing from Hlobane. They were cold and wet. Worst of all, very few had eaten anything for two days. One of "Wood's irregulars," a friendly Zulu, spent the night with them. Under the cover of a heavy early morning mist he slipped away and ran back to Kambula. He told Wood what he had heard: The Zulu army would attack about noon.

Although Wood's Natal native troops and the Boers had run away during the night, Wood was still confident. He held a fortified position along a ridge top. The main position was hexagonal in shape, about 200 yards across; almost 200 yards to the east there was a smaller position, 100 yards long by 30 to 40 yards across. In between was the Royal Artillery battery, well entrenched, and just south of the smaller position there was a large cattle laager. The positions were fortified by heavy wagons chained together, as well as by trenches, earthen walls, and a wooden palisade. Within the fort, Wood baked bread every day, held band concerts, and built his men a cricket pitch. Despite the desertions, Wood still had two thousand European troops. There were more than

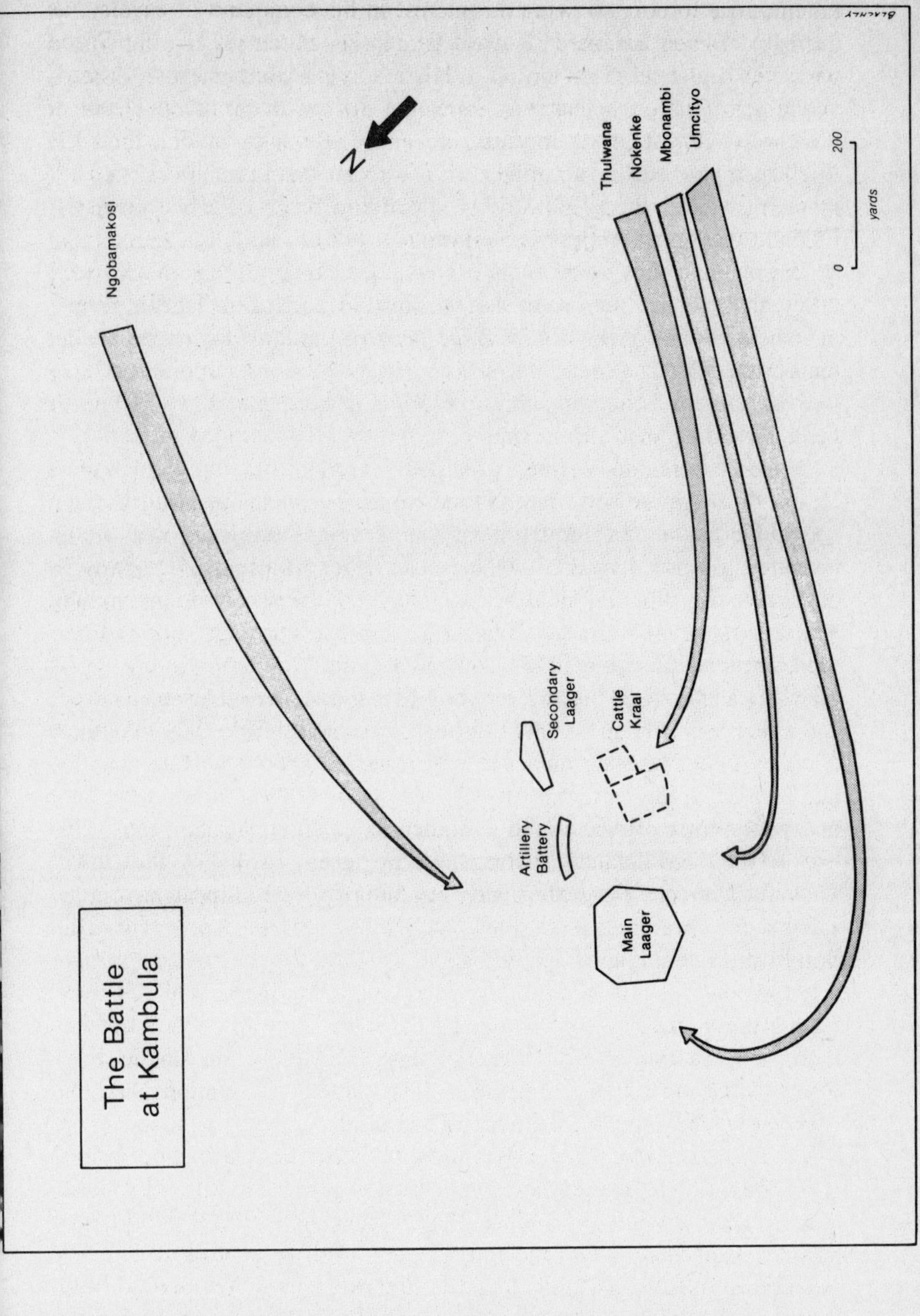


The Battle at Kambula

six hundred colonial horsemen and 121 artillerymen and engineers, but the backbone of his defense was his imperial infantry, two battalions of the 13th and the 90th, in all 1,238 men. The men of the 13th were veterans who had seen service in South Africa since 1874. Those of 90th were almost all youngsters, new to the service. When they left England a year earlier an officer who watched them embark wrote, "A more miserable, limp, half-grown shambling batch of boys never left England inside her Majesty's uniform."[30] Wood had commanded them for a year, and they were tougher now. The two battalions looked very different: the older, bearded men of the 13th in tattered and faded uniforms, their helmets a dirty brown, and the boys of the 90th with their scarlet tunics and white helmets almost as good as new. As different as they looked, they had one very important thing in common: They had never before stood against a Zulu charge.

Wood had trained his men to strike their tents (to give the troops a clear field of vision and fire and to protect the tents against bullet holes) and to get to their positions in less than seventy seconds, so he was in no hurry to order his men to the walls. Instead he sent out a party to cut firewood so that his field bakery could bake fresh bread, an amenity Wood thought essential (his men said the bread was half corn and half sand and tasted terrible). He also sent his cattle out to graze. At 11:00 A.M. his scouts rode in and reported that the Zulus were on the way, and as British officers watched through their field glasses, five columns of Zulus could be seen maneuvering in the distance—the chest formed up, and the right horn ran off at a rapid pace, the left horn hooking out more slowly. When Wood's scouts first encountered the Zulus, they had taunted the white men, saying, "We are the boys from Isandlwana."[31] They also yelled, "Don't run away, Johnnie, we want to speak to you."[32] Zulus called all British soldiers "Johnnie." All the regiments from Isandlwana were there, spreading out as they moved toward another battle with the "red soldiers." There were a few gaps in their ranks, but not very many, as most of those who had fallen earlier had been replaced. In addition to their spears, clubs, old rifles, and new Martini-Henrys, many Zulus wore British white leather ammunition belts and pouches taken from the dead men of the 24th.

As the Zulus approached, Wood recalled the firewood detail and retrieved the cattle. But before he ordered his troops to arms, he insisted that they eat dinner, which they did, apparently steadied by Wood's imperturbability even though their battalion officers tried to hurry them. A few of the eighty-eight wounded and sick men in hospital joined their comrades, including an officer commanding one company who insisted on being carried out to his men so that he could cheer them on. Wood gave the order to strike the tents at 12:45, and the Ngobamakosi of the Zulu right horn instantly picked up speed in their charge. They had interpreted the striking of the tents as an indication that the British were retreating, and they were eager for the kill. They were well ahead of the other Zulu formations, and Buller saw a chance to goad them into charging prematurely. Wood agreed, and Buller's horsemen teased the Zulus, opening fire before withdrawing slowly, firing, and withdrawing again. The young men with single red feathers came on with a rush.

Although no one knew it yet, the precipitous charge of the Ngobamakosi committed the Zulus to an attack on Wood's fortified position, and it cost them any chance they may have had for victory. Mehlokazulu, a junior officer with the Ngobamakasi, recalled:

> Our regiment, the Ngobamakosi, was so anxious to distinguish itself that we disobeyed the King's orders, and went on too fast, without waiting for our supports. When we got to the camp we were so tired that we could do nothing, and by the time our supports came up we were beaten back. Had we waited properly for our supports, we should have attacked the camp on three sides at once, and we should have taken it.[33]

Wood watched through his binoculars as the Ngobamakosi charged. He saw a "fine, tall chief running on well in front of his men." The man fell, was helped up, and was hit again. He was replaced, but three more chiefs fell as the British fire knocked the Ngobamakosi down. As Mehlokazulu told the story, the Zulus lay down and returned the British fire, waiting for the rest of the Zulu army to enter the battle: "[W]e were lying prostrate, we were beaten, we could do no good. So many were killed that the few who were not killed were lying between dead bodies, so thick were the dead."[34] From the British lines it didn't seem quite so one-sided. There was so much smoke that it was difficult to see the effect of the fire, and when the Ngobamakosi lay down at distances of 200 to 400 yards away and opened a heavy fire with Martini-Henrys, it seemed to the British like a planned tactic. The Zulu firing increased as other regiments finally came up and occupied a ravine on the south of the camp. Soon the camp was surrounded on three sides, and the Zulu crossfire was doing damage.

The British infantry in the cattle kraal were taking such heavy losses that they began to withdraw. This was a dangerous moment, so Wood ordered two companies of the young 90th to counterattack with bayonets.

They did so with such dash that they drove back the Zulus, but so many of them were being shot down that Wood ordered them to retreat. That was the turning point of the battle. If the Zulus had charged, Wood thought, they might have broken the British position.[35] Zulu officers urged their men on, but there was no charge. Wood himself shot three Zulu officers as they exposed themselves in frantic efforts to inspire their men. The courage of the Zulu leaders was not enough. There would be no last organized charge. Even so, some Zulus had fought their way into the cattle kraal. Wood sent two companies of the 13th to charge them with bayonets. Two hundred bearded red soldiers charged and the Zulus were routed. The Zulus were so hungry that many of those killed were found with their mouths stuffed with corn meal meant for the cattle.

A warrior named Sihlahla, who had fought at Victory Hill on January 22, was with the *umXhapo* regiment, which was part of the right horn. He described the battle much as Mehlokazulu had:

> Everyone in the Ngobamakhosi lay down as the safest, for the bullets from the white men were like hail falling about us. It was fearful, no one could face them without being struck. . . . I found myself near a large white stone placed there by the white people [a range marker?]; behind this I got, and there remained until the force gave way and fled. We were then pursued by the horsemen from the camp, who rode after our retreating army and turned them about like cattle. We were completely beaten. . . . Not one of our force doubted our being beaten, and openly said that they had had enough and would go home. Mnyamana, the induna in command, tried to collect the force and march it back to the King, but he could not.[36]

Most Zulus fought much more resolutely than Sihlahla, who was one of the "coastal" Zulus Mehlokazulu scorned, but by 5:30 P.M., after more than four hours of fighting, the Zulus were wavering, and Buller's horsemen were ordered out to charge them. He pursued them until it was dark, killing mostly men of the Qulusi, who had arrived just in time to be swept back by the Zulu retreat. But Zulus from royal regiments were killed, too. Many died bravely. George Mossop said that when many Zulus were overtaken, they turned and exposed their chests saying, "*Dubula M'lungu*" ("shoot, white man")—and the white men did. Lieutenant Cecil D'Arcy, a colonial officer who earned a Victoria's Cross the day before at Hlobane, was still remembering his men's terrible cries for mercy as the Zulus speared them the day before while he rode out after the retreating Zulus. He ordered his men to remember Hlobane and to give no quarter.[37]

Private John Snook, a mounted infantryman from the 13th, joined the pursuit: "Then we let our mounted men out of the laager wagons, and I can tell you some murdering went on. They followed them up for about nine miles, and killed about 700."[38] The killing continued the following day, as Snook described: "On March 30th, about eight miles from camp, we found about 500 wounded, most of them mortally, and begging us for mercy's sake not to kill them; but they got no chance after what they had done to our comrades at Isandhlwana."[39] When the Zulus ran, Lieutenant D'Arcy ordered his horsemen to follow. They pursued the Zulus for eight miles, "butchering the brutes all over the place." D'Arcy estimated that his men killed over 2,300 Zulus.[40]

When it came time to examine the Zulu dead, expressions of admiration for Zulu courage began to emerge. One British private wrote, "I never saw the like, nothing frightened them, as when any of their numbers were shot down others took their places." Sergeant Edward Jervis of the 90th added, "I confess that I do not think that a braver lot of men than our enemies in point of disregard for life, and for their bravery under fire, could be found anywhere."[41] A colonial officer who had fought bravely at Hlobane was also impressed by the Zulus' courage: "We all admire the pluck of the Zulus. I wish you could have seen it. Under tremendous fire they never wavered, but came straight at us."[42] Another officer added: "There is no doubt the Zulus fight splendidly. They rush straight up, and don't seem to fear death at all. The cannon worked first-rate; so differently to the firing at Isandlwana."[43] As Mossop inspected the Zulu bodies, he saw a "big powerful dead" Zulu lying on his back with "a good portion of his head blown away." The man had a beautifully carved snuffbox on a string around his neck, and Mossop thought it would be a nice souvenir. When Mossop reached for his prize, the "dead" man kicked him in the stomach. Mossop was bowled over, his wind knocked out. When Mossop recovered, he took possession of the snuffbox. He did not mention taking the Zulu to the hospital. Wood's men buried about eight hundred Zulus found lying within 300 yards of the camp. It was not pleasant work. Sergeant Jervis said: "A more horrible sight than the enemy's dead, where they felt the effects of shellfire, I never saw. Bodies lying cut in halves, heads taken off, and other features in connection with the dead made a sight more ghastly than ever I thought of."[44]

Not all the Zulus were butchered by Wood's horsemen. Wood ordered that the horsemen bring him at least one member of every Zulu regiment represented in the battle. The next morning Wood interrogated fifteen or twenty "grand specimens of savage humanity." When he had finished,

Wood mentioned that before the battle of Isandlwana the British had treated wounded Zulus in their hospital, only to have those men attack them when the camp was attacked. He asked, rhetorically, if anyone among them could tell him why he shouldn't kill them. A Zulu with an "intelligent face" answered: "There is a very good reason why you should not kill us. We kill you because it is the custom of the Blackmen, but it isn't the White men's custom."[45] Impressed by the Zulus' appeal to the force of custom, Wood gave the men safe passage through the British forces. Perhaps neither Colonel Wood nor the Zulu prisoners knew that British troops had already adopted the Zulu "custom" of killing without mercy, and that they would continue to do so.

The Zulu army at Kambula was defeated by one of its greatest strengths—the rivalry between regiments. At Isandlwana the umCityo regiment was first to enter the British camp—first "into the tents," as a Zulu officer put it. Since then, the Ngobamakosi regiment was not permitted any relief from the boasts and taunts of its rival regiment. At Kambula, when the Ngobamakosi saw a chance to be first into the British camp, they charged without a thought for their king's orders. Despite their courage, they were stopped cold. If all the Zulu regiments had charged at once, they might have had a chance to break into the British camp, but it would have required a terribly costly charge, and once inside the camp the Zulus would have faced a counterattack by more than six hundred horsemen. But there was no coordinated charge. Zulu spears never became a factor in the battle. Instead, the Zulus exchanged rifle fire with the British before they retreated. During more than four hours of battle, the Zulus killed only three British officers and eighteen men; they wounded sixty-five more. Probably three thousand Zulus were killed during the battle and the subsequent pursuit. Many others must have died later of their wounds.

After the battle Mehlokazulu offered an excuse for his regiment: "It was unfortunate for the Zulus that the Ngobamakosi regiment should have marched quicker than was expected; we had no intention of attacking the camp, but were drawn on to do so by the mounted men, before the main body of the Zulu army came up."[46] A warrior from the Thulwana who had survived Rorke's Drift told the same story, attributing the Zulu defeat to the mad rush of the "horns" to be the first into the camp. Instead of getting into the camp, as each rival regiment had boasted it would be the first to do, the men were simply exhausted and played no significant role in the battle. It was the men of the Zulu chest, including the Thulwana, who fought their way into the cattle kraal; two unmarried regiments of the Zulu chest—the Nokenke and Umbonambi—were virtually annihilated in the effort. This veteran warrior concluded by saying that "the Ngobamakosi and umCityo acted like fools."[47]

When remnants of his defeated army returned to Ulundi, King Cetshwayo was furious. His men had disobeyed his orders and had suffered a terrible defeat at little cost to the British. The warrior from the Thulwana regiment described the army's return: "The King was very angry when we went back; he said we were born warriors, and yet allowed ourselves to be defeated in every battle, and soon the English would come and take *him*."[48] Cetshwayo threatened to kill the officer who commanded the Ngobamakosi, but nothing came of it, perhaps because so many of the officers were killed in the battle, perhaps because the man was Sigwelewele, one of the king's most loyal supporters.[49]

Many Zulus believed that their losses at Kambula were the heaviest they had yet suffered.[50] The king had no time to mourn his losses. On the same day that his army had been decimated at Kambula, Lord Chelmsford invaded Zululand with the largest British army yet to take the field. To oppose Chelmsford, Cetshwayo had nothing but the second-rate local men who had been defeated at Victory Hill two months before. To reinforce them, Cetshwayo dispatched orders to the men of five young regiments who lived in the coastal area plus the coastal men of the Thulwana, who were still led by Dabulamanzi on his white horse. This army was less than one-third as large as the 35,000-man force that had been ready to oppose Chelmsford on March 13. This time only about 10,000 men were assembled at a place called Gingindhlovu—"the place of elephants" in Zulu, "Gin gin I love you" to the British.[51]

## GINGINDHLOVU

Pearson's men at Eshowe were near the end of their rope. Food was in very short supply, many men were sick, and medical supplies were exhausted. Chelmsford had delayed marching to Pearson's relief as long as he could. Since Isandlwana, Chelmsford had become a model of caution, but now even he had to admit that he had enough force. In truth he had too many men to supply, 5,670 in all, 3,390 of whom were white. Chelmsford ordered all units to march close together, but with their transport wagons they spread out for almost 3 miles as they marched slowly into Zululand. Chelmsford and his officers were afraid that the Zulus would attack while they were on the march. So was John Dunn, who was also skeptical about the fighting qualities of the young British troops. Except for two companies of the veteran "Buffs," the four British infantry battalions contained many raw recruits. They had never seen warfare before, and many were barely familiar with their weapons. To make matters worse, one of the regiments, the 57th, which had only recently arrived from Ceylon, was physically unfit for any hard campaigning. Once again, Chelmsford's luck was good. Much of his good fortune can be attributed to the presence of 540 sailors and one hundred Royal Marines from the Naval Brigade. These were older men, experienced in war in many parts of the empire. A photograph taken at the time shows one contingent of those men from the H.M.S. *Tenedos*. One of the sailors was black, probably a West Indian.[52] The Royal Navy sometimes recruited black West Indians as buglers or drummers, but this black man would do more than make music, he would stand shoulder to shoulder with white sailors and fire against the Zulus. The weakest points of any square were its four corners, where it was most difficult to bring massed rifle fire to bear on an attack. Chelmsford put either a Gatling gun or a cannon in each corner and backed them up with sailors and marines. They were a colorful lot, the sailors in their middie blouses and straw hats, and the marines in bright new scarlet tunics. Whatever they wore, those men would stand up to a Zulu charge.

The Zulu army had a new commander named Somopo, who would do nothing to eclipse the memory of Shaka. Instead of ambushing the long, strung-out British column or driving off its cattle herds, he waited on a hill just north of Gingindhlovu for the British to approach. They arrived the night of April 1. Instead of waiting for the British to resume their march and once again be vulnerable to attack, he ordered an attack for the next day at dawn, when the British would still be secure behind the laagered wagons and in the trenches that they now prepared every night. Just before 6:00 A.M., British scouts rode back to the laager with word that the Zulu army was moving toward them. That came as no surprise to John Dunn, who had scouted the Zulu camp the night before and knew that there would be an attack. Dunn urged Chelmsford to send out cavalry to provoke the Zulus into a charge, but there was no need to bait them. As more than five thousand men inside the British laager watched, the Zulu army deployed into its classic crescent formation—its *only* formation—and charged.

If the Zulu will to fight had been crushed at Kambula, as historians have argued, there was no evidence of it yet.[53] Captain (later General Sir Edward) Hutton wrote:

> The dark masses of men, in open order and under admirable discipline, followed each other in quick succession, running at a steady pace

through the long grass. . . . The Zulus continued to advance, still at a run, until they were about 800 yards from us, when they began to open fire. In spite of the excitement of the moment, we could not but admire the perfect manner in which these Zulus skirmished. . . . In spite of our steady fire the Zulus continued their advance nothing daunted, the force attacking our front utilizing cover.[54]

Led by a Gatling gun that fired into a mass of Zulus at a range of only 300 yards, the British opened a tremendous fire. Fortunately for the Zulus, who were taking terrible losses as it was, most of the British rifle fire was high. John Dunn, who was calmly putting his superb marksmanship to use by sitting on a wagon and picking off Zulu officers, whom he knew and disliked, noticed that the fire of the British infantry was passing far over the heads of the charging Zulus. Dunn pointed out to Chelmsford (who was commanding his forces while wearing a bright red nightcap) that the Zulus were then only 300 yards away, but the young infantrymen still had their sights set at 1,000 yards. The men of the Naval Brigade fired more accurately, and once the infantry was commanded to lower their sights, the Zulus suffered terrible losses. Even so, about one hundred Zulus got to within 20 yards of the laager before they were killed. A few Zulu officers actually seized British rifles before they were shot or bayoneted. Dabulamanzi was seen leading one charge that got to within a dozen yards of the British line.[55] A British officer was amazed: "Fancy, there were some of them twenty yards from the trench. Talk about pluck! The Zulu has all that. They were shot down one after the other, and they still came on in hundreds."[56] The war correspondent "Noggs" Norris-Newman, a former Imperial officer himself, who was rumored to have been emasculated by Britain's enemies in an earlier colonial war, was a witness, and he too was enormously impressed: "No praise can be too great for the wonderful pluck displayed by these really splendid savages, in making an attack by daylight on a laager entrenched and defended by European troops with modern weapons and war appliances."[57]

There were fewer than half as many Zulu warriors in this attack as at Isandlwana or Kambula, and there were many more British guns firing against them. Even so, they charged the British guns so hard that they almost broke the British line. Maori Hamilton-Browne described the battle with what was, for him, understatement:

It must have been about 6:20 A.M. when the Zulus made their first great effort to storm the front, right, and rear faces of our defenses, and their advance was indeed a splendid sight, as just at that moment the sun came out and shone full on the lines of plumed warriors, who, with their arms and legs adorned with streaming cow-tails and

> each brandishing his coloured ox-hide shield and flashing assagais rushed forward to what he fondly hoped to be an orgie of blood, with a dash and elan that no civilized troops could have exceeded. This magnificent charge, beautiful as it was as a spectacle, was a trifle too enervating for the over-worried, unfed and somewhat nervous youths who had to face it, very many of whom more than wobbled in the shelter trenches. In fact it was only the frantic efforts of the officers of one regiment that, on the death of their Colonel, prevented their men from making a clean bolt of it, and that just at the most critical moment when the charging Zulus were within one hundred yards of the shelter trenches. Troth it was a near call and for a few minutes it was a toss-up whether the laager at Ginginhlovu was not to be a second shambles like Isandlwana.[58]

It was the 60th Rifles, a regiment that wore *green* coats and fought this battle lying in a shallow trench, that wavered when their commander, Lieutenant Colonel Francis Northey was shot, but other units felt the pressure of the Zulu assault too. One Gatling gun was almost taken by charging Zulus, and one Zulu actually fell dead draped across the sailors' machine gun. In another charge, a Zulu actually leaped into the laager. He was a ten-year-old udibi boy, a sleeping mat carrier, who was swept up in the passion of the Zulu attack (a Naval brigade sailor sat on the boy until the battle was over, and later the boy entered the Royal Navy). After about one hour and twenty minutes, the Zulus were beaten, and Chelmsford ordered his horsemen out in pursuit.

Although the foot soldiers and sailors were under orders never to step outside the laager, the commander of the Naval Brigade, Commodore Richards, could not restrain himself. Vaulting the parapet, he began slashing with his sword in all directions. "The sailors, mindful of the threatened penalties, never stirred, but yelled with delight, 'Go to it Admiral!' and, 'Now you've got 'em! Look out, sir, there's one to the right in the grass!' till they were all roaring with laughter."[59]

As the cavalry pursuit was beginning, one Zulu refused to run. Armed with only his spear, he stood with his back to a large thorn bush, ready to fight anyone who dared. A British horseman was about to shoot him, but a sergeant who had been a saber instructor waved to the man not to fire and rode at the Zulu with his sword. A crowd gathered to watch the combat. No details of the fight were recorded, except that it lasted a long time before the mounted British sergeant finally impaled the Zulu on his sword.

Hamilton-Browne was part of the mounted pursuit. As usual when he was in a fight, he was in high spirits:

> Now it came to pass as I, riding my own line and being very busy using only the point [of his saber], chanced to notice a big fine Zulu louping along through the long grass, and had half a mind to go for him, but at the same moment he was charged by a M.I. [mounted infantry] man, who galloping recklessly past him made a most comprehensive cut at him, which however, although it failed to annihilate or even wound the Zulu, still drew blood, as it lopped off the ear of his own horse, a proceeding that the animal resented by promptly kicking off its clumsy rider. The Tommy was however true grit, for in a moment he regained his feet and hanging on to the reins which, good man, he had never let go, he turned on to the astonished Zulu and discharged on to the latter's hide shield such a shower of blows that the noise sounded like a patent carpet-beater at work and effectually prevented him from using his assagai. Again, I was on the point of going to our man's assistance and had swung my horse ready to do so, when up from the rear galloped another Tommy who, holding on to the pommel of his saddle with his left hand, flourished his sword and shouted, "Let me get at the bleeding blighter, Dick," and then delivered a terrific cut which in this case missing the crow etched the pigeon as it nearly amputated poor Dick's sword hand, who might well have ejaculated, "Lord save me from my friends." This, nor any other pious cry he did not use, as his remarks, on receiving the wound, were of a decidedly declamatory nature and were sufficiently comprehensive so as to embrace not only his enemy and his rescuer but also all things animate and inanimate within the district. The blighter had however come off badly for he had been knocked end over end by the rescuer's horse, and before he could regain his feet the rider, whether voluntary and involuntary, was precipitated on to the top of him and without further delay, discarding his sword, grabbed the Zulu's knobkerrie with which he proceeded to bash its owner over the head, so seeing they were all right I devoted my attention to my own work.[60]

Like many war stories, this one may have been improved in the telling, but it illustrates the profound difference that existed between young British recruits who tried to run away and veteran soldiers who fought with something that amounted to intense pleasure.

"Maori" Browne's "work," like that of the other mounted men, was killing. The experienced horsemen, followed by the clumsy mounted infantry and the Natal natives on foot, pursued the fleeing Zulus for 7 or 8 miles, killing them the entire distance. Sergeant Edwin Powis, formerly of the 24th, was now a mounted infantryman. He wrote: "We were cutting them down like grass, they were that thick." Powis and the other mounted men gave no quarter. When the bugle signaled "cease fire,'' Powis found three wounded Zulus. ''We cut off their heads, the three of them, and let them lay,'' he wrote without comment.[61]

According to Fleet Surgeon Henry F. Norbury, who was inside the laager throughout the battle, only one Zulu prisoner was taken, a warrior of the Thulwana who had been wounded in the leg. He told Norbury that the Zulus had been ordered by Cetshwayo to attack where they had because it was the site of a great victory on a former occasion. Norbury wrote that the wounded Zulu was asked why he had fought for a king whom the British thought was despotic and feared by his people. ''He answered, somewhat nobly, as I thought, 'And what would you think of a people which would desert their King?' ''[62] As events were to prove, most British officers failed to see anything noble in the Zulus' loyalty to their king.

After the battle, the British found rifles stamped ''24th'' and a sword that had belonged to Lieutenant Francis Porteous, who had died with his men at Isandlwana. More than two thousand Zulus had been killed. Almost a thousand of them lay in rows near the laager where British fire had stopped their charge. The Zulus removed many of their dead during the night, but many still remained. The British tired of burying them after counting to 580. British losses amounted to two officers and eleven men killed, with forty-eight wounded. It was an overwhelming victory, and Chelmsford marched into Eshowe justly proud of himself. The first troops to reach Eshowe were the 91st Highland Infantry wearing their tartan trousers (or ''trews'' as they were called) and led by their pipers playing ''The Campbells are Coming.'' As Chelmsford's troops marched back to Natal in escort of Pearson's thin and sickly garrison troops, his column had to detour around the Gingindhlovu battlefield to avoid the appalling stench of decomposing Zulu bodies. Although 580 had been buried, many others lay rotting. The following night the young green-coated soldiers of the 60th Rifles panicked again. Mistaking men of the 91st Regiment for Zulus at night, they shot fifteen of them, twice as many as the Zulus had shot in the battle. Then seeing some real Zulus, they went at them with their bayonets, killing three and wounding eight more. The Zulus were the unarmed scouts of John Dunn, who wept for ''his children,'' as he called them. Dunn thought that the Naval Brigade had professional fighting men, but he cursed the British ''boy'' soldiers.[63] Hamilton-Browne was simply appalled. He could not understand how the defense of the Empire had been entrusted to ''children'' like these.

The battles at Kambula and Gingindhlovu had proved that Zulu courage, however incredible it might seem to British observers, was not enough to defeat British troops in a fortified position, even if many of those troops were scared boys who couldn't remember to lower their sights. As the Zulu warriors straggled home to their kraals, many knew beyond further doubt that they could not defeat the British, at least not in battles like these.

# Chapter 7

## "Fight Us in the Open": The Last Battle

The Zulu warriors who Chelmsford's panicky young troops imagined were gathering in the darkness were in fact straggling back to their homesteads. The wounded hobbled along, helped by their friends and young udibi boys. Many of them died along the way. They were buried in shallow graves or left in caves or the thick brush. Somopo's men did not have as far to go; they were already in their home district. Some headed for Emangeni, the royal homestead, where Cetshwayo had lived as a boy. The men of the royal regiments dispersed throughout Zululand, mingling with the dispirited and wounded survivors of the battle at Kambula. When the tired and suffering men reached their homes, their women greeted them in the traditional welcome: Faces covered with white clay, leaves around their ankles, the women swept a path for their sons, brothers, and husbands with little handbrooms, singing, "Ki, ki, ki, ki, ki, ki—*kuhle kwetu!*" (Oh! oh! oh! Joy in our homes!)[1] Their joyous welcome quickly turned to grief for those who had died. Men and women alike sobbed uncontrollably, rolling on the ground in their anguish. All over Zululand families mourned for their dead. Older men admitted that they were afraid to fight again, and even young warriors lost their enthusiasm for washing their spears in the blood of the red soldiers. Thousands of Zulus had died at Kambula and Gingindhlovu, and not one British soldier had been killed by a Zulu spear.

Cetshwayo felt his nation's grief, and with his counselors he desperately sought a way out of the war. Zulu men were worried about their herds and fields; it was not safe for them to leave their homesteads for long. Wherever they could, the British were burning kraals and stealing cattle. There were signs of political dissention. Hamu, the king's half-brother and the former commander of the Thulwana, had defected to the British, and Cetshwayo's cousin Zibhebdu, a powerful young chief and counselor who controlled a vast area of northeast Zululand, was becoming more and more independent. Zibhebdu had commanded the Dloko at Isandlwana, where he had been slightly wounded. (It was said that his ''wound'' was a result of being hit in the eye by the cork from a champagne bottle found in an officer's tent). He was healthy now, and he had fought at Kambula, but there were rumors that he wanted to overthrow Cetshwayo. Although some of Cetshwayo's young regiments still wanted to fight, Cetshwayo and his counselors wanted an end to the war. The king's most brilliant counselor, his prime minister, Mnyamana, was a distinguished war leader (he had more than once stood up to Shepstone and was known as the only Zulu the Thulwana would stand in awe of), but he had long recommended a policy of peace. He had been in command at Kambula and had seen the defeat. Now he again urged the king to seek peace. Messengers were sent to find someone among the British who would negotiate. The messengers were shot at, arrested, or ignored.[2] As late in the war as June 12, King Cetshwayo still did not know the name of the British commander or, for that matter, that there even was a single supreme commander. As a result, his messengers walked more than 150 miles in a futile attempt to arrange a peace conference. They needn't have bothered: The British knew that Cetshwayo wanted peace, but Chelmsford was not interested in negotiation.[3] He was determined to have a smashing military victory.

When Lord Chelmsford returned to Natal early in April after relieving Pearson at Eshowe, he found the colony awash with British troops. In addition to growing numbers of mounted volunteers from Cape Colony and literally hundreds of unattached ''special service'' officers who had one way or another managed to get leave from their regiments to fight the Zulu, there were more than seven thousand armed Africans and almost 17,000 Imperial British troops called from the farthest corners of the empire. There were no fewer than fifteen full battalions of infantry and two regiments of cavalry—the 17th Lancers and the 1st King's Dragoon Guards. If Chelmsford could have found a way to supply all those men in Zululand, he could have fielded an army larger than anything Cetshwayo could mobilize, but supply was still Chelmsford's greatest problem. He had lost most of his transport at Isandlwana, and the profit-minded colonists of Natal were not making it easy for him to replace his wagons and oxen. Even when transport could be found, Chelmsford had massive administrative problems. London had sent him no fewer than four major-generals, two of whom scarcely spoke to one another, but it had not sent food for the troops or forage for the horses. (English cavalry horses did not graze; they had to be provided with fodder.) The British were forced to purchase mules from as far away as Texas. One of the mules later kicked Hamilton-Browne, breaking his leg and putting him out of the rest of the war.[4]

Among the reinforcements sent to South Africa was Captain W. E. Montague of the 94th Regiment. The greatest fear of officers like Montague was that the war would end before they would have their chance at glory. A remarkable illustration of their zeal to reach the war zone came at a recoaling stop when the artillery officers on Montague's troop ship actually stripped to the waist and joined their men in shoveling coal. When their ship arrived in South Africa, they encountered so many horror stories about the Zulus that they named Cape Town "great funk-land." The officers bought postcards of Zulus, which they referred to as "hideous savages," before the 94th Regiment set off for Natal. When they arrived, they were amazed to learn that even officers could carry no more than 40 pounds, so a gigantic pile of luxuries (beds, rubber mattresses, easy chairs, and so on) piled up in Durban. There would be no cricket pads in officers' portmanteaus this time.

The new arrivals were told to be on the alert for Zulu attacks everywhere, even in Durban, where Zulus were rumored to be prowling about and planning to sabotage the lighthouse. The men were ordered to dye their white helmets and belts brown for camouflage. They also learned that there would be no alcohol on the campaign, except for officers, of course, who could choose among "Dry Monopole" champagne, Hennessey brandy, Bass beer, Hollands gin, and some smuggled bottles of whisky. The Natal settlers were making a fortune supplying the troops, but as Montague and the 94th marched up-country, people merely stared at them. There were no cheers, and no flags were waved. Montague marveled at the butterflies, birds, and wildflowers. He was fascinated by a "war dance" put on by some Natal native soldiers, but he was repelled by the drunken colonists, who drank gin instead of water. Like everyone else, he made absolutely no mention of East Indians. They were invisible.

As Montague and his men slogged closer to Zululand, many other officers used the time on their hands to attend dances and dinners, to hunt, and to flirt with farmers' daughters. Meanwhile, Chelmsford and his no longer meager staff tried to sort out his army and its transport. As usual Chelmsford insisted on doing everything himself, and he would not be hurried. This time, he would be even more meticulous in his preparations to invade Zululand. While he gathered his supplies and made his plans, his newly arrived young infantrymen learned what it meant to march in the African sun, how to laager a camp, and how to live through the day without gin or rum. Cavalry mounts, which came off their ships so thin that they looked like greyhounds, slowly regained their strength. All the new men heard terrifying stories about the Zulu army, and the young soldiers became openly apprehensive.

Troops were kept busy escorting supply convoys through Natal to the Zulu border, where more troops guarded the growing supply dumps. A newly arrived officer of the 58th Regiment described what the period of waiting was like:

> Camp life here is dreary and monotonous. The number of men in the convoy, say, 1,000, may look very large on paper; but when you have this number distributed among 100 or 200 waggons they do not look so imposing. Every waggon on the road must have its guard, as none can say when an attack is likely to be made. . . . The civilians here wonder how in such a climate, with seventy rounds of ammunition, belts, water bottle, haversack filled, rifle and bayonet, an English soldier can march twenty miles a day under a roasting sun. After a march we have to laager the convoy. On drawing all the wagons together . . . these are entrenched . . . we act always on the assumption that the Zulus may be upon us at any moment.[5]

This description of routine precautions against Zulu attacks referred to supply columns that marched through Natal to a supply dump that was still nine miles away from the Zulu border! Before Isandlwana, Chelmsford had joined his staff officers in snickering at Colonel Bellairs for writing general orders that required laagering every night. "Bellair's mixture," the orders were called, punning on a well-known patent medicine. But Chelmsford had not taken any chances since. His general orders required every soldier to sleep with his boots and ammunition belts on, his rifle at his side. All the men stood to, ready to fight every morning an hour and a half before daylight. There would be no repetition of Captain Moriarty's failure to laager at Myer's Drift. But the effect of the continual state of alarm—while the troops were still in Natal—was to terrify many of the teenage recruits who made up much of the force of Chelmsford's new regiments. For example, the 58th would later find itself involved in a panic, or "funk" as the British called it, when its men, under the orders of its officers, opened fire on phantom Zulus in the middle of the night. They even fired two shells from their cannon. Five British soldiers were wounded. There were no Zulus anywhere nearby. Other regiments were even more panicky.

While Chelmsford was building up transport and supplies for his "grand army'' of Natal, as some of his officers called it, some of his men were continuing to raid Zulu kraals. A mounted patrol from the 80th Regiment, the regiment whose men had died in Mbilini's attack at Myer's Drift, shot two Zulus during a raid on April 5. One of them proved to be Prince Mbilini, the victor at Myer's Drift. Redvers Buller's horsemen were seldom inactive, and neither were ''Maori'' Browne's. Zulus in Sihayo's district often sniped at British troops on the Natal side of the Buffalo River, and Browne regularly retaliated by raiding into Sihayo's territory. Those were more than bloodless diversions from the boredom of camp life. One incident should be enough to convey the casual horror of those days. A Zulu sniper had been firing at Hamilton-Browne's camp on the Natal side of the river, so Hamilton-Browne and a few men crossed the river, lay in ambush, and caught the man (Browne actually tackled him). The Zulu was wearing a red cloth around his head, which he freely admitted was intended to deceive the British (a red headband was used to identify natives who fought *for* the British, not against them). We pick up Hamilton-Browne's account:

> I almost felt sorry for the poor chap, but a scout must have no feelings and years of savage warfare had blunted any I might have ever possessed, so as soon as he had recovered his wind a *rheim* [rope] was passed round his neck and we trotted back to camp. On our arrival there we handed over the prisoner to the main guard, which during the day used a wagon outside the laager for a guardroom, and I at once reported to the O.C.
>
> He ordered me to return to the prisoner, question him and then to report anything I might find out. This I did but of course could get nothing out of him, though he owned up readily he was a spy and that he wore the piece of red stuff round his head as a disguise. I was turning round to return to the O.C. when I struck my shin, which I had badly bruised a few days before, against the boom of the wagon. The pain was atrocious and I had just let go my first blessing when the Sergeant-Major, a huge Irishman, not seeing my accident, asked, ''What will we do with the spoy, sor?'' ''Oh, hang the bally spy,'' I ripped out and limped away, rubbing my injured shin and blessing spies, wagons and everything that came in my way. On my reporting to the O.C. that I could get no information, but that the man owned up to being a spy, he ordered the Camp Ajutant to summon a drum-head courts-martial to try him. Paper, pens and ink were found with difficulty; true, there was no drum but a rum keg did as well. The officers, warned, assembled and the Sergeant-Major being sent for was ordered to march up the prisoner.

> He stared open-mouthed for a few seconds, then blurted out, "Plaze, sor, I can't, shure he's hung, sor." "Hung!" exclaimed the O.C., who was standing within earshot. "Who ordered him to be hung?" "Commandant Browne, sor," replied the Sergeant-Major. "I ordered him to be hung?" I ejaculated. "What do you mean?" "Sure, sor, when I asked you at the guard wagon what was to be done with the spoy did you not say, sor, 'Oh, hang the spoy,' and there he is," pointing to the slaughter poles, and sure enough there he was. There was no help for it. It was clear enough the prisoner could not be tried after he was hung, so the court was dismissed and there was no one to blame but my poor shin.[6]

Hamilton-Browne was hardly the only man on the British side to take the killing of Zulus lightly. Lieutenant (then Captain) Charlie Harford was also leading patrols near Rorke's Drift. One morning he and Major Wilsone Black were startled to discover the body of "a wizened-up grey-headed" Zulu hanging from a scaffold. A private from the 24th explained to the concerned officers that the dead man was a spy. "Good Heavens!" said Black. "By whose orders was he hung?" "Captain Harford, sir" was the reply. Astonished, Harford, who had given no such order, investigated but never found out who had hanged the elderly Zulu or why.

As April and May dragged on, the only fighting and killing was done by small groups of jaded veterans like Browne and Buller. Soldiers in camp were exhausted by their predawn vigils and by continually loading and unloading wagons. There was still no rum for the men, whose discipline deteriorated, and floggings increased. Supplies piled up, but not until the last day of May was Chelmsford ready to begin his advance toward King Cetshwayo's homestead at Ulundi. In the tradition of European invasions, he meant to defeat the Zulu army, burn Cetshwayo's "capitol," and bring back the king in captivity. Once again Chelmsford divided his forces into three columns. Chelmsford would again command the central column. Wood would command a reinforced left column, which would join Chelmsford's force inside Zululand. A third column, led by General Crealock, would march up the coast.

Major General Henry Hope Crealock, like his younger brother, John North Crealock, Chelmsford's supercilious military secretary, was a talented artist who had once left the army and tried to make a living as a painter. He was to become the most ridiculed officer to serve in the war. Crealock's orders were to march up the soggy and malarial coast, burning kraals as he went, before moving inland to join with Chelmsford and Wood for a final, concerted assault on Cetshwayo's kraal. He commanded more than nine thousand men, who were more or less assembled at Fort Pearson on the Natal side of the Tugela River. Unfortunately for Crealock's plans, more than eight hundred of his men were seriously ill (Colonel Pearson himself had typhoid), there were few competent doctors, and despite everyone's recognition that malaria was endemic, there was no quinine available, perhaps because most officers, and some army doctors, believed that malaria was caused by air poisoned by the rotting flesh of men and horses.[7] Few wagons and cattle were available either, and Chelmsford kept most of those for his column. When Chelmsford was finally ready to march, his column had 10,000 oxen!

Crealock slowly, very slowly, gathered transport and supplies and bridged the Tugela River. There was excitement when a sailor fell in the river and was eaten by a crocodile, but there was no invasion. Crealock was almost three weeks late in beginning his advance, and once he began he went nowhere, partly because he had such severe hemorrhoids that he could not ride a horse. He blamed his transport, the rough terrain, and disease, all of which were problems, but his force became the laughing stock of the army. They were known as "Crealock's Crawlers," and a great joke in Natal was, "Have you heard the news? They've found Crealock." Crealock was not easy to love. His men were embarrassed by his lack of drive and his love of comfort. Wolseley later wrote that Crealock was a "vain swaggering snob," that he spoke to his men as if they were "dogs," and, worst of all, that he was "afraid to advance." "He has no dash and judging from his past history is very careful of his own hide and not likely to expose his valuable person to any dangers."[8]

Major (later General Sir) Bindon Blood served with Crealock's 1st Division in command of the Royal Engineers. He was embarrassed by the division's lack of purpose:

> When the 1st Division was formed, it was 9,215 strong, of all ranks, and when Lord Chelmsford told me at Durban of my appointment to it, he said, "You will get to Ulundi long before any of us—yours is far the easiest route." As things turned out, the division sat at the mouth of the Tugela for about three months, then advanced some thirty miles (measured in a straight line), halted there while the action at Ulundi was fought, went back thence (without me!)—and was broken up.[9]

Actually by far the shortest and best route to Ulundi was the same one Chelmsford had taken in January, but he adamantly refused to march near Isandlwana this time. The alternate route he chose was longer, and the terrain was much more difficult, but that is the way he would march. Chelmsford could not confront the skeletons and ghosts of

Isandlwana. Chelmsford also wanted to spare his men the sight of the field at Isandlwana. Partly because the British were unwilling to risk more lives burying their dead, and partly because the 24th Regiment wanted to bury its own dead, and it was a long time before the 24th had their losses replaced, it was not until late June that all the bodies at Isandlwana were buried. By then the bodies had been so dessicated by the sun that they looked like mummies, but oddly only a few had been disturbed by vultures or animals. Even after the months of delay, the burials were shoddily performed. Bodies were so haphazardly tossed into shallow graves that arms and legs were left sticking into the air as ghastly reminders of the battle. Perhaps it is just as well that Chelmsford spared his young soldiers a return to Isandlwana. But Chelmsford was not thinking only of his men's feelings. Even if the bodies at Isandlwana had not been fully buried, Chelmsford had to try to bury his memories. The route he chose to Ulundi involved a detour of about 100 miles and month's delay, but no one could persuade Chelmsford to take the direct route through Isandlwana.[10]

London was furious about Chelmsford's lack of progress. The war was becoming tremendously costly. The Government had sent Lord Chelmsford overwhelming forces and had nothing to show for it. Chelmsford tried to explain that he had too few wagons, that the ones he had were continually breaking down, and that oxen used to one kind of grass would sicken and die when they encountered another kind on the march. His men and horses needed "toughening" too, he wrote. Chelmsford had no doubt that he would eventually win a great victory, but London's patience ran out. On May 26, the Government appointed Sir Garnet Wolseley to relieve him. Wolseley was made a full general and given plenary civil and military powers that made him the supreme commander not only of British forces but of Natal, the neighboring colonies, and "native affairs," including the Zulus. It was just what Wolseley had dreamed of. Quickly gathering his favorite officers from his West African campaign of 1874, he set sail for South Africa.

News of Wolseley's appointment was a painful blow to Chelmsford, especially as it came on the heels of a calamity so terrible that some officers thought it would unhinge the general. The last thing Chelmsford needed as he attempted to orchestrate his second invasion of the Zulu Kingdom was the responsibility of playing nursemaid to the French Prince Imperial, Louis Napoleon, heir to the Bonaparte throne. While young Louis was growing up in exile, he attended the Royal Military School, Woolwich, where he was popular with the British cadets and tops in his class in both fencing and horsemanship. As heir to the French throne he could hardly be commissioned as an officer in the British army, but he loved the adventure of war and asked to be allowed to go to South Africa. The British Government was aghast! It was bad enough having the future king of perhaps Britain's foremost enemy in attendance at the British artillery and engineering school, but it would be unthinkable to have the last Bonaparte killed in a British war. Royalty ignored such trifles. Louis's mother, the Empress Eugénie, interceded with Queen Victoria, and Louis, a charming but bumptious twenty-two-year-old, soon arrived in Chelmsford's camp riding a huge gray horse named Percy, which he'd bought in Natal.

Everyone who met the Prince Imperial liked him, but he soon proved as recklessly adventurous as everyone feared, and the British officers who tried to protect him were driven to distraction by his daredevil antics. On June 1 he rode off to sketch with a very small escort under the command of a French-speaking British officer. Ignoring signs that Zulus were approaching, Louis refused to hurry away from a potential ambush. Twenty or so Zulus, led by a subchief named Sabuza burst, out of 6-foot-high grass, and before Napolean could mount his terrified horse he was speared. Everyone else, including the British officer, rode off pell-mell. Napoleon fought with his sword, and died with the hair from a Zulu's head in one fist. There were seventeen wounds in the front of his body, none in his back. He had not tried to run. Neither had his pet terrier, which was found speared at his feet. Not only had Lord Chelmsford failed to protect the prince, but the British officer who should have protected him had run away. When Chelmsford heard the news he was distraught. Major Lord Grenfell found him with his head on a table "in a state of absolute despair." First Isandlwana, now this. It was several days before Chelmsford would recover sufficiently to command his army.

Wolseley and his entourage reached Durban on June 28. Wolseley was horrified to discover that Chelmsford had once again divided his invasion forces into three divisions. Sir Garnet had considered Chelmsford a nitwit before, and now he was beside himself. He sent off peremptory orders to Chelmsford to consolidate his forces. By the time Lord Chelmsford received the orders he was camped only 16 miles south of Ulundi. He ignored Wolseley and moved on toward his climactic battle. As Wolseley tried to get a grasp of the situation, he was bombarded by rumors. When it comes to vicious gossip, nasty insinuation, and outright lies in the service of bitter rivalries, it would be difficult to match the British officers in this war, who wrote and said outrageous things about one another.[11] Wolseley's staff happily plunged into the swirl of intrigue, sure of their own virtue and eager for glory. As Sir Garnet Wolseley sat at dinner with Sir Bartle Frere and others, he listened and learned, delighted to confirm his conviction that everyone associated with Chelmsford was hopelessly incompetent. Only Wood and Buller were spared his contempt. Wolseley's diary records his musings.[12] It is not a noble document.

Three days before Sir Garnet's arrival, Natal was thrown into turmoil by a Zulu raid across the Buffalo River. More than a thousand Zulus, led by a defector from Natal, crossed into Natal, burning African kraals and killing. They returned to Zululand with thousands of cattle and in high spirits. Although no whites had been hurt, Natal was in an uproar. Cetshwayo was blamed. In reality, Cetshwayo knew nothing about the raid. It was mounted primarily by the Cube people, who had never taken orders from Cetshwayo and hadn't even fought against the British armies. The only other raid into Natal during the entire war was made on the day of the battle at Rorke's Drift, and Cetshwayo had specifically forbidden that.

Except for small-scale raiding, there had been no fighting for months. The army was inactive, its men engaged in their ordinary daily activities at their home kraals. In some border areas, the British had burned kraals, destroyed crops, and stolen stock, all of which worried the wealthy men of those districts no end. They and the king's counselors urged Cetshwayo to end the war, but as we have seen, the king's peace emissaries were unsuccessful. By late June, as Chelmsford's army approached Ulundi, Cetshwayo made almost frantic attempts to avoid a battle, sending messages (written in halting English by the Dutch trader Cornelius Vijn) to Chelmsford. Chelmsford knew that Cetshwayo wanted peace, but he responded by setting conditions for surrender that were almost as impossible to meet as those Frere had imposed to start the war. Still trying, Cetshwayo sent two hundred head of cattle and two huge tusks of ivory to General Crealock. The tusks were a traditional Zulu form of earnest money, a pledge that Cetshwayo would do his best to meet Chelmsford's demands. Crealock sent the peace emissaries on to Lord Chelmsford, who did not understand the meaning of the enormous tusks, and no one seems to have explained it to him. At any rate, it is unlikely that Chelmsford would have accepted a peace settlement on any terms short of abject surrender. Chelmsford wanted to defeat the Zulus in a climactic battle fought in an open field. He believed that only after such a defeat would the Zulus stop fighting. He wanted a victory to restore his reputation, and he knew that he had the forces to win. He put up the Zulu emissaries for the night, then sent them back with new demands for surrender. Captain Montague said that the Zulus scowled incessantly.[14] They had reason to.

While Chelmsford waited for a last message from Cetshwayo, he completed a strongly entrenched laager. On July 3, British scouts saw a large herd of royal white cattle on the far side of the river being driven from Ulundi toward Chelmsford's camp. Even Chelmsford knew that this herd of cattle represented a large peace offering. Before the cattle got to the river, men of the umCityo regiment—the ''sharp-pointed ones''—intercepted the cattle and turned them back. Cetshwayo's soldiers were determined to fight. As the king later said,

> I sent a number of cattle to try to get the English to make peace; but the uMcijo [umCityo] regiment drove them back and said they would fight. . . . I then asked them why they would not allow the cattle to be taken to the English. And they said, ''We will all rather die.'' I said, ''What is going to kill you all? Do you not know that the English will kill me for your doings and let you go free?''[15]

Shortly after noon, Chelmsford decided that Cetshwayo was not going to negotiate further. He ordered Buller to take his Frontier Light Horse across the White Umfolozi River and scout the route to Ulundi. With Buller rode Captain Lord William Leslie De la Poer Beresford. Known to his brother officers as ''Bill,'' Lord Beresford could not bear the thought of missing a good battle. He had managed to get leave from his regiment in India, the 9th Lancers, and had arrived in Zululand just in time to win a Victoria Cross and to take center stage in what Victorians would have considered the perfect adventure. Buller's men swept small parties of Zulus ahead of them, and when one Zulu lagged behind, Beresford spurred his horse into a charge. The Zulu raised his shield over his head in a sign of surrender, but Beresford knew nothing about that and ran the man through with his sword. Flipping the body off the sword, he cantered back to the other mounted men with a happy shout of ''first spear, by Jove!'' Beresford was an avid hunter of wild boar, and this traditional pig-sticking cry seemed appropriate to him.

Before Beresford could celebrate his ''good hunting'', some three thousand Zulus erupted from a hidden gulley and charged, firing as they came. One trooper fell out of his saddle dead, and another hit the ground wounded. As the Zulus rushed in to spear the wounded trooper, a sergeant named Fitzmaurice, Lord Beresford wheeled his horse around and galloped back brandishing his sword. Although Beresford's courage was admirable, his judgment was questionable, because there were dozens of Zulus close to the dazed sergeant. Fortunately for Beresford and

Fitzmaurice, Sergeant Edmund O'Toole rode right behind Beresford firing his carbine. While O'Toole kept the Zulus at bay, Beresford beckoned to Fitzmaurice to get up behind him. The sergeant was too dazed to understand. Beresford then *ordered* him to mount! Still, Fitzmaurice sat on the ground. Furious, Beresford next threatened to punch Fitzmaurice if he did not get on the horse. Fitzmaurice still did not obey. Instead, he collapsed. With O'Toole still holding off the Zulus, Beresford leaped off his horse and tried to lift Fitzmaurice up on the horse. The sergeant was more than 200 pounds of now dead weight, and Beresford couldn't lift him. O'Toole jumped off his horse, and the two men together somehow managed to fling the more or less conscious Fitzmaurice on to Beresford's horse. With the Zulus now close enough to throw spears, Beresford got in the saddle, told Fitzmaurice to hold on, and rode off with O'Toole right behind. After riding only 300 yards or so, Fitzmaurice passed out again and pulled Beresford off the horse. O'Toole and Beresford again struggled to push the inert Fitzmaurice back on the horse. Again they finally succeeded and rode off just ahead of the still pursuing Zulus. Again, as if playing a part in a bad melodrama, Fitzmaurice fell off the horse, toppling Beresford to the ground with him. Amazingly, the now exhausted Beresford and O'Toole got Fitzmaurice back on the horse for a third time, and they made it safely back across the river. While Beresford and O'Toole were acting out their suspenseful rescue, another trooper named Raubenheim had been shot off his horse. Captain Cecil D'Arcy, a colonial officer who had already won a Victoria Cross at Hlobane, went back for him. All alone, D'Arcy tried to lift the wounded man on to his horse but sprained his back so badly that he had to abandon Raubenheim. D'Arcy's back was so badly injured that he was barely able to ride back to camp. He had acted as bravely as Beresford, but there had been no one to help him.

That night, July 3, Chelmsford issued his battle orders. His force would march out of camp in the early morning, cross the river, and form a square on the plain beyond at a spot Buller had chosen during his foray. If the Zulus did not attack him there, he would march toward Ulundi until the Zulus finally gave battle. There was no reason to worry about that. The spot Buller chose for battle was the same one chosen by Cetshwayo. Colonel Evelyn Wood urged Chelmsford to stay in his laagered camp and wait for the Zulus to attack him, but Chelmsford refused. He insisted that the Zulus would never accept defeat until the British met them in the open, without walls or trenches. He concluded by saying, "they've called us ant-bears long enough," referring to the Zulu jibes that the British burrowed into the ground like aardvarks, or ant-bears as the British then called them. It was obvious to his officers that Chelmsford was determined to prove the defeat at Isandlwana was due not to his failure to laager the camp but to Durnford's and Pulleine's failure to have their men fight "shoulder to shoulder." Chelmsford would fight that way tomorrow: in the open, in a square, shoulder to shoulder.

Chelmsford's decision to march out of his laagered camp and fight in the open meant that some troops would have to stay behind to guard the supply wagons. In a colossal irony, he chose the 24th! The officers of that star-crossed regiment were outraged, and they pleaded for a chance to redeem the honor of the men who died at Isandlwana. Chelmsford explained that the troops of the 24th were all boy recruits who weren't ready to be risked in battle. It is true that the 24th had been reconstituted with brand-new recruits, and they had panicked the night of July 1, leaving their rifles behind and hiding under wagons when it was thought that the Zulus were attacking. Some officers said that the 24th was being punished by being left behind,[16] and its young soldiers certainly had behaved shamefully, but it may also have been true that Chelmsford simply did not want the 24th in "his" battle, just as he did not want to see the field at Isandlwana where the original 24th had died. The 24th would watch the battle from the safety of an entrenched camp. Their ignominy was lessened only slightly when four soldiers who had been court-martialed and sentenced to be flogged for their cowardice had their sentences remitted.

The British army spent a bitterly cold, sleepless night listening to the Zulus prepare for the next day's encounter. Colonel Arthur Harness was there with reinforced artillery batteries. He later wrote:

> You may fancy we all went to sleep that night with many thoughts of what the next day might bring us; our sleep was not improved by being roused about midnight by the fiendish chanting of the Zulu army being prepared for fighting by the witch-doctors, etc., and also—as we have since learnt—of an additional army which had arrived that night from near Crealock's division, singing on their way to the king. It all seemed so unpleasantly close that one could hardly believe we were to be left alone that night.[17]

Many soldiers didn't believe it. Twice the young soldiers panicked, thinking they were being attacked. Colonel Lowe, who commanded the Lancers, was stamped on the head as he slept by a frightened soldier's hobnailed boot. It is fair to say that so far the young soldiers were not doing well at all.

The men's spirits were not improved when Wood's friendly Zulus loudly interpreted distant screams in the night as trooper Raubenheim being tortured by Zulu women. Sergeant Edward Jervis of Wood's 90th Light Infantry wrote to his mother that the Zulus were "yelling like demons."

> They were preparing for the fight for the next day, which, I suppose, they knew would take place. Well, mother, there seemed to be as if there were thousands of voices, and we could see their fires very plainly. I could not sleep, so I lay awake thinking of home, and you, old Ted, and Dick, wondering how you all were, and if I should be alive the next night. The next morning saw us all up before daylight, and having had coffee and a bit of biscuit we fell in silently for the march.[18]

As the men of the 24th watched through the cold morning mist, Buller's Frontier Light Horse led Chelmsford's army across the shallow White Umfolozi River. It was a formidable force. There were twelve cannon and two Gatling guns. In addition to Buller's mounted men, Chelmsford had a troop from the 1st Dragoon Guards, the entire 17th Lancers, thirty-three companies of Imperial Infantry, and more than a thousand men from the Natal Native Contingent. In all, there were 4,165 white troops and 1,152 Africans marching in a huge square across the plain toward Ulundi. The red coats and the green grass made a pretty sight for newly arrived Lieutenant Colonel Charles Robinson, who watched and listened to the regimental bands playing.[19] The festive mood changed early in the march when Buller's men found the body of trooper Raubenheim. He had been scalped and disemboweled, and his nose, right hand, and genitals were missing. Whether he had been mutilated by war doctors or vengeful women was unknown, but angry murmurs rippled through the ranks as the news spread.

The Zulu army that waited for Chelmsford's huge red square to advance was as large as ever. All the famous regiments were assembled, most of their losses made up by young men. After such terrible losses at Kambula and Gingindhlovu, it seemed certain that the Zulu army had lost its zest for battle, but many veterans had joined the young men in answering their king's call to battle. The umCityo regiment had made certain that a battle would take place by turning back the cattle Cetshwayo had sent to Chelmsford. After the battle, several Zulu warriors said that they had been confident that they could defeat the "red soldiers," and four Zulus who were taken prisoner the night before the battle told the British soldiers that they "pitied" them. Zibhebdu was there once again leading the Dloko, Mehlokazulu was there with the Ngobamakosi, and Dabulamanzi still led the Thulwana. Cetshwayo had already gone into hiding, but many of his counselors, along with Cornelius Vijn, watched from a distant hill as the Ngobamakosi rose out the long grass to face the British square. Slowly, all the other regiments rose to form a perfect crescent. More than 20,000 ostrich-plumed warriors began their angry buzzing sound, rattling their spears against their shields and stamping their right feet in thunderous unison. As the enormous British square marched closer, the Zulus were shaken by its size. One of the few Zulu prisoners taken just after the battle expressed his dismay:

> The King himself personally placed the different regiments and gave us our orders. We were watching and expecting that the [British] army would leave the laager and march for the King's kraal. We saw the force as it started to cross the river, and surrounded it as we had been told to do. . . . We had no idea the white force was so strong in numbers till we saw it in the open . . . and we were startled by the number of horsemen.[20]

Buller was ready with his horsemen to goad the Zulus into charging, but there was no need. The Zulu army was already moving forward. Chelmsford refused to dismount, so his staff officers also had to remain on horseback, exposed to Zulu fire. Buller, who never left his horse in any battle, sat mounted next to Chelmsford, smoking a cigarette while he watched the battle through a telescope. This time Chelmsford did not wear a red nightcap; he was in full uniform. The British artillery opened fire, and as shells exploded among the Zulus, officers with binoculars saw the warriors jab at the smoke with their spears. The inexperienced Zulu soldiers did not understand artillery. As the Zulu lines drew nearer, the artillery switched to canister, and the Gatling guns and rifles joined in. It was 8:35 A.M.

Leaving several large reserves behind out of range of British guns, the Zulus advanced with their usual speed and precision. Lieutenant Colonel Sir Charles Robinson watched their charge:

> They gradually came down in the long grass, running round to try to surround us. . . . Our men's infantry fire did not check this at all at first, and at the corner of the square between the 21st and 58th, where I stood principally, the Zulus came on steadily in spite of it working round at a sort of half run (fired at by case shot and musketry) in the most determined way. . . . It surprised one enormously . . . to see them come on thus in the face of a withering fire . . . up to less than 100 yards of us. Any nearer and it would have become a bayonet and assegai affair. As it was, 2 or 3 officers drew their swords or revolvers expecting a hand-to-hand fight of it.[21]

So many Zulus fell dead that it appeared to one British corporal as if they had been "tipped out of carts."[22]

Melton Prior, an artist for the *London Illustrated News* and a veteran of seven wars, described what he saw from his position close to Chelmsford:

> At a distance of 800 yards the enemy was seen advancing in skirmishing order in the front, and large masses behind them as supports. On they pushed in face of a perfect hailstorm of lead, steadily and unflinchingly, as only a brave and determined soldier can do. But for the coolness which was shown by our troops, from the officers in command down to the bugle boys, it would have been hopeless to stand against the intrepidity which the Zulus displayed. In the course of all the campaigns at which I have been present, I can state without hesitation that I have never come across an enemy which I have felt more pride in seeing beaten. For over half an hour they faced a fire so searching and so deadly that almost any other troops would have flinched before it; and at one moment it was a grave question whether they might not succeed in a rush on one of our faces. As it was, from 2,000 to 3,000 formed up about thirty deep, and with a piercing war-cry made a dash for the corner, which was being held by the 58th and 21st, and two guns of Major Le Grice. Lord Chelmsford, who during the action was seen riding first to one point and then to another, on seeing this, rode to the corner threatened, and the words from him, "Cannot you fire faster?" were answered by one continuous rattle from the whole of the infantry in that direction. In a few moments it was evident this had had the desired effect of checking this rush, and almost immediately after they were observed to waver, turn, and finally to fly in all directions.[23]

This last attack was made by the umCityo, who made good their boasts of bravery.

Lord Grenfell saw a Zulu induna who led that attack against the corner of the British square where two Gatling guns were firing. Grenfell saw the man fall with a bullet in the head. After the battle, Grenfell measured the distance between the man's body and the machine gun at 18 yards. Two years after the battle, Lord Grenfell returned to battlefield.

> I again paced the eighteen yards and came to my old friend, a splendid skeleton, his bones perfectly white, his flesh eaten off by the white ants. I felt I could not part with him, so I put his skull into my forage bag, and brought it home with me. It now adorns a case in my collection of curiosities.[24]

Grenfell was a kindly and sensitive man, so it is possible, although only just, that he took the skull as a gesture of respect. Be that as it may, to put a brave man's skull in one's "curiosity" case is an unusual way of showing respect.

A Sergeant of the 17th Lancers, waiting with the other Lancers inside the square, also described the Zulu charge:

> They advanced yelling like madmen, in all about 25,000, the place was black with them, and they kept up a tremendous fire, but fortunately high; still, men and horses were dropping all round, and it was hardly a place for a nervous old gentleman to take a stroll. The infantry, who carried a hundred rounds per man, kept up a fire like one continual blaze, but not withstanding this the Zulus got to within fifty or sixty yards of us.[25]

This attack was driven off when the British artillery fired canister into the Zulu ranks at 50 yards. Chelmsford thought the Zulus were beaten and was on the verge of sending his cavalry out after them when the Zulu reserve charged again, the married men of the Nodwengu regiment getting to within 30 yards of the square. In another incredible episode from this storybook war, the men of the veteran 13th Regiment, who had fought with bayonets at Kambula, actually stopped firing at the Zulus and beckoned to them to "come on" and fight with spear against bayonet.[26] After thirty minutes or so of courageous charges, as often by head-ringed married veterans as by the young, unbloodied warriors, the Zulus broke. This time Chelmsford did send out the Lancers, shouting, "Go at them, Lowe!"

Lieutenant Colonel Drury Curzon Drury Lowe was commanding the 17th Lancers only because its colonel, Thomas Gonne, had shot himself in the foot at pistol practice. Lowe was anything but a brainy officer, but then Lancers were supposed to charge, not think, and Lowe was certainly willing to charge. He wheeled his gold-braided, blue-and-white-coated regiment into line, red-and-white pennons fluttering on the tips of their 9-foot-long lances. Their ornate uniforms prompted one of their officers to say the men looked like a "lot of damned tenors in the opera."[27] No sooner had Colonel Lowe ordered his men to advance than he was knocked off his horse by a spent bullet. His men rode on without him. Lieutenant Viscount St. Vincent had what he described as a splendid time leading his troop into the Zulus, some of whom lay in the grass to avoid the deadly lances, sometimes trying to stab a horse, sometimes leaping up to grab a lance and try to pull the Lancer off his horse. They were usually sabered or shot by other cavalrymen who followed the Lancers. Occasionally the fleeing Zulus turned and fought as units. The son of a nobleman, Captain the Honorable Wyatt-Edgell, was killed in one such stand. But most Zulus simply ran, as Lieutenant Colonel Robinson unfairly observed, "like sheep," trying to escape the Lancers and Buller's colonial horsemen.

Young George Mossop, who rode with Buller, was awed by the Lancers' charge:

> On their great imported horses they sat bolt upright, their long lances held perfectly erect, the lance heads glittering in the sunshine. They formed into line. In one movement the lances dropped to the right side of the horses' necks, a long level line of poles . . . the steel heads pointing straight at the mass of retreating Zulus. As the big horses bounded forward and thundered into them, each lance point pierced the Zulu in front of it; the man fell, and as the horse passed on beyond him the lance was withdrawn, lifted and thrust forward into another Zulu in front. The movement of withdrawing the lance and again getting it into position was very rapid. . . . It was a grand sight to see them at work, but they did not appear to me to be humans and horses—just a huge machine. A handle was turned—and it shot forward; a button was pressed—up went the spears, and it reformed in line; another button was pressed—down went those awful spears, and again it shot forward.[28]

A Lancer wrote this account to his brother:

> You should have seen us. With tremendous shouts of "Death, Death!" we were on them. They tried lying down to escape, but it was no use, we had them anyhow, no mercy or quarter. . . . We only stopped when we could go no further and the horses were completely done up. . . . The Zulus lost about 2,000 or 3,000, our loss was small, about twenty five killed and hundred wounded. . . . The fellows we charged were all young men, splendidly-made fellows, and all stripped for fighting.[29]

The most experienced European infantry ran in terror when pursued by Lancers, and the Zulus had no previous experience with this kind of warfare. They ran, but not like sheep, as Colonel Robinson so disparagingly said. Many fought back bravely with the weapons they had, and one man left a lasting impression. When some Lancers were about to run him down, he turned and, spreading his arms out, presented his bare chest to their Lances. The Lancers killed him, but they spoke of him for a long time afterward.[30]

Most of the cavalrymen stopped their pursuit because their horses were exhausted, but a few, including Lord Beresford, rode on to Ulundi. In addition to sticking pigs, Beresford was a champion steeplechase rider. When he put his horse over the king's thorn-bush fence, he became the first Briton to enter Ulundi. He was known as "Ulundi" Beresford the rest of his life. Right behind Beresford was the son of a Lord, the Honorable William Drummond, Chelmsford's civilian interpreter. In another of this war's eerie coincidences, Drummond was riding Louis Napoleon's former horse, the large gray named Percy. Percy vaulted the thorn fence with ease, but later he was found riderless. After looking for treasure without success and settling for a few souvenirs, the British burned Ulundi. Its more than 1,500 grass-roofed houses in the 500-yard-across circular kraal made an enormous blaze. "It was a splendid sight," one officer wrote. Drummond was listed as missing. He was the brother of one of Queen Victoria's maids of honor, and the Queen anxiously wrote an inquiry as to his welfare. Months later Drummond's body was found in the ashes of King Cetshwayo's kraal.

Chelmsford had defeated the Zulus in an open fight and had burned Cetshwayo's "capitol." His forces had driven the Zulu regiments off the field of battle, killing at least 1,500 of them and probably many more. Evelyn Wood counted no fewer than sixty dead Zulus within seventy paces of one of the Gatling guns, and it had jammed no fewer than six times during the forty-minute fight.[31] Still, Wood rather pettishly said that the Zulus hadn't charged nearly as well as they had at Kambula. It is possible that Wood was right. The Zulu attack at Kambula had lasted more than four hours, and this one ended after "only" forty minutes. But for forty minutes these Zulus attacked a force more than twice as large as the one Wood commanded at Kambula. The Zulus were defeated, but their last charge against the British still stands as a monument to their courage.

The British losses were only ten dead and sixty-nine wounded. It was a crushing victory, and the Zulus knew it. The same Zulu prisoner who said that the Zulus were shocked by the size of the British square said, "The army is now thoroughly beaten, and as we were beaten in the open, it will not reassemble or fight again." Lieutenant Colonel Robinson wrote that the British native allies saw it the same way:

> [O]ur having gone out and fought and beaten the Zulus (20,000 and all the best regiments were there) fairly in the open, has had an immense effect on our natives and morally has done 10 times as much good for our prestige with them as a victory from a laager would have. They, as well as the Zulus, always half believed that the [Zulus] could overwhelm us in the open field.[32]

Evelyn Wood had urged Chelmsford to entrench the square, and Chelmsford had refused. According to Wolseley, Wood said that Chelmsford wasn't "fit to be a corporal,"[33] and in some respects he was a poor general, but this time he was right and Wood was wrong.

The war was over as far as General Chelmsford was concerned, and to the surprise of even his strongest advocates, who thought he should pursue King Cetshwayo, he promptly marched his army away from the smoldering ashes of Ulundi back toward Natal. Chelmsford sent his resignation on ahead to Wolseley. He would leave the job of capturing Cetshwayo to Wolseley. Disgusted with Chelmsford, Sir Garnet Wolseley nevertheless took on that task along with the rest of his duties. He organized several small mounted columns to search for the Zulu king, who was somewhere in the still hostile northern half of Zululand. Patrols from each column rode out looking for the Zulus' fugitive sovereign. The ensuing search showed a few of the British at their best—and many others at their very worst.

Northern Zululand is a very large area of mountains, forests, ravines, and impenetrably thick bush. The chances of a British patrol's just stumbling across the king's hiding place were nonexistent. Without help from the Zulus themselves, the British could never find the Zulu king. Wolseley had been assured by Frere and Shepstone that the Zulus hated their despotic king. He was shocked when no Zulu could be found who would give the British information about his whereabouts. The patrols were urged to try harder. Ambitious young officers like those who had volunteered for glory in Zululand needed little urging.

One patrol, led by Captain Herbert Stewart of the Dragoon Guards, had Charlie Harford as its interpreter. Stewart and Harford rode for 300 miles through northern Zululand without finding so much as a clue to Cetshwayo's whereabouts. The kraals they found had no men, and the women and children who were there offered neither information nor food. Harford was persistent but polite in his search for information. He also showed respect for the Zulus he met. On at least one occasion he displayed great courage. That happened when he and Stewart rode unarmed into the kraal of an old chief, Somkele, who was a relative of Cetshwayo. They were confronted by a thousand armed warriors and an insolent Somkele. Ignoring the fact that they were still at war with the Zulus, Harford brazened it out, demanding respect as representatives of the "Great White Queen" and exchanging jibes with Somkele. Eventually Somkele softened, and the British officers were treated to Zulu beer. They reciprocated with a flask of brandy (which Somkele loved). Finally they were presented with a cow, two sheep, and some goats. In return they gave Somkele a cheap mirror. Somkele was delighted with the mirror, but he gave Harford no information about the king. When the British rode away, Somkele was still admiring himself in the mirror, saying, "Ow! I never knew I was so ugly!"[34] Ugly or not, he had not betrayed the king.

Other patrols took a less gentlemanly approach. Wolseley was determined to punish the Zulus, whom he referred to as "those interesting niggers," until they surrendered Cetshwayo. Writing "perhaps I am brutal, but . . ." Wolseley angrily ordered his patrols to burn kraals and take away the cattle.[35] They did so with enthusiasm, but not until they had first indulged themselves in looting:

> I have seen a soldier with four milking-bowls over his shoulders, two in front and two behind, four or five girls' bead-fringes [worn around their buttocks] round their waist, three men's tail-pieces slung over one shoulder and below the other, like a shawl, a number of bangles on his wrists, on his hat a Zulu's ball of feathers, four or five assegais in one hand and six or seven knobkirries in the other. Many of the officers also wore copper and brass bangles as the spoils of war.[36]

One patrol dug up the grave of King Mpande, Cetshwayo's father, and took away his remains.[37] Earlier in the war, when British working parties were harassed by small parties of Zulus, they had rigged dynamite booby traps. A reporter from the *Natal Daily Telegraph* wrote with satisfaction that one of those booby traps "blew about six Zulus to atoms."[38] After the defeat at Ulundi, many Zulus, along with their women and children, took refuge in caves. Sometimes they sniped at British troops. When called upon to surrender, most refused. When eight head-ringed Zulus did decide to surrender after being promised safe conduct, they were immediately killed by native soldiers, whom the British were too slow in restraining. Not surprisingly, word of the incident spread, and several groups of Zulus refused to leave their caves and continued to resist. British troops sealed the mouths of the caves and threw dynamite inside. Many hundreds of Zulu men, women, and children were killed.[39] Much of that devastation was carried out by men of the veteran 13th Regiment, some by the newly arrived 94th. Natal newspapers reported the use of dynamite against women and children without critical comment. Wolseley was delighted when patrols led by John Dunn found 500 kilograms of powder hidden in a cave. On another occasion Dunn led Wolseley to a kraal where rifles were repaired and bullets were cast from lead. Dunn also captured many royal cattle, which Wolseley happily confiscated.[40]

Still, no one betrayed King Cetshwayo, not even after being tortured. The British had beaten and flogged Zulus from the very first days of the war in search of information.[41] Now they did so with exceptional brutality. The men who ordered and personally supervised the application of torture were not white colonials or private soldiers, nor were they the traditional African enemies of the Zulus—they were imperial officers, including men of high social standing. Captain Ederic Frederick, Lord Gifford, for example, relied on torture in his search for Cetshwayo. Lord Gifford was one of Wolseley's favorite officers. He had led a detachment of scouts for Wolseley during the Asante War, when his daring exploits had made him a national hero. He was undeniably brave, but he was also ruthless. Lord Gifford arrived in Zululand too late to see any fighting at Ulundi, but he joined the search for Cetshwayo with his usual vigor. Gifford commanded a patrol of 1st Dragoon Guards under the experienced Zulu fighter Major Percy Barrow, another of Wolseley's men. They regularly used threats against any Zulu, including women and children, whom they suspected might know the whereabouts of Cetshwayo. Some Zulu men were beaten, and others were tied up to tree limbs and flogged. A senior chief was kicked to his knees and burned with firebrands. Several times Zulus were threatened with death and taken out into the bush to be shot. While other Zulu prisoners listened, a shot would ring out, and the British officer would come back to say that the execution had been carried out. In addition to the use of terror, the British also offered large bribes for information. Still no Zulu would betray their "despotic" king. A civilian from Natal who was the patrol's interpreter and knew the Zulus well was surprised and perturbed by the Zulus' devotion to Cetshwayo: "Nothing would move them. Neither the loss of their cattle, the fear of death, nor the offering of large bribes would make them false to their king."[42] Many Zulus opposed Cetshwayo and his uSutu faction, but political opposition was one thing, and betraying the Zulu king to the red soldiers was another.

Finally, Gifford found a homestead where Cetshwayo was thought to have slept the night before. Gifford's interpreter, W. H. Longcast, described what happened: "Two lads were found there, and, as they denied all knowledge of Cetshwayo's whereabouts, they were blindfolded, and a volley fired into the air. The ruse succeeded, and one, exclaiming 'My brother is shot!' promised to lead Lord Gifford to the King's retreat."[43] Various writers have referred approvingly to Gifford's success in "tricking" a Zulu boy.[44] That same "trick" used against white children would be more likely to be considered a war crime than a "clever ruse," as it was called then. The newspaper reporter Norris-Newman wrote that Gifford "had a wonderful way with the Zulus."[45] It is unlikely that the Zulus would have put it exactly that way. Cetshwayo was captured the next day, August 29. He said that he was a very old man. He was forty-seven. Almost two months had passed since Ulundi had been burned. Cetshwayo's capture ended the British military campaign. The now "former" king was sent to house arrest in Cape Town, and most of the British troops sailed away.

Although the British routinely exaggerated the numbers of Zulus who attacked them,[46] they consistently underestimated Zulu casualities. That is so because the Zulus removed many of their dead and wounded before the British could attempt to count bodies, and when the British did count bodies they rarely went beyond 200 or 300 yards from their defensive perimeter. Many Zulus lay dead outside that area. For example, while the official British count of Zulu dead at Gingindhlovu was 580, whom they buried, Norris-Newman noted that when a more extensive search of the battlefield was made, 1,100 dead Zulus were counted.[47] Apparently most Zulus who were wounded later died—so many, in fact, that the Zulus persisted in their belief that the British bullets were poisoned. Zulus told the border agent Eustace Fannin that even the slightly wounded "nearly all died."[48] After the war, a few British observers met Zulus who had survived their wounds (Harford met one man who had recovered from eleven wounds, several of them serious), but most white observers were surprised that so few of the Zulu warriors they met after the war had *any* wounds.[49]

About 10,000 Zulus had been killed on the war's various battlefields. Perhaps as many more died later of their wounds. How many cattle, sheep, and goats were lost to the British is unknown. On the British side, seventy-six officers and 1,007 men were killed in action; others died of wounds or disease. How many of their Natal African allies were killed was never determined. The war had cost the British Crown over more than £5 million. Britain was eager to declare the war at an end, and so it did. The war had begun at all only because British forces had invaded Zululand; now that they were gone, there was no reason for the Zulus to continue the warfare. They had their fields and their cattle to look after, and it was time to plant next year's crop.

The red soldiers came and fought, then they left. The Zulus really had no idea why. Wolseley did. They came to destroy Zulu power, and Wolseley was the man for that job. Lieutenant Governor Sir Henry Bulwer tried to persuade Wolseley not to destroy the Zulu nation. Wolseley would have none of it, recording in his diary that Bulwer "goes in however for being a lover of the human race: humanity before Nationality is his cry which I would always reverse."[50] Wolseley was as good as his word. He divided the former Zulu Empire into thirteen chiefdoms, one of which was given to John Dunn. The result was civil war. Despite reports of widespread bloodshed (John Dunn's forces killed several hundred in one fight, earning him the title of a "little white Shaka," and another chief killed more than a thousand a little later), the British Government ignored Zululand. It had gotten what it wanted, the destruction of Zulu power. Natal need no longer worry about a Zulu invasion. Instead it would now benefit from the creation of a destitute population available for wage labor. Each of the thirteen new district chiefs, who swore allegiance to Wolseley, was required to agree that the people in his district would be allowed to work in Natal and the Transvaal. Wolseley also forced some chiefs to provide Zulu men as "bearers" to carry British supplies back to Natal. That kind of labor was demeaning for Zulu men, as Wolseley was informed, but he was not swayed.[51] Despite the British victory, there was no triumph for British High Commissioner Sir Bartle Frere. There would be no seat in the House of Lords, not even praise from his Government. He had destroyed Zulu power, but the disaster at Isandlwana and the cost of the war had destroyed Frere's career. He was recalled from South Africa in May 1880.

When King Cetshwayo was first captured, his legs were too badly chafed for walking, so along with several wives he was carried to Durban in a wagon. There is a famous photograph of the Zulu king taken at that time. He is sitting on the deck of a British ship that is about to carry him into captivity in Cape Colony. Except for his polished headring, the king is wearing nothing but a small fur loin cover and a bracelet on his right wrist. His massive, powerful legs, along with his ample belly, leave no doubt of his royal heritage. His face, with a small mustache, is strikingly handsome, but it is his expression that makes the photograph so memorable. He is looking directly into the camera and smiling, but it is no ordinary smile. He seems to be giving the British a condescending royal smirk.

Cetshwayo was a problem for the British conscience. The former king had given up his leopard skins and cow tails for European clothes, and with the change he had lost much of his regal bearing. He had also been slow to grasp the complexities of some British customs. Lieutenant Charlie Harford, who was once again serving with his old regiment in South Africa and spent considerable time with Cetshwayo, was amused by the king's passionate interest in Lady Robinson. Lady Robinson was "an uncommonly pretty" woman, according to Harford, but she was married to the British High Commissioner, and the king's offer of fifty head of cattle for her was neither appropriate nor, probably, sufficient.[52] Despite gaffes like that, which betrayed the king's unfamiliarity with

British customs, Cetshwayo quickly grasped many of the niceties of British etiquette and foreign policy, and he impressed those who knew him best, like his interpreter, R. C. A. Samuelson, with his dignity, intelligence, and compassion.[53]

Cetshwayo was majestic and even autocratic at times, as Samuelson noted, but he was hardly insensitive. Major Ruscombe Poole became a close friend of Cetshwayo. When Poole was killed in the Anglo-Boer War of 1881, Samuelson had to break the news to Cetshwayo. "As soon as the bad news had been interpreted by me, Cetshwayo's head drooped downward and tears rolled down his cheeks."[54] Not only was Cetshwayo liked by his captors, but the deposed king was gathering adherents in the British Government, too. When he wrote letters to the Colonial Secretary like the following, it was difficult not to listen: "Do you kill me like this because I am a black man? My country would not have been destroyed and I would not have been taken captive if the Zulu matters had been from the very first properly looked into by the Imperial Parliament." Again:

> Who could be a greater friend of the English than I, who remained quiet in my country till I was attacked and taken captive. I fought when I was attacked, just to ward off a falling tree, as it were, even as any other person would do. I request you to look to my case and not my colour, and not leave me to die here while my family is being scattered and is dying off on the hills.[55]

When Lord Elcho called Cetshwayo a "cruel and crafty gorilla" in Parliament, he was shouted down and forced to substitute more moderate language.

In 1882 Cetshwayo was allowed to visit England. Accompanied by three Zulu chiefs, he met the Prince and Princess of Wales and Queen Victoria. He also strolled along Bond Street and walked in Hyde Park. Once he visited Lord Granville, who was sympathetic to Cetshwayo's restoration.

> Having passed the statue of Achilles in Hyde Park Cetshwayo asked Lord Granville whom it represented; on learning that it had been erected in honour of the great Duke of Wellington he turned to one of the chiefs accompanying him and remarked, "You see it was not so very long ago since they fought as we do, without clothes."[56]

In January 1883 Cetshwayo was allowed to return to Zululand, and the thirteen chiefdoms were replaced by three political divisions. The extreme south was held as British Crown land, the central region was given to Cetshwayo, and the north went to his former ally Zibhebhu. The result was intensified fighting.

Zibhebhu was related to Cetshwayo and had fought bravely in the royal army leading the Dloko Regiment. In fact, he was the only high-ranking Zulu officer to be wounded leading his men against the British square at Ulundi. But Zibhebhu had been a prosperous and independent chief of the Mandlakazi people for years, and since Cetshwayo's capture he had become even more prominent and ambitious. Cetshwayo's return threatened his gains. Cetshwayo's adherents, the royal uSutu faction, lost no time in confirming Zibhebhu's fears. First they raided Zibhebhu's territory, then they sent a large army against him. Zibhebhu's much smaller force retreated skillfully before it sprang a terrible ambush. More than four thousand uSutu were killed. Zibhebhu lost only about a dozen men. Later, Zibhebhu attacked Cetshwayo's homeland and in a single battle killed over more than five hundred uSutu, including fifty-nine of Cetshwayo's most senior chiefs and counselors. Jolly old Chief Sihayo was among the dead.[57] Cetshwayo himself was speared but escaped, only to die a little later, apparently poisoned by Zibhebhu.[58] Only three months later, in May 1884, Frere died.

After that, Zululand was relatively quiet for many years. Even during the Boer Wars the Zulus were quiet, defending themselves only when Boers rode into Zululand to steal cattle. Unbeknownst to the Zulus, however, their military reputation was still serving British interests. By 1897 the British and French were approaching a military confrontation for control of West Africa. In an effort to intimidate the French, information was leaked to the French military attaché in London that the British were preparing to ship Zulu troops from Natal to Nigeria.[59] A few months later the French signed an agreement with the British. The British bluff with Zulu warriors may not have been decisive, but it was an interesting symbolic use of a "disarmed" and "demilitarized" people.

Although Zululand was generally peaceful, it was neither a happy nor a tranquil place. There were endless political intrigues, and growing poverty—many Zulus who had fought bravely against the British were now pulling rickshaws in Durban[60]—but there was no serious fighting until 1906, when the government of Natal imposed a poll tax on the Zulus. The tax was "fair"—Zulus would pay the same tax as European residents of Natal—but it was anything but equitable, since the Europeans in Natal had far larger incomes than the Zulus. Europeans could also vote to change the law; in 1905 exactly three Zulus were registered to vote.[61] The tax was a spark, and an aggressive leader named Bambata fanned it into an explosion.[62] Twenty-seven years after Ulundi, the Zulus went to war again against a white army.

The rebellion of 1906 was very different from the Anglo-Zulu War. For one thing, only about 12,000 of the 300,000 Zulus then in Zululand actually took an active part in the rebellion, and the white soldiers were all colonists from Natal. No Imperial British troops were involved. Even so, there were some startling similarities to that earlier war. At the beginning a white sergeant was killed, and his genitals were used to "doctor" the Zulu warriors. Many of the old Zulu ritual precautions were followed, and new ones were added, some of them similar to the Maji-maji rituals used to the north in Tanganyika a year earlier. As before, many Zulu elders urged restraint, pointing out that the rebels would be defeated just as their seniors had been in 1879; the young men of 1906 responded with a derisive boast worthy of their grandfathers: "*We* were not there!"[63]

The government of Natal sent 10,000 men with modern weapons against the Zulus. The white troops had heavy artillery and modern machine guns. They also had magazine rifles that would fire five or seven rounds before reloading. If all of that modern weaponry were not enough, the whites fired dum-dum bullets (These soft-nosed bullets that expanded on contact were illegal in "civilized" warfare). The massive colonial army eventually forced the Zulus to fight a guerrilla war, but at times the Zulus launched frontal attacks using the traditional Zulu formation. The chest advanced against machine gun fire, while the horns tried to envelop the position. The young Zulus shouted "uSutu" as they charged, and some got close enough to stab with their spears. When those semi-Westernized young men of 1906 were wounded, they lay waiting for death as their fathers and grandfathers had done. E. A. Ritter was there:

> When a part of the Zulus rebelled in 1906 the author fought against them as a trumpeter in the mounted Natal Carbineers. This enabled him to witness their bravery in battle, and although their regimental training had been suppressed for a generation it was amazing to see how well they kept their traditional battle formations and faced a hail of bullets with nothing but assegais and shields. From a fifty-foot-high precipice flanking the Mangeni Valley the author had a grandstand view of the epic encounter between Captain Lonsdale's Natal Native Contingent, armed with shield and spear, and similarly armed Zulus. The Zulus were a remnant broken by several encounters with Colonial troops lower down, yet in ones and twos they attacked the advancing line of Lonsdale's force, and several times scattered their attackers until, one by one, collapsing from their wounds, they would lie, an elbow on the ground and their head supported on their hand, proudly awaiting the traditional *coup de grace* and disembowelling.[64]

Most of the Zulu rebels, including the fifty-two-year-old Mehlokazulu, were killed when their forces were surrounded in a gorge:

> Then commenced a merciless slaughter which lasted sixteen hours. Shells and shot rained down into the gorge from every side and as this fire ceased the troops came in mowing down everyone in sight. No opportunity was given for surrender, for no prisoners were taken. Those who fled into the forests and tried to take shelter by climbing the trees were ruthlessly shot down; dum-dum bullets were extensively used.[65]

The Natal government reported that six hundred Zulus were killed in the battle. The correct number was undoubtedly much higher. The government estimated that 2,300 Zulu rebels were killed during the rebellion. That number, too, was probably low. Colonial forces hanged some Zulus more or less at their whim and flogged others unmercifully, sometimes to death. Rape was also commonplace. General Jan Christian Smuts, who would later serve as President of the Union of South Africa, said sadly that the 1906 campaign was "simply a record of loot and rapine."[66]

White colonial doctors and nurses refused to care for Zulu wounded, so that task was left to Indians, who were organized as stretcher bearers and medical aides. The Indians wore khaki uniforms, puttees, slouch hats, and Red Cross armbands. They were led by an Indian with the rank of sergeant major, who was sympathetic to the Zulus and their suffering, but who had volunteered out of a sense of loyalty to the British Empire.[67] The sergeant major was named Mohandas Gandhi. He could not speak Zulu, but he tried to comfort the suffering men.

# Chapter 8

# The Experience of War

Any attempt to understand what it was like to fight in the Anglo-Zulu War, or why those men fought as they did, must begin by acknowledging that there can be no simple or sovereign answers. There are few things more complex than the feelings and motivations of men in battle. One reason why the question is as vexing for the Anglo-Zulu War as it has been for every other war is that there are so many different kinds of battles. There are short battles and long ones, small ones and large. Fighting from behind a stone wall is not the same as charging the men protected by that wall. Facing cannon fire is not the same as facing a cavalry charge. Skirmishing with long-range rifle fire is not the same as fighting face-to-face with spear, sword, or bayonet. Fighting alone is not the same as fighting in a group. The differences are as great as day and night; incidentally, fighting during the day is not the same as fighting at night.

A second reason why the feelings of men in battle are so complex is that even when men are engaged in the same kind of battle, they will not all experience the fighting in the same way. At best, a soldier experiences only a small portion of a battle's complexity, and every man's experience of that small portion is affected by fatigue, hunger, thirst, fear, smoke, dust, noise, and much else. As a result, all battle experiences are partial and personal. Again, some experiences are recalled clearly, others as if in a dream, and some not at all. Veteran soldiers are likely to differ from novices, just as officers are likely to differ from men in the ranks, older men from young men, tired men from fresh ones, confident men from frightened ones, and so on. What is more, even when the men of a unit are alike in those and other characteristics, they will still differ so greatly in personal motivation that one man may sacrifice his life recklessly while another may go to equal extremes to avoid danger. The meaning of bravery may also vary from one group of soldiers to the next, just as it may vary within a single small group. A man may be brave in one kind of fighting and shrink from another, just as a man who is surpassingly brave in one battle may lack courage in another. Bravery is only one issue in men's experience of war, but it is a central one, and in its complexity it exemplifies the subject: Why men sometimes fight so bravely and at other times run away is not a question that has been answered easily in the past, and it will not be answered easily here.[1]

To complicate matters even more, it would be absurd to assume that the Zulus and British were exactly alike in their experience of battle. Zulus and Britons came from dramatically different cultural worlds in which the meanings of life, of fighting, and of dying were not the same. One of the tasks of this chapter will be to explore those cultural differences. At the same time, however, it would be wrong to assume that Zulus and Britons were so different that their experiences of battle were utterly incomparable. In fact, while there were important differences between Zulu and British soldiers in their experience of battle, when it came to fighting, those very different men were often more alike than they were different.

## TYPES OF COMBAT

First, we should distinguish three different kinds of fighting that took place frequently during the Anglo-Zulu War. There were encounters between small groups such as scouts; there were large battles between defenders and an attacking force; and, finally, there were pursuits in which men of one side ran for their lives while those of the other pursued them. To begin with small groups, both the British and the Zulus used Zulu spies to infiltrate each other's armies, and we know that both sides sometimes caught and killed those men. It goes without saying that those men were brave, even foolhardy, but we know so little about who they were or why they acted as spies that we can say no more than that. We know more about the men who scouted for both sides. Some Zulu scouts went ahead individually or in pairs to observe and report back with information. Zulus said that scouts had to be brave but not rash, because it was their job to report back with information, not to take chances with their lives. Mpatshana confirmed that the men chosen to scout were "men of courage."[2] Sometimes boys barely into their teens played this role bravely, too. Other scouts acted more like skirmishers, moving in groups of a score or even more. It was a common tactic of such scouts to let themselves be seen, then retreat in what appeared to be panic, hoping to draw the enemy into range of the entire Zulu impi. That tactic was relatively safe against enemies on foot who were armed with spears, but the British sometimes pursued on horseback and fired their rifles accurately at considerable distances. The Zulus countered by using mounted scouts who were armed with rifles too.

British scouts were always horsemen. If they were careful, they could ride away from an ambush with little risk. However, the terrain of Zululand could be treacherous for even the most experienced British mounted scouts. Zulu warriors could easily hide in deep gullies or in grass that grew as high as 10 feet in some areas. When ambushed, a horse might step in an aardvark's hole and throw its rider. As we saw, several British officers and men risked their lives to save men thrown from their horses. Although a few British officers, both colonial and Imperial, were less than courageous in this form of warfare, most of them did very well. Those men had ridden all their lives, and this sort of irregular fighting, like that in the American West, attracted adventurous officers in droves. It was an exciting way to spend a day, and, except for a rare ambush, there were few chances of being killed. It must quickly be said that Zulu scouts thrived on adventure too. Considering that they were often on foot and not as well armed as the British, they took remarkable risks. Brave men on both sides fought in many small skirmishes, but if the war had consisted of nothing more than skirmishes, it would have attracted little attention. What made this war so remarkable was its large battles in which so many men fought and died.

Over the six-month duration of the war, the Zulus and British fought seven major battles, and in all but one—the fight on top of Mount Hlobane—the Zulus attacked and the British defended. In all six Zulu attacks, thousands of Zulus charged across hundreds or thousands of yards of open ground while British rifles, Gatling guns, and artillery fired into their ranks. As we have seen, at least 10,000 Zulus, and perhaps many more than that, died. To defend against charges like those required both skill and courage, but no form of warfare requires more courage than an infantry charge over open ground into heavy fire.

Troops from many countries have shown great bravery in their frontal attacks. Almost every country remembers at least one epic example of astonishing heroism by its men charging into enemy fire and dying, sometimes to the last man. But there is no army that has not recorded at least one instance in which its best troops attacked, only to break before the enemy's fire, running back in panic or surrendering in abject submission. There is no need to single out any troops in this regard. Men of *all* countries and races have failed in their attacks and have run away in disorder. We sometimes forget that most European armies knew perfectly well how horrible it was to charge a strong enemy position and therefore took pains to leave its troops no choice but to advance or die. Sometimes officers shot or sabered anyone who refused to advance; sometimes cavalry or picked infantry followed the attacking ranks with orders to kill any man who ran back toward them. We think of heroic charges like that of Pickett's division at Gettysburg in terms of brave men, not men who trudged forward numbly because they had no choice, but both kinds of men took part. Pickett's nineteen-year-old Virginians had never been in battle before that day, and they charged into massed cannons four times before they were almost all killed or wounded. Their courage cannot be diminished, and many of them needed no encouragement, but this Confederate division, like most on the North side, used "file-closers"—hundreds of men with fixed bayonets who followed the attacking ranks under orders to kill any man who ran.[3]

Men of many armies have tried to describe what it is like to walk, trot, or run forward across open ground against rifles, machine guns, and cannon, with men in front of you or to your side being blown apart, dismembered, or flung into the air as blood-spouting bits of formerly human creatures. Men hunch their shoulders against the fire, bunch together, and die with screams that once heard can never be forgotten. Most accounts of battle, at least until recently, when "blood and guts" description became acceptable, have ignored those terrible realities of war. Except at Isandlwana, where only a few regiments withdrew in the face of British fire, every Zulu attack against the British ultimately failed and the Zulus broke away, usually running for their lives. The Zulus did not have any equivalent of file-closers.

It was terrifying to attack British fire power, as a warrior who fought at Kambula put it, with Zulu "arms, legs, and heads" flying in every direction.[4] Yet, as horror-evoking as these words are, the images still lack meaning. *We* were not there. Perhaps the closest we can come is by recalling the chilling account of a Zulu who charged against the British with the umXhapo regiment in the *relatively* bloodless battle of Victory Hill, fought on the first day of the war against Pearson's men at the Inyezane River:

> We were told to advance and, grasping our [weapons] we went forward packed close together like a lot of bees. . . . We never got nearer

> than 50 paces to the English, and although we tried to climb over our fallen brothers we could not get very far ahead because the white men were firing heavily close to the ground into our front ranks while the [cannon] was firing over our heads into the regiments behind us. . . . The battle was so fierce that we had to wipe the blood and brains of the killed and wounded from our heads, faces, arms, legs and shields after the fighting.[5]

It is difficult not to be impressed by a battle in which the survivors were covered by the blood and brains of the killed and wounded, especially considering that this was not one of the longest or bloodiest battles that the Zulus fought. In an attempt to understand what the Zulus had to endure in their attacks against massed British firepower, let us try to re-create an attack from the Zulus' side. Zulu attacks began with ten or more regiments maneuvering into positions that would allow the two horns to swing out ahead of the chest. In every battle those complex movements of thousands of men were carried out with such amazing precision that they appeared to be choreographed. The precision is particularly remarkable when it is recalled that those deployments of masses of men usually took place while the British were firing explosive shells into the Zulu formations. After Isandlwana, the British artillery no longer withheld its fire for fear of frightening the Zulus away. British gunners placed shell after shell in the midst of the Zulu regiments at ranges of 1 mile and more. The shrapnel from each explosion could kill or maim a score of Zulus. Perhaps because the British rarely had more than six cannon available in any battle, the artillery fire never slowed or disrupted the Zulu advance.

As the Zulus neared the British position, a Gatling gun or two often began to fire, sending up to seven hundred bullets a minute into the Zulu ranks while they were still more than 1,000 yards away. That fire sometimes decimated large groups of Zulus, but because the British usually had only one or two Gatling guns and they typically jammed after a few minutes of firing, no Zulu attack was stopped by the long-range fire of Gatling guns. Nevertheless, substantial numbers of Zulus were killed and wounded by this long-range fire. As the Zulus drew nearer, they fanned out into ten or twelve ranks, each hundreds of yards long, and one after the other, like waves in the green grass, rows of Zulus trotted toward death. Volleys of rifle fire knocked down the front ranks, and the following ranks had to jump over the torn, bleeding, disfigured bodies of friends, relatives, and countrymen, only to be hit themselves. When the British artillery began to fire canister, the devastation in the Zulu ranks was appalling, as dozens of men were torn to pieces by each shell. Eventually, so many Zulus in the front ranks had been killed that the rear ranks lay down looking for cover. Those who had rifles fired them, mostly with little effect.

The initial Zulu charge was usually blunted, and the Zulus were forced to take cover in the first few minutes of the battle. It was then that Zulu courage was put to the ultimate test. As the Zulu survivors lay in gullies or behind rocks, where they were relatively safe from the British bullets that continued to fly over their heads, Zulu officers urged the men to leave their positions and once again run toward the British guns. Time and again, Zulu regiments rose and advanced to be shot down again, sometimes within a few yards of the British guns. In some battles the fighting went on for hours before the Zulus were no longer willing to go on dying and ran away from the guns that had killed so many. Then the terrible pursuits began.

It is impossible to say why some Zulus stayed in the rear ranks or only charged a few hundred yards before taking cover, while others actually charged directly into the fire of a Gatling gun, falling dead across the gun itself. We shall explore this question further later in the chapter. The point here is that there were many reasons for the Zulu attacks to fail. The death of leaders could stop a charge, and so could physical exhaustion. Most important was the intensity of British fire, which forced attacking Zulus to take cover. It seems to be a universal of warfare that once men take cover, it is very difficult for them to expose themselves to heavy fire again.[6] Unless the fire slackens, as it did at Isandlwana, men continue to shelter themselves in gullies or depressions, and even the bravest leaders cannot urge them on. At Kambula, for example, you will recall that when Colonel Wood ordered two companies of his troops to retreat he was concerned that if a large body of Zulus pinned down in a nearby gully were to follow the urgings of their officers and charge, the outcome of the battle would have been in doubt. The Zulus stayed in the gully, and their officers were shot down.

The most remarkable fact about the Zulu attacks against British positions is not that all but one of them failed (keep in mind that the charge of Napoleon's elite Imperial Guards broke in the face of British fire at Waterloo),[7] but that their attacks were pressed for so long in the face of such heavy losses. The British were unanimously impressed by the Zulus' "pluck," and some British officers explicitly wondered whether British troops would charge as bravely. Their question could not be answered during the Zulu War. Small numbers of British troops did charge with fixed bayonets at Isandlwana, Rorke's Drift, Kambula, and Victory Hill, and they did so bravely, but what they did was not the same as charging into massed rifle and artillery fire. The heaviest fire faced by British troops was by the previously mentioned two companies of men who sallied out of their laager at Kambula and were rapidly recalled by Colonel Wood because of their losses. Except for the chaotic fight on Hlobane, British horsemen did not face heavy fire either. It is fair to say that throughout this war, the Zulus attacked and the British defended. For that reason alone, it can be said that the Zulus were compelled to show consistently greater courage.

Except at Isandlwana, where British units were widely separated; at Hlobane, where the mounted British forces were routed in a chaotic running fight; and at Myer's Drift, where most of the British were killed in a surprise attack, the British forces fought in a tightly closed formation. In three major battles (Kambula, Gingindhlovu, and Rorke's Drift), their position was fortified by a combination of walls, wagons, and trenches that partially protected their bodies, and at the last battle outside Ulundi they fought shoulder to shoulder in a huge square. We shall discuss the psychology of this kind of defensive fighting later, but it is obvious that fighting shoulder to shoulder with other men, encouraged and steadied by officers and NCOs, is very different from charging against such a position. British soldiers fired volleys on their officers' command, often by small sections so that the smoke could clear before the next section fired. Few of those men fell to Zulu rifle fire, so unless the Zulus approached to spear-thrusting range, there was little reason for the British soldiers to waver or, for that matter, to be terribly frightened. As the Zulus so often lamented, when the British were in a solid defense that covered their flanks and their rear, the Zulus "could not find a way in."

The final form of fighting involved retreat and pursuit. Traditional Zulu tactics involved the shock of a surprise attack (like Myer's Drift) and a reckless pursuit of the routed survivors. That happened at Isandlwana and Hlobane when the British fled in disorder. The Zulus fled from the battlefield after three major battles (Kambula, Gingindhlovu, and Ulundi). The British had an advantage in both retreat and pursuit because of their horses and firearms, especially revolvers. When a Zulu army was defeated, it was expected that its men would run in panicky disarray; it was not expected that defeated British soldiers would flee in disorder. Nevertheless, even though Zulu armies were routed more often and more catastrophically than the British were, the British did experience panic, and both officers and soldiers did run away from battle in terror. It may be significant that whenever men on one side ran away, men on the other side pursued them with reckless abandon. In this war, at least, men were never more reckless with their own lives than when they were pursuing a fleeing enemy.

This, then, is a summary of *how* the two sides fought. Why they fought as they did is a question that is both more intriguing and more complex.

## THE BRITISH

So much has been written about the British army in Victorian times that there is no need to counter-march over most of this familiar ground. Still, it may be useful to mention a few points that may not be quite so obvious and some others that contradict popular misconceptions about British soldiers and officers in the Zulu War. The most obvious point, yet one that must be reiterated, is that officers and men fought for very different reasons. Officers fought because they wanted to, because the army was their chosen career, and because it was by fighting that honors and promotions were achieved. With very few exceptions, private soldiers went to war because they were ordered to do so. Let us consider first why private soldiers fought against the Zulus.

Six battalions of infantry were serving in South Africa when the war broke out (the 3d, 1/24th, 2/24th, 1/13th, 80th, and 90th). These men were familiar with Africa and, to a lesser extent, Africans. They knew the rigors of campaigning, and most of them had little fear of the Zulus before the war began. As far as one can judge from their letters, they were far more interested in being quartered in Cape Town, where there were bars and women, than in marching all over Africa just, as one soldier put it, "to keep the Zulu buck back."[8] Shooting Africans could be good sport for them, but booty was sacred to infantrymen, and there was no booty to be had fighting "Kaffirs," only hard work marching, pushing wagons out of the mud, eating hardtack, and doing without life's pleasures, namely liquor and women. Many soldiers wrote that they hoped their regiment would be sent back to England. Officers, on the other hand, hoped to be sent *from* England to war, *any* war. Private soldiers fought where and when they were ordered to fight; whether they enjoyed fighting or were terrified by it was irrelevant as long as they did their duty. They were disciplined soldiers who marched, loaded their weapons, aimed, and fired by command. Unlike their officers, most privates did not refer to combat as a "grand adventure" or life's most "delicious" and "thrilling" experience. They didn't care about medals, either. For example, the best-known of the private soldiers who won a Victoria Cross in the war was the veteran Private Henry Hook, who fought so bravely at Rorke's Drift. He spent the rest of the war on guard duty at Rorke's Drift, where he saw no more combat, and made no fuss about wanting to do so. He did not receive his medal until August 3. He was not exactly overwhelmed by the honor: "It was curious, but until then I had scarcely ever thought about the Victoria Cross, in fact we did not know or trouble much about it, although we had a V.C. man in the regiment—Griffiths, they called him. He was killed, with the rest, at Isandlwana."[9]

Like British soldiers in other wars before and since, most of these veteran soldiers had pride in their regiment, confidence in one another, and respect for their officers. There was variation among them, of course, from born fighters to more retiring religious men, but with rare exceptions the veteran infantrymen, like the sailors of the Naval Brigade and the Royal Marines, were steady and reliable fighters. Some, like Wood's Bugler Walkinshaw, were seemingly fearless. All in all, it is remarkable how well those veteran soldiers fought against the Zulus. In the first round of battles—Victory Hill, Isandlwana, and Rorke's Drift—British soldiers, sailors, and marines followed orders with discipline, shot accurately, and fought savagely with the bayonet. In more recent wars, European soldiers—including the British—have rarely been willing to fight with their bayonets. Those men who fought the Zulus not only fought willingly, but it is fair to say, based on Zulu accounts, that a British soldier with a bayonet fixed on his rifle was more than a match for a Zulu warrior armed with a stabbing spear. Those veterans not only fought desperately when their only choices were to fight or die, as at Isandlwana and Rorke's Drift, they attacked ferociously with the bayonet in such battles as Victory Hill and Kambula.

We can only speculate about their motivation, but three factors stand out. They fought in part because of peer pressure within their company. Not to fight bravely was almost unthinkable for these men, who had soldiered together for years. But it must also be said that they fought because they liked to. They liked to fight with their fists or with whatever else was handy against civilians, sailors, or soldiers of other regiments. Many of them, perhaps even most, enjoyed "potting" Africans, as they put it. Another, less often discussed reason for fighting was their profound sense of racial superiority. Those veteran British soldiers shared a firm sense of their superiority to Africans. Zulus were "kaffirs" or "niggers," and although they might be brave men, they were still inferior. When veteran British soldiers yelled "come on, you black bastards" they were reasserting their racial superiority. Many of them would literally die before they would submit to black men.

The young recruits who were sent to Natal as reinforcements for Chelmsford's depleted forces may have believed in the inherent superiority of white Britons to Africans, but they did not believe that they were better fighting men than the Zulus. Most of the recruits were young, small, physically weak, and poorly drilled. They were not at all proficient with either rifle or bayonet, and they were terrified of the Zulus. From the day they were ordered aboard ships for South Africa, they had heard about the now legendary invincibility of the Zulus. Once they arrived in Natal, veteran soldiers told them horror story after horror story. As if to prove that the stories of Zulu supermen were true, British officers made those boy soldiers sleep in full combat gear, laager every camp, even in Natal, and stand to at their battle stations every morning long before dawn. It is not surprising that the rookie soldiers did not believe they were better warriors than the Zulus, and they had little confidence in the young soldiers who would fight next to them. Some of the new units, like the 2d Battalion of the 24th, were virtually all recruits, and so were the 58th and 60th. Like the 60th, another veteran regiment, the 91st Argyllshire Highlanders was filled with recruits; to bring the 91st up to strength, 374 recruits from eleven different regiments were added to the regiment. The new men were neither Scots nor well-trained, and they did not know one another or their officers.

The result was a series of panics in which the newly arrived regiments fired at night sounds, sometimes killing their own outlying scouts and sentries. In battle, they sometimes shot recklessly, not obeying their officers' commands, and when Zulus came close to their lines they wavered and some ran.[10] Several were court-martialed; others were flogged. With their rifles, machine guns, artillery, and the support of more veteran regiments, they were able to hold off the Zulus, but they did not fight well, and they certainly did not charge the Zulus with bayonets. It was just as well for them that they did not have to do so. Those young men lacked everything that made veteran soldiers fight so well—confidence in themselves and in their comrades and officers, and an arrogant sense of superiority. Major Tucker, who had to sort out the mess at Myer's Drift, later said what everyone was thinking[11] and many were saying: "These young soldiers are more bother than they're worth!" Even when their officers provided superior leadership, the young soldiers were, as more than one officer summed it up, "no good."

When Lieutenant Q. McK. Logan of the 2d Battalion of the 24th Regiment marched to Rorke's Drift with Chelmsford's tired and apprehensive men the morning after Isandlwana, he looked over the carnage and said, "The men have the pluck but without a good officer they are like sheep."[12] Outrageous as that comment may sound to modern ears, it was largely true. Even though the officers who led at Rorke's Drift were hardly inspiring leaders, they seem to have fought bravely enough, and after the battle the private soldiers praised them extravagantly and gave them enormous credit for their survival. The importance of a British officer to British soldiers at the time of the Zulu War can hardly be overstated. Soldiers obeyed their officers because they had no choice, but they also wanted to believe in them as men from a higher plane of existence. When they found one who behaved as if he were, they would fight beyond themselves. A soldier at Kambula wrote this about Colonel Wood:

> He is as cool and collected in action as if he were in a drawing-room. Walking down from the fort to the laager under a heavy fire, swinging a stick and whistling, then going past the wagons he has a pleasant look and a smile of encouragement for everyone he meets, let him be private or officer, it matters not. The men here I am sure would follow him anywhere, they are so fond of him.[13]

For the most part, the British officers in the Anglo-Zulu War did nothing to tarnish their reputation for personal bravery and for steady leadership of their men. They lived for war and the chance for active service, and despite the many horrors of this war, they were in their glory. Without active service in war, an officer's career could not be fulfilled, and his life would not be complete. In their search for combat and a chance for glory, British officers might draw the line at invading Yorkshire, but then again they might not. The motto of the 4th Dragoon Guards in World War I was, "We'll do it! What is it?"[14] Like many other regiments, the Dragoon Guards wanted to fight, and almost any adversary would do. They would just as soon have fought the Belgians or the French as the Germans. During the Anglo-Zulu War, even officers who liked Zulus and were sympathetic to their cause eagerly fought against them. Charlie Harford was one example. Colonel Durnford was another. Durnford had served on the Boundary Commission that had found in favor of the Zulu land claims versus those of the Boers. He often said that the missionaries in Zululand were "at the bottom of all evil" in Zululand and the Zulus had done nothing to instigate hostilities. Shortly before the war, Durnford wrote this about King Cetshwayo: "Poor devil! He is really doing all he can to keep peace; but the white man wants his land, and alas for Cetshwayo!"[15] Durnford was also one of a very few British officers to prohibit the use of the epithet "nigger" by men under his command. But when war came, he was as frantically eager to see action as anyone in the British army.

British officers knew that the conspicuous display of bravery in battle was essential, but gallantry had to be witnessed before it could be rewarded. Winston Churchill, then a young lieutenant in India, wrote candidly to his mother what many of his fellow officers were probably thinking: "I rode my grey pony all along the skirmish line where everyone else was lying down in cover. Foolish perhaps but I play for high stakes and given an audience there is no act too daring or too noble. Without the gallery things are different."[16] As we have seen, Evelyn Wood displayed the same kind of disdainful gallantry throughout the Zulu War, and he was as aware of the "gallery" as Churchill. Like Churchill, he wanted medals and promotions in reward for his courage, and he complained bitterly when he felt that recognition was too slow in coming.

All officers felt the pressure to be—or to appear to be—brave, and most of them performed their roles admirably. So powerful was the expectation that officers would behave gallantly under fire that when Bromhead and Chard—considered by all to be hopelessly dull and lethargic—rose to the occasion at Rorke's Drift, no one was surprised at their bravery, only at their enterprise in organizing the defense. After that battle, neither officer made any effort to see further combat or, for that matter, to perform any other duty. There may have been some truth in Thomas Fuller's words in 1732: "Many would be cowards if they had courage enough."

Fuller's cynical observation did not apply to some British officers, who repeatedly behaved with reckless disregard for their own lives, even when there was no audience. Among those men were Durnford, Buller, Harford, Hamilton-Browne, and Churchill's uncle, Lord Beresford. Men like these may have had medals on their minds, but they didn't act like it. For various reasons they were at their best in combat. It has been suggested that for Redvers Buller, who was from a particularly wealthy and socially prominent family, war substituted for sex: "Letters that Redvers wrote to his wife reveal that for him, fighting brought relief to a terrible lust for which he candidly expressed shame."[17] It might not be far wrong to say that Hamilton-Browne fought because he enjoyed doing so. The reasons why Charlie Harford fought so bravely lie beyond conjecture. Despite Harford's rash courage, he was not decorated until his retirement in 1907.

In spite of the pressures that virtually forced officers to fight bravely, some British officers did not distinguish themselves, and a few were accused of cowardice. The journals of several officers refer to several brother officers—usually unnamed—who "funked it" by avoiding danger or simply running away, "skedaddling," as it was called.[18] Bindon

Blood, who wrote that he had "frequently seen men lose their nerve on active service," described an incident in which an officer friend of his rode away in panic when the Zulus began to fire. "My friend always used to look unhappy afterwards when we met, although I never said a word about the occurrence to him, or anyone else, for at least fifty years."[19] Most officers were not as circumspect as Blood. They gossiped, they tormented suspected cowards in the mess, and in extreme cases they brought officers to trial. As we have seen, Captain Gardner was ridiculed mercilessly for his flight from Isandlwana, and Colonel Weatherly probably would have been had he not been killed at Hlobane. Colonel Russell was shuffled off from his combat command to a supply depot, and several officers who "lost their nerve" were sent home for "medical" reasons. Lieutenant Curling, who survived Isandlwana, was one of those, and so was Lieutenant Colonel Wykeham Leigh Pemberton, who commanded the 60th Regiment after Colonel Northey was killed at Gingindhlovu. Two officers, Lieutenants Harward and Carey, were brought before courts-martial. Even generals were not above suspicion. Although no one questioned Chelmsford's courage under fire, several officers, including Wolseley, openly said and wrote that General Crealock was less than eager to risk his life in battle.

Even men who were later judged to be heroes might fall under suspicion of failing in their duty. For example, when the Zulus burst into the British camp at Isandlwana, several mounted officers (including Smith-Dorrien, who went on to become a field marshal) who were not in direct command of troops rode for their lives. One who rode away was Lieutenant Teignmouth Melvill, Colonel Pulleine's adjutant. Melvill carried with him the "Queen's Colours," presumably on Pulleine's orders. With him went another staff officer, Neville Coghill. Both men escaped the camp area, but Melvill was unhorsed as he tried to cross a flooded river. Melvill was exhausted by carrying the cumbersome flag, so despite a badly sprained knee (ingloriously suffered trying to catch a Zulu chicken for the stew pot), Coghill dismounted and went to his assistance. Both men were shot dead by Zulus. Melvill, you will recall, was one of the few Imperial Officers who believed that the Zulus would charge into the camp at Isandlwana unless the British stood shoulder to shoulder. Melvill, who had a B.A. from Cambridge University and spoke seven European languages, had a future in the army. He also had a wife and small children. Coghill was one of the least scholarly of British officers, but he was a charming, handsome man who would have succeeded to a baronetry. Both men had a great deal to live for, but Melvill gave his life trying to save the colors, and Coghill gave his for Melvill and the colors he was trying to carry to safety.

The two men were generally regarded as heroes by their fellow officers. Although there was no provision for the posthumous award of the V.C. in 1879, the medal was sent to both men's families in 1907. In 1879, however, Sir Garnet Wolseley was not impressed. After a visit to the site where the men had died, he wrote, "I am sorry that both of those officers were not killed with their men at Isandlwana instead of where they were: I don't like the idea of officers escaping on horseback when their men on foot are killed."[20] Neither Melvill nor Coghill was in command of troops, but Wolseley may have thought that they should have tried to rally the fleeing redcoats. It was men like Wolseley, whose own bravery in battle had been established beyond doubt, who set the standards other brave men tried to meet.

There is nothing mysterious about why British officers fought bravely. It was obvious to all of them from their earliest days in the army that only conspicuous bravery could be relied on to advance their careers, and any sign of cowardice would bring disgrace not only to the individual but to his family as well. How they felt about the experience of battle is a little more difficult to determine, because what they said or wrote about their feelings may have been colored by their knowledge that they were expected to glory in battle. Nevertheless, a few men admitted to being were nervous and frightened, and many others must have felt fear without saying so. But more often, officers wrote that they were so busy with their duties that they simply had no time to experience fear. A few, like Churchill, admitted to being aware that their coolness and bravery under fire was being observed, but they also said, no doubt correctly, that by showing indifference to danger they were steadying their men.

It is strange that so few seem to have been deeply affected by the death of a brother officer. Seventy-six officers were killed in the war against the Zulus, and often their bodies were terribly mutilated. Others were horribly wounded, yet even those officers who were closest to these unfortunate men seem not to have been much affected, except, in some cases, by an increased desire for revenge. But since most officers were extremely combative—"bloodthirsty," as Colonel Harness, who commanded British artillery, said about several of them—these men hardly stood out from the rest. Several officers, including Wood and Buller, fought on although they were physically exhausted, refusing to admit it until after the battle at Ulundi. Some—Hamilton-Browne is only one example—seem never to have lost their craving for close combat, and while most officers were a little less enthusiastic than Browne about hand-to-hand combat, most of them looked upon the war against the Zulus as a grand adventure. It was, to use the word that appeared most often in their letters, journals, and reminiscences, "fun," an experience not to be missed.

The British experience of battle against the Zulus was probably no different from that of British soldiers and officers in other late Victorian colonial wars. Why they fought and how they felt about it is still fascinating, even if it is not mysterious. On the other hand, why the Zulus fought so hard and how they experienced battle is still largely unexplained. For the British they were worthy, if inscrutable, opponents. In most accounts of the war, they have remained little more than a dark backdrop on a stage where British heroism and tragedy were played out.[21]

## THE ZULUS

For the Zulus, like the British, there was no single experience of battle. Some men avoided battle altogether by becoming diviners, for example, or simply by spending the war in remote forests or mountains. Others reported for duty but fell out on the march, arriving too late for battle (there were many sarcastic Zulu jokes about the tenderness of such men's feet). A surprising number deserted to the British. Larger numbers of men lagged behind and never quite came under British fire, while others ran away as soon as the firing began. But most Zulus who fought in royal regiments charged hard, risking their lives again and again as they approached the British guns. Some among them took unbelievable risks, charging to the muzzles of British guns and trying to wrest them away. A few, like the young man who single-handedly charged the British as the two forces passed by one another after the battle at Rorke's Drift, would surely have deserved a VC if they had been British. It was said that warriors who, like this man, had a "lust for war," as one Zulu put it, were often exceptionally combative and ungovernable when they were children. There was a place for such individuals in Zulu culture in the front ranks of their regiments.[22]

Not all Zulus had a natural lust for battle, but the majority of them fought with such courage that the British were startled. As Lieutenant Curling said after his escape from Isandlwana, the British were not concerned early in the battle, even though they could see that they were being attacked by large numbers of Zulus. They had seen equally large numbers of African warriors advance against them in the 9th Frontier War of 1877–78, but those men had not pressed their attacks. As the British prepared to fire against the advancing masses of Zulus, they "never dreamed the Zulus would charge home!"[23] The Zulus "charged home'' in half a dozen major battles, and every British eyewitness account of those battles praised their courage. Several battle-experienced British officers wrote that no European troops would have charged against British fire as bravely as the Zulus did. They were speculating, of course, but their point was made. The Zulu soldiers were exceptionally brave men.

In attempting to explain the reasons for their courage in battle, we must keep in mind that before the reforms of Dingiswayo and especially Shaka, the Zulus had been indifferent warriors. Shaka's changes in weapons, tactics, military organization, and rewards for bravery converted these men and other less than warlike peoples who joined their ranks into the scourge of southern Africa. Shaka's armies fought often, but for over two decades prior to the Anglo-Zulu War their only opportunities for combat were the brief civil war of 1856 and some regimental brawls. Despite that long period of inactivity, when the Zulu troops could win no honors and capture no booty, somehow their martial spirit remained intense. Some of the reasons why that was possible are to be found in Zulu culture itself.

After Shaka, warrior virtues were exalted. Boys thought of great feats of war and practiced battle skills. Adults encouraged them, and other children teased them if they cried or ran away. As they grew older they served as udibi boys, and later as young warriors. Everything in their young lives focused on their martial valor. Even today in some of the more rural parts of Zululand, middle-aged men enjoy stick fights; as women and children look on, these paunchy oldsters belabor each other with hardwood sticks for the sheer pleasure of displaying their skill and courage.[24] As young men competed with one another and with older men for recognition, they were encouraged by young women. For a brave warrior there was the hope of rewards from the king in the form of cattle, praise, or insignia of honor. For a coward there was no longer as much fear of being put to death as there had been during Shaka's rule, but there would certainly be ridicule and scorn. As we saw in Chapter 3, the Zulus made bravery in battle a primary virtue, and most Zulu warriors displayed an arrogant pride in their military superiority. No doubt different men were affected in different ways by various aspects of the Zulu warrior culture, but two sets of factors stand out as basic sources for the reckless courage that Zulus displayed. The first is the rivalry complex that underlay so much of Zulu military motivation, and the second is a set of prebattle activities that renewed and heightened men's appetite for battle.

Rivalry among warriors was at the very heart of the Zulus' quest for battle. Young warriors competed among themselves and with older married men. In one form or another, women were always involved. When young men did not display sufficient zest for war, their girl friends taunted them mercilessly. Often their manhood was questioned, as for example by songs in which young men were ridiculed by mocking suggestions that they use the small gourds that covered their penises as snuff boxes, as they were clearly not needed where they were.[25] Much of the rivalry was generated among young men and women who resented the war honors of older warriors and their right to marry, but older warriors did nothing to reduce tensions. For example, the Thulwana regiment was fond of stopping men who were traveling on the road and humiliating them by forcing them at spear point to dance, play children's hopping games, sing the very private and intimate songs their wives composed at the time of the consummation of their marriage, and, if the wife was present, to have sexual intercourse with her in public.[26] Unmarried men were abused as well.

In 1878, before the annual first fruits ceremony at Ulundi, a young regiment—the Ngobamakosi—was quartered with the Thulwana. Because not enough housing had been prepared, young men and married warriors actually were obliged to share the same sleeping quarters. When men of the Thulwana felt like having sexual relations with their wives, they ordered the younger warriors to wait outside. The young men, who did not enjoy sitting outside in the cold listening to the sounds of love-making, began to yell for the men of the Thulwana to "hurry up . . . we want to come in and sleep."[27] During the ceremony at the king's kraal, the angry young warriors attacked the Thulwana with hardwood fighting sticks. When it became clear to Hamu, the leader of the Thulwana, that his men were being battered by the stronger young warriors, he ordered them to use their spears. In the ensuing brawl, sixty or seventy of the young Ngobamakosi were killed (see Chapter 3). Coming only a short time before the Anglo-Zulu War, that was a well-known incident, but it was only one example of the rancorous rivalry that existed in Zululand. It was one of the great strengths of the Zulu military system that when it came time for war the inter-regimental hatred could be redirected toward the Zulus' enemies.

As we have seen, while the Zulu army was being ritually protected and strengthened prior to battle, the king paired off men from different regiments in dancing competitions, which often concluded with an exchange of insulting challenges in which one warrior boasted to another that he would exceed the other in bravery in the coming battle. The intensity of the feelings that resulted could drive entire regiments to rush into battle prematurely with disastrous results, as happened at Kambula. As a means of provoking men to fight without concern for their lives, however, rivalry was remarkably effective.

Other practices may have contributed as well. It has been suggested that the Zulus' courage may have been enhanced by the use of narcotics before battle.[28] Such a practice would not have been foreign to the British, whose troops, like those of other European armies of the eighteenth and nineteenth centuries, often went into battle roaring and fighting drunk,[29] although they seldom did so against the Zulus. Some East African societies, like the Maasai, may have used several narcotics before going into battle,[30] and some other societies may have used *cannabis sativa* for this purpose.[31] *Cannabis sativa* (known to the Zulus as *insangu* and to most Americans as marijuana) was known in southern Africa before the arrival of the first European explorers. It was eaten and smoked, but its effects were more often said to be soporific than aggressive.[32] At the time of the Anglo-Zulu War, Zulu men smoked insangu almost every day (in a cow's horn water-pipe),[33] and sometimes they added it to their snuff, but the daily use of cannabis was not associated with violence, much less with war. Nevertheless, some Zulus did say that insangu acted as a stimulant. The emetic preparation that Zulu warriors drank as a preparation for battle may have contained cannabis or other psychoactive substances, because many Zulus reported that the drink made "their hearts feel very bad indeed, full of cruelty and daring."[34] Whether it was the drink or their own expectations that made them feel that way cannot be determined, nor can we know for certain whether the snuff they inhaled just before going into battle contained cannabis or any other drug.[35] To what extent the Zulus' courage was a response to a drug must remain an open question, but the bulk of the evidence suggests that if narcotics played a role at all, it was a minor one.

Dancing, on the other hand, definitely contributed to the Zulus' readiness to engage in battle. There were many kinds of dances in Zulu culture.[36] Some were joyous, some solemn, others erotic, but some were explicitly related to warfare. The intricately synchronized movements of several dances must have helped to develop the Zulus' remarkable ability to coordinate their maneuvers as they deployed for battle. There were also war dances that created great excitement. In 1880, a British observer described one such dance, on this occasion intended to prepare men for a community hunt rather than war:

> They stand in a semicircle several ranks deep, with their shields and knob-kerries, the master of ceremonies with his small white shield in front. He gives the signal; a kind of weird quartet is heard in the

> ranks, first very softly, then taken up by one after the other, but still softly, all keeping time with their feet; presently it grows louder and louder, and the whole crowd seems labouring under the intensest of suppressed excitement. . . . The earth shakes beneath the thunder of their feet as they bring them to the ground like one man. They clash their knob-kerries and shields together; they roar like wild beasts; but never for a moment do you lose the modulation of the fantastic harmony, the rhythm of the strange, fierce, thrilling chant to which you feel yourself unconsciously beating time; and an irresistible longing comes over you to seize a kerrie, throw yourself into the rout, and stamp and howl with the best of them.[37]

Men became so excited during dances that as recently as the 1950s Zulus were known to attack one another with deadly weapons simply because they bumped into one another during a war dance.[38] During the Anglo-Zulu War, war dances helped to inspire men as they began their long marches toward battle. Dances held near dawn before an assault must have helped to prepare warriors for the charge that was to follow. At Rorke's Drift, the Zulus renewed their fighting spirit by holding ten- to fifteen-minute war dances between each of their many charges. Dances that could drive the old and tiring warriors at Rorke's Drift to throw themselves at almost certain death, time after time, were powerful machines of war.

Yet the Zulu willingness to "charge home" was not the result of any single belief or practice. It resulted from the experience of living within a warrior tradition that created a sense of invincibility, from participation in a dramatic panoply of ritual preparations, and from an unquenchable feeling of rivalry. Drugs and dancing were only adjuncts to a larger complex of factors. Like the British officers against whom they fought, everything in the lives of these Zulus prepared them for bravery in battle. One of the greatest early-twentieth-century authorities on Zulu history and customs, the Reverend A. T. Bryant, offered what was then a common explanation of Zulu bravery: The "nervous system" of the Zulus (and other Bantu people) "was notoriously obtuse, and, feeling less pain, they feared death less."[39] Racist beliefs of that sort have long since lost credibility, but the idea that the Zulus feared death less than the British still remains. The Zulus' profound fear of death has already been described, and their readiness to charge massed rifle fire was all the more remarkable because they feared death so much. That leads to a second perplexing question.

In every battle against the British, even Isandlwana, Zulu charges wavered and eventually broke in the face of British fire. In four major battles, they eventually fled in disorder. Despite the Zulus' unquestioned courage, at some point in every battle they were unwilling to risk their lives any longer, and in most battles, courageous attack was followed by disorderly retreat. Why did their courage fail? Why did they run away in such panic? There are no simple answers. Lord Moran, a British physician with experience in two world wars (he was later Churchill's personal doctor), observed that courage was a finite and expendable commodity, and, as later research has confirmed, eventually all men reach the point where their supply of courage has been exhausted.[40] But how rapidly the courage of Zulu warriors was depleted depended on a number of considerations—the pride of the regiments involved, their degree of physical exhaustion, the number of casualties who fell among them, and the loss of hope for eventual victory, among others.

Some regiments fought more resolutely than others in battle after battle. That, presumably, is true in most armies. But despite their vaunted ability to run 50 miles and then attack, at times even the most audacious Zulu regiments were too exhausted physically to fight any longer. That was true at Rorke's Drift and at Kambula. Even at Isandlwana, where they won such a great victory, several Zulus reported that the Zulu army was too exhausted to fight any longer if Chelmsford's column had returned earlier. A few Zulus in every battle charged to their certain death, but most were more cautious. It was seldom that large bodies of Zulu troops charged until all were shot or bayoneted to death. Except for Rorke's Drift, where perhaps 20 percent of the Zulus who engaged in the battle were killed on the battlefield, Zulu battlefield deaths were usually not more than 10 percent, although many others later died of their wounds. Other troops, including British regiments in many battles, have continued to attack despite suffering a much higher percentage of casualties than that. What was remarkable about the Zulus was their persistence. Most Zulu regiments fought in three major battles and took heavy losses in all three. European military units that suffered comparable losses typically took much longer to recover their willingness to fight.[41]

For the Zulus, the loss of will to continue the fight undoubtedly had to do with their assessment of the magnitude of their losses, but it also was affected by their sense of hopelessness when they realized that they were unable to charge close enough to the British to use their spears. There may be another reason as well. Some Zulu survivors referred to their own exhaustion, and most mentioned the deadliness of British fire in explaining their inability to charge into the British ranks, but several insisted that the main reason that the Zulus lost heart was British superiority in *supernatural* protection! As Zulus died by the hundreds, they rapidly lost confidence in the protective rituals that had been carried out to protect them, but they suspected the British of using magic effectively when they discovered monkeys (which were kept as pets) in the British camp at Isandlwana. For the Zulus, monkeys, particularly baboons, were thought to possess supernatural powers, including powers for evil. In later battles the British were seen to have not only monkeys but human skulls, suggesting to the Zulus that even more sinister magical practices were taking place (the British were inveterate collectors of skulls as trophies). After Kambula, Zulus asked Cornelius Vijn, who was still in Zululand:

> ''What is meant that at the beginning of the battle so many white birds, such as they had never seen before, came flying over them from the side of the whites? And why were they attacked also by dogs and apes, clothed and carrying fire-arms on their shoulders?'' One of them even told me that he had seen four lions in the laager. They said, ''The whites don't fight fairly; they bring animals to draw down destruction upon us.''[42]

In subsequent battles, beginning most noticeably at Kambula, Zulus began to complain that British magic had made them invulnerable to Zulu bullets. Given the enormous volume of Zulu rifle fire, the obvious fact that few British soldiers fell *was* puzzling. The Zulus did not realize that their sights were set to fire too high, so another explanation had to be found. The British must have protective magic! A Zulu who fought at Ulundi had the following story to tell, as recounted by Montague. It illustrates the Zulus' sense of rivalry as well as their belief in British magic:

> ''Myself and three friends determined to get nearer to your guns than any other Zulu, and we did''—three or four men actually got within thirty yards of one face of the square. ''Then my three friends were killed,—pouf—pouf—pouf''—and he imitated the bullets whistling, and his head bobbing.—''so I ran away; but you had put iron palings in front of your men, and hung red coats on them, so that our guns could not kill them. I saw myself the bullets fall off them.'' Everyone said this same thing; it was only that which beat them.[43]

Once the Zulus gave way, whether after one hour of battle or five, they fled with every man running for his life. Why men who approached battle in such disciplined formations and then stood bravely against devastating British firepower should suddenly run away as a disorganized mob is puzzling. With the partial exception of the flight after Ulundi, when some Zulus did resist, there was no attempt to organize rearguard actions to slow the mounted British pursuit. Although a few individuals fought for their lives, the vast majority of Zulus simply ran. To be sure, for men on foot to be pursued by cavalry was a terrifying experience, and knowing that prisoners would only rarely be taken must have added to the panic. Even so, the British horsemen were never in great numbers, and a disciplined stand by Zulu riflemen could have kept the British horsemen at bay. To make matters worse, once the Zulu regiments ran from battle, they refused to reassemble as fighting units. Instead, to the despair of their king and his counselors, they dispersed to their homesteads.

The Zulus recognized that if their warriors once gave way, the battle was lost. Captain J. W. Shepstone, Sir Theophilus's son, reported that he conversed with several Zulu chiefs and warriors shortly after the war:

> They said that, though they had carried everything before them at Isandhlwana, they were fully convinced on that day that they were no match for the white man. I asked how, and they replied: "You know what we are, when we once give way and run. There is no stopping us to fight with the pursuer. But your people, when, as in several instances, only numbering three, would stand back-to-back and defy us to approach. While the ammunition lasted, we did not attack; but took advantage of them when their powder failed."[44]

Tired and dispirited men are likely to retreat and then run, and panic, once started, is contagious. That is true in all armies, including the British, but in most armies a panicky rout is the exception. In the Zulu army it was the rule. Cetshwayo and his indunas could gnash their teeth all they wished, but they could not feign surprise. They knew that except for men of high rank who would never run away for fear of losing their privileges, if the Zulu armies were stopped, they would run away. The reasons for their precipitous flights are not clear. It may be that because the only legitimate expectation in traditional Zulu war was to attack and vanquish, there was no military tradition to support an orderly withdrawal. But that is conjecture. It seems paradoxical to us that men who were so brave in their attacks would run away in panic when their attacks eventually failed. It did not seem paradoxical to the Zulus. They expected to run away if their attacks failed. Like British officers who hoped that their heroic actions would be seen by others, the Zulus "performed" their heroism for other Zulus to witness and admire. If heroism were not seen by others, there would be no praise, no honors, no reputation. And so as Zulu warriors ran into battle their eyes were on one another. When most of those among them who could report deeds of courage had been killed, when no officers were still alive to goad them on, and when there was little hope of reaching the British lines, the survivors of a company looked to one another and by a tacit understanding began to withdraw. Once a body of men began to run away, the effect on other men was contagious, as it is in most armies. Shaka's regiments sometimes ran away like this too.[45] It was the traditional end to a Zulu battle. They either destroyed their enemies or ran away. It is not what the king wanted and not what Zulu officers wanted, but it is how the Zulus fought.

Another puzzle is the Zulus' failure to modify their tactics when it became clear that massed attacks in their "charging buffalo" formation could not defeat the British. After the battles of January 22, most senior Zulus and many of the men in the ranks were reported to have said that they knew they could not defeat the British. Mnyamana, the king's prime minister and a senior military officer, advised Cetshwayo to make peace. Cetshwayo tried, but his emissaries, as we saw, were rejected or mistreated. In reality, the Zulus might not have had to sue for peace. They had opportunities to inflict terrible losses on the British had they modified their tactics. After they captured about 1,500 modern rifles along with ample ammunition at Isandlwana, they clearly had the means to make the war so costly that the British might very well have been unwilling to continue it. It is possible that after the defeat at Isandlwana, the British people would have refused to accept anything less than a "victory" over the Zulus, but Prime Minister Disraeli had never wanted this war, and its cost was an enormous burden to his Conservative Government. Moreover, the fighting tied down troops that would be needed in Afghanistan if the crisis there worsened. If the Zulus had chosen to fight a guerrilla war, the British might well have accepted one of King Cetshwayo's peace envoys and agreed to a negotiated settlement, which could always be portrayed to the British public as yet another righteous demonstration of imperial progress.[46]

Even before the capture of so many Martini-Henrys, the Zulus could have ambushed advance parties of British troops and attacked their advancing columns as they were strung out over miles. The use of ambush was not unknown to the Zulus. Shaka had won his greatest victory against the Ndwandwes by leading them on to ground of his choosing, and Zibhebhu, who fought throughout the Zulu war, later ambushed the uSutu troops with devastating effect. Advance parties of Zulus tried to set up ambushes during several battles in the Anglo-Zulu War, but the main Zulu forces never relied on an ambush. Also, there were repeated opportunities for large numbers of Zulus to approach unseen through the 6- to 10-foot grass to points of attack virtually on top of almost defenseless columns of foot soldiers and wagons, strung out along miles of trail. To the amazement and relief of British officers, they never did so. It would have been even easier—and almost equally devastating—for the Zulus to have driven off the British cattle herds. Without cattle, the British forces would have been even harder pressed than they already were to remain in the field long enough to sustain a campaign. With one exception, when the Zulus drove off over more than nine hundred head of weakly guarded cattle that Colonel Pearson was trying to send back to Natal from his fortress at Eshowe, the Zulus did not attack the British herds. Instead local men tried to defend their own herds against British raids, while the royal regiments assembled for their massed assaults.

In the war's first battles on January 22, the Zulus surprised the British by the volume of their rifle fire, but the Zulu guns were fired at long range and with spectacular inaccuracy. Although the Zulus had some Martini-Henrys before the war, most of their weapons were obsolete muzzle-loading muskets. After the Zulus had captured so many modern rifles, however, they could have used those weapons to devastate the British as they stood or knelt, partially exposed, in their laagers. In the center of every laager were unprotected horses, cattle, and men, and from even a slight elevation the backs of men on the far side of the laager would be exposed as well. A few Zulus did enfilade the British laager at Kambula from a small hill, forcing two companies of the 13th to take new positions, but that was a rarely used tactic. Some Zulus were skilled marksmen, having worked previously for hunters such as John Dunn. There were also some white men, including Boers, who could have helped to teach other Zulus how to shoot a Martini-Henry with reasonable accuracy. If that was done, there was no evidence of it in the ensuing battles. Zulus continued to blaze away, always firing high and rarely taking an elevated position from which their fire could be effective. Apparently, the king made no effort to reorganize "rifle regiments" or to train his royal troops in the use of those viciously kicking, hard-to-aim weapons. If he did, Cornelius Vijn, who was with the Zulus throughout the war, saw no sign of it. Instead, it appears that each Zulu warrior treated his captured British rifle as his personal property, and he shot it in battle when and how he chose.

Mehlokazulu said after the war that some warriors did practice firing their rifles, but there was no discernible improvement in their marksmanship as the war went on.[47] For example, it is almost inconceivable that

20,000 or so Zulus at Ulundi, at least half of whom had rifles, including more than a thousand Martini-Henrys, could have fired at over more than five thousand British troops standing shoulder to shoulder in the open for over an hour and yet kill only ten and wound only sixty-nine. The British heard thousands of bullets passing over their heads. If that volume of fire had been more accurately aimed throughout the war, the British would have suffered great losses and might even have been beaten, as they were a year later by Afghan tribesmen who were better marksmen.[48]

Finally, from the beginning of the war to the very end, British officers feared night attacks. As the new regiments with their young recruits arrived, these men proved to be unsteady in the daylight and utterly terrified at night. Many of their officers believed that if the Zulus were to attack at night, the British could not hold them. There were no night attacks. It was not traditional for the Zulus to attack at night. Although Zulu forces sometimes raided at night, Shaka's armies preferred to attack at dawn, partly because it would have been too difficult to distinguish friend from foe at night, but also because daylight was necessary to observe brave deeds.[49] However, it was certainly not the case that the Zulus could not or would not fight at night. One of Shaka's greatest victories was a night battle, and although the battle at Rorke's Drift began in the late afternoon, it lasted all night. Perhaps the Zulus were not aware how panicky the young British soldiers were at night, but the most likely explanation for their failure to launch night attacks or ambushes, or to use riflemen as sharpshooters, is simply that none of those techniques fitted well with their traditional attack formation. That formation called for thousands of men to maneuver themselves into position, then charge until they could stab with their spears. Trapped by this tradition, there was only one honorable way for royal troops to fight. After Louis Napoleon had been killed in an ambush, the king returned his sword, and several Zulus, including Mehlokazulu, apologized for that less than gallant way of fighting.[50] Mpatshana, who fought at Isandlwana, commented scornfully on the use of ambush by some Zulus in the rebellion of 1906, saying that such men were not real Zulus: "Zulus would have taken up a position *in the open* [italics his] and come face to face with the foe. They waylaid Europeans wherever they could. We laughed at them for this."[51] Ambushes, well-placed sharpshooters, and night attacks might be all right for others, but brave Zulus wanted to meet their enemies man-to-man in the light of day.

That the Zulus persisted in the use of their traditional method of making war even though other tactics would have been more effective is hardly unusual in the history of armies. The British were at least as tradition-bound as the Zulus. Hamilton-Browne thought that "English" officers, brave as they were, were incapable of learning *anything* new about war. So it proved to be when many of the officers who served against the Zulus fought the Boers in the Transvaal during 1880 and 1881. They marched grandly into the massed fire of Boer rifles and were shot to pieces. In the second Boer War, beginning in 1900, the British still changed nothing. They marched steadily, shoulder to shoulder, across open ground into the fire of Boer rifles, machine guns, and artillery, suffered appalling casualties, and sometimes fled in panic. For much of the war their commander was the now very stout and bibulous cavalry leader Sir Redvers Buller, who had every reason to know better. And later, in World War I, the British refused to modify their suicidal massed frontal attacks against fortified German trenches.

A final question remains. Why did the Zulus agree to stop the fighting? The British believed it was the only reasonable response to the Zulus's devastating defeat at Ulundi. There was something to that belief. The Zulus were "frightened," as Mehlokazulu said, before the battle, and after it many of the warriors were willing to concede victory to the British. They said repeatedly that the British had fought in the open and won, and as a result they were the better warriors. King Cetshwayo also helped to terminate hostilities by making little effort to rally his scattered regiments. Instead, he went into hiding, and the common warriors went home to their herds, fields, and families. For the Zulus the war could not be prolonged much longer without the risk of economic disaster. War was only an interlude in Zulu life. Now it was time to plant the crops.

For the British, war was not only a glorious adventure, it could be a mission, even a crusade, to be fought, as the Victorian poet Thomas Macaulay wrote, "for the ashes of their fathers and the temples of their gods." The Zulus did not share that vision of war. Zulu warriors did not fight for religious vengeance or for political goals. The battles they fought might sometimes serve the political interests of their king or his counselors, but for the ordinary Zulu fighting man going to war was an enjoyable episode, a chance to capture booty, win honors, and return home to the admiration of women. They longed for "praises" describing them in the grandest terms, such as "he who is wet with yesterday's blood." But the battles had gone badly, and further fighting served no purpose for the Zulus. With a few exceptions, the warriors accepted their defeat with good grace. It is unlikely that the British would have done so, but the Zulus were willing to say that it had been a good fight, they had lost, and there were no hard feelings. After Ulundi, Charlie Harford was riding with a patrol looking for King Cetshwayo when he was approached by a Zulu warrior who

> . . . came up and asked if any of us had been at Isandhlwana, and on telling him that I was out with the [Natal Native] Contingent at Isipezi at the time of the fight, he caught hold of both my hands and shook them firmly in a great state of delight, saying it was a splendid fight. "You fought well, and we fought well," he exclaimed, and then showed me eleven wounds that he had received, bounding off in the greatest ecstasy to show how it all happened. Rushing up towards me, he jumped, fell on his stomach, got up again, rolled over and over, crawled flat, bounded on again, and so forth, until he came right up to me. His movements being applauded by the warriors squatting in the centre of the kraal with a loud "Gee!"
>
> I now had a look at his wounds. One bullet had gone through his hand, three had gone through his shoulder and had smashed his shoulder-blade, two had cut the skin and slightly into the flesh right down the chest and stomach, and one had gone clean through the fleshy part of the thigh. The others were mere scratches in comparison with these, but there he was, after about eight months, as well as ever and ready for another set-to. Could anything more clearly show the splendid spirit in which the Zulus fought us? No animosity, no revengeful feeling, but just sheer love of a good fight in which the courage of both sides could be tested, and it was evident that the courage of our soldiers was as much appreciated as that of their own."[52]

Shortly after the war Bertrand Mitford, a British civilian who traveled throughout Zululand, was greeted by a Zulu carrying a spear:

> The one with the assegai was a fine, tall fellow, with a cheery countenance and hearty manner, and we speedily became friends. But he of the assegai . . . belonged to the Udhloko regiment, and had been present at the attack on Rorke's Drift, which battle he proceeded to fight over again for my enlightenment with an effusiveness and pantomimic accompaniment thoroughly Zulu; going into fits of laughter over it, as though one of the toughest struggles on record were the greatest joke in the world.[53]

Mitford also met Mehlokazulu and asked him if he had regretted having fought:

> No, he couldn't exactly say that; he was a young man and wanted to prove himself a warrior. He had been in all the principal engagements: Isandhlwana, Kambula, and Ulundi, and now he wanted to "sit still."
>
> Always?

> Well, that he couldn't say either; he liked a fight now and then; there was no mistake about it.[54]

He could not resist the chance for a fight again in 1906.

Only a few days after the end of hostilities in 1879, Captain Ned Montague led a small patrol into remote areas demanding that the Zulus give up their arms. He did not get their weapons, but he captured their view of the fighting beautifully:

> They said out, without the smallest hesitation, "What more do you English want? You have beaten us fairly—we own that you are better at fighting than we are—so now go away!" As to compensation sought for by us, we might as well have asked for the moon. Like boys at a public school, they had had a fight to see who was the "best man": that decided, nothing was left but to be the greatest friends, and be off.[55]

In addition to the pleasure they took from fighting well against a formidable enemy, the Zulus took pride in their ability to force the British to "hide" behind the walls of their laagers and forts. A year after the war, warriors pointed to the abandoned fort at Eshowe as a monument to their prowess.[56] It was an imposing fortress to point to—stone and earthen walls, deep ditches, spikes, wire barriers, and gun emplacements. All this, the warriors boasted accurately enough, was necessary to keep the Zulus at bay.

Still, most Zulus did not pretend that the battles with the British had been nothing but manly sport. One warrior complained that the British really hadn't fought fairly as they had "killed too many."[57] By the time of the last great battle at Ulundi, many Zulus felt that it was futile to continue the war. Even so, many Zulus did not attribute their eventual defeat solely to superior British fire power. They admitted that the British had fought in the open and that the Zulus had run away, but a story spread throughout Zululand that the reason for the Zulu defeat was once again supernatural: The British had fought behind a fortress of sheet iron.[58] Umsweanto said: "There was metal—iron sheeting—which protected the white men. The Zulus hit it. It resounded with a sharp clang."[59] It is possible that when the British troops fixed bayonets the sun reflected brightly, suggesting to some Zulus the presence of a metal barrier. When British officers after the war scoffed at the idea of a metal roof and asked how the British could possibly have carried so much sheet metal with them, the Zulus were not convinced. It is not unlikely that the belief that the British used "unfair" magical means to defeat them made it easier for Zulu warriors to end the war.

There were other reasons as well. Large portions of Zululand had been ravaged by British raids, as crops were burned and livestock driven away. Many Zulu families were in serious economic distress. Even young men who had no immediate stake in the wealth of Zululand could see that the war was jeopardizing their future. Another important factor was the Zulu belief that if they stopped fighting, the British would leave them in peace. Zulus knew that the Boers were land-hungry, but they perceived the British as warriors who for some unknown reason were in Zululand for a good fight; once the Zulus acknowledged them as the winners, they would go away. A British officer recorded what was a common belief among the British about the Zulus. ''The Zulu will bear us no ill will; he is perfectly ignorant of revenge, as also of gratitude. He loves fighting when he is ordered up by his chief, otherwise he is peaceful and very contented—a really noble savage; plenty of wives to do all the work and kafir-beer for himself.''[60] And so the British made ready to sail away, pleased that they had defeated such ''noble savages'' and understanding no more about the Zulus and their way of life after the war than they had before it began.

The great chiefs pledged their allegiance to the British, surrendered a few old guns—it seemed that no Martini-Henrys existed in Zululand—and returned to their kraals and their political intrigues. The British troops did go home, as the Zulus expected, but Wolseley's partitioning of Zululand made civil war a certainty. There was no peace, and the colonists in Natal eventually annexed Zululand, as many of them had always wanted to do. For the Zulus, their war with the British was just one rather brief episode in their history. The civil disorder that followed was much more catastrophic.[61] Their war with the red soldiers would be remembered. The fighting itself was worth remembering and boasting about, but most Zulus could not say what the war had been about. It was different for members of the royal lineage and for the district chiefs. For them the war meant the end of empire and the beginning of civil war.

As the British left, they remembered the Zulus as worthy opponents—''plucky fellows''—who made it possible for many officers to win medals and gain promotions. The British did not try to understand the Zulus, but they did remember their bravery. They went home to their honors, told tales of the war, held reunions, and displayed their souvenirs. But they had other wars to remember and more wars to look forward to, and so the skull of the brave Zulu that Lord Grenfell had picked up on the battlefield at Ulundi became just one of many memorabilia in his case of ''curiosities.'' Without a thought about the Zulu dead and without curiosity about the Zulus' future, the British fighting men waited for their next call to arms.

# Chapter 9

# Colonial Wars in Africa

In 1914, as World War I opened in Africa, a British task force sailed from India to invade the German colony of Tanganyika (now Tanzania). In German hands, Tanganyika was a threat to British Kenya, its neighbor to the north, but the British were short of troops who could be diverted from the war in Europe to fight in Africa, and there were not many colonial troops available throughout the Empire either. The best troops of the Indian army, for example, had already been shipped to France, and all that remained in India were poorly trained, physically unfit, and deplorably led battalions of Indian soldiers. Undeterred, the British gathered up some eight thousand of those men, added one English regiment—they called the result "Force B"—and shipped the lot to Africa. After all, they reasoned, the German forces in Tanganyika were almost all African soldiers—*askaris*—and although trained and led by a few German officers, they were *only* Africans. The British commander, Major General Arthur Edward Aitken, was warned by one of his junior officers who had spent years in Kenya commanding African soldiers that the askaris were excellent fighting men and that their own Indian troops were a good deal less than that. The British general curtly dismissed the idea: "The Indian Army will make short work of a lot of niggers."[1] As it happened, those contemptible African soldiers routed Force B, whose troops fled for their ships leaving their dead, wounded, and weapons behind. It would be four long and bloody years before overwhelming British power would finally force those African soldiers and their German officers to surrender. Like most British officers, General Aitken apparently had no acquaintance with the Anglo-Zulu War in his background.

To underestimate the fighting qualities of Africans was nothing new, nor was it unique to the British. Until very recently, European and

American scholars neglected most aspects of African history, dismissing African culture as well as Africans themselves as inferior. African religions were discounted as pagan, their customs as barbaric, their governments as despotic, their architectural achievements as nonexistent, and their minds as, well, to be charitable, more like those of children than adults. As recently as 1963, Hugh Trevor-Roper, the Regius Professor of Modern History at Oxford University, wrote: "Perhaps in the future, there will be some African history . . . But at present there is none; there is only the history of Europeans in Africa. The rest is darkness . . . and darkness is not a subject of history."[2] That kind of dismal and arrogant ethnocentrism has been rendered laughable by anthropological and historical research, as well as by the accomplishments of contemporary Africans, but with the possible exception of African art, much of the reality of African life and the European experience with it is still poorly understood even by well-educated Westerners. Even though the European experience with Africans was often characterized by armed conflict, the military prowess and achievements of African soldiers have continued to be largely unknown. Africans fought one another for centuries before the Europeans arrived, and despite the Europeans' superior weapons, Africans fought them too. Africans won more of those battles than European colonial history has chosen to remember.

Not all African societies had a zest for war. Some small societies had virtually no military organization at all; they tried to avoid making enemies of their neighbors and, if attacked regardless, fled into nearby forests, mountains, or deserts. Some societies took up permanent residence in those inhospitable environments, where they were usually able to avoid warfare. For example, the Bushmen took refuge from the warlike Nguni in the mountains of Zululand. In many other small societies, all young men served as part-time warriors, fighting for their families, property, and glory. Like the Nguni before Shaka, however, the wars those men fought were seldom very bloody. The purpose of war was the capture of animals or women or the display of martial virtue, not large-scale killing. However, a few societies, like the great kingdoms of West Africa or the East African lake regions, maintained huge standing armies (sometimes including women), developed prestigious professional military castes, and conducted devastating and profitable wars of conquest.

Before the spread of firearms, the weapons of war were similar throughout most of Africa. Except in the northern desert regions, where horses and camels were common, men fought on foot, usually behind shields. They threw spears or stabbed with them and carried a variety of clubs and swords. Bows and arrows (sometimes poisoned) were widely known, of course, but were more often used in hunting than in warfare.[3] While the technology of war was pretty much the same throughout Africa, African armies differed tremendously in size, martial spirit, discipline, leadership, training, and tactics. Some depended on stealth and ambush, others on massive frontal assaults. Even so, it is fair to say, as the African historian Ali Mazrui has, that in most of Africa warfare and the warrior tradition were inseparably linked to property, politics, religion, esthetics, and sexuality. Symbolically, emotionally, and economically, warfare was central to much of Africa, so central, in fact, that a man's virtue was often inseparable from his valor.[4] African warriors were often called upon to die for their honor, their family, their clan, their king, their way of life, or the spoils of war. Like soldiers everywhere, they sometimes ran from danger, but very often they fought with immense courage.

In addition to the wars that took place between one African society and another, and one kingdom and others—wars that were sometimes remarkably chivalrous and sometimes terribly cruel, wars fought for land, cattle, women, territory, or revenge—Africans also fought against foreigners. In search of gold, ivory, hides, and slaves, lighter-skinned men came to Africa from China, Indonesia, India, the Arab world, and Europe. Some, like the Chinese, Indians, and Malays, were willing to confine themselves to more or less peaceful trade carried out from trading posts on the coasts. Others were more aggressive. The Arabs used armed caravans that sometimes marched thousands of miles into the interior of Africa. With as many as a thousand soldiers, the caravans could fight when necessary, but most often they traded guns to powerful tribes in exchange for slaves or ivory. When the European traders came to Africa, they tried both approaches. When peaceful trade was unsuccessful, they used force. For example, the Portuguese, who were the first Europeans to explore Africa in search of wealth (and converts to Christianity), wasted little time using armed force in Angola. From the mid-sixteenth century until 1680, when they finally established their rule, regular soldiers of the Portuguese army fought at least one major battle every single year. The stakes were high. The Portuguese eventually shipped perhaps 8 million slaves to Brazil, the majority of them from Angola.[5] However, in West Africa, where the Portuguese were seeking gold as early as the fifteenth century, force was not a successful strategy.

For one thing, the West African kingdoms were enormously powerful. As early as the eleventh century some kingdoms, especially in Ghana, could raise large armies for their campaigns. Later, as war became more specialized with the use of cavalry and guns, professional armies were created. One kingdom, Songhay, even had a full-time navy that patrolled the Niger River. By the fifteenth and sixteenth centuries, many West African states could put armies of twenty or thirty thousand men in the field. Given that strength, not to mention the African weather and endemic diseases to which the Europeans had no resistance, it is unlikely that any fifteenth- or sixteenth-century European state would have had an easy time winning a war against one of them. Fortunately for the Europeans, trade relationships were so well developed that European traders could usually achieve their ends peacefully. The monetary system of the great Mediterranean states and Europe had been based on West African gold since the Middle Ages.[6] There were trade goods in West Africa from all the states of the Mediterranean and even, surprisingly, from Medieval England. By the time of the Portuguese arrival, West African miners had produced several hundred *tons* of gold. Mineral wealth like that was an irresistible attraction to Europeans; slaves were another. The Portuguese were soon followed and supplanted by the Dutch, French, Prussians, Danes, Swedes, and British.

By the late eighteenth century, various Europeans wrote vivid accounts of West African armies and their wars. They described huge armies armed primarily with Danish guns—called ''Long Danes''—and powder that surprisingly was made in the United States. Many African soldiers also had pistols and swords, but spears and bows and arrows were not common,[7] although some armies did use crossbows and most had a few cannon. The soldiers were hardy (they could march 40 miles in a day carrying a load on their heads), and many were well disciplined. They often fought sieges against their opponent's cities, which were fortified by walls and ditches. Some of those fortresses were immense. The one at Kano in northern Nigeria, for example, enclosed an area half the size of Manhattan with a 30- to 50-foot-high wall 40 feet thick at its base; the entire wall was surrounded by two wide ditches.[8] The purpose of those wars was not to annihilate the opponents; they were fought for captives or to conquer new territories whose farming populations could be taxed. Even so, hundreds, sometimes even thousands, of people were killed.

In the nineteenth century, France became the dominant imperial power in West Africa. Although French interests clearly lay in Europe, not Africa, France nevertheless devoted enormous resources in men and money to the conquest of African territories.[9] In addition to Morocco and Algeria in the North, France conquered French Somaliland and Madagascar in the East and most of west Africa, including Mauritania, Senegal, Guinea, Mali, the Ivory Coast, Upper Volta, Niger, Togo, Dahomey,

Chad, Congo, Cameroun, Gabon, and the Central African Republic. In all, French military expeditions gave France an African empire of almost 4 million square miles. Although the graves of French Marines and Foreign Legionnaires are scattered over much of this vast area, most of the actual fighting was done by African soldiers—*tirailleurs*—who were trained, equipped, and led by French officers. Despite their superior weapons, sometimes it was all the French-led armies could manage to defeat their African opponents. For example, in the Western Sudan (now Mali) the French fought a series of battles against the black cavalry of the Tokolar Empire, whose leader declared a holy war against the "infidel" Christians. After one battle in 1857, General Louis Faidherbe reported with concern: "They march against our fire as if to martyrdom, it is clear that they wish to die."[10] A few decades later, the British would fight in the Eastern Sudan against other Muslim Africans who were equally brave.

Eventually France extended its control over much of West Africa through the fighting prowess of its French and African soldiers. Those men fought for loot, including slaves, and as a result French officers and administrators became protectors of the slave trade. Regular slave markets were held under the walls of French forts, and slave caravans were taxed throughout the nineteenth century and into the twentieth. And like the other European powers (most of which had rejected the slave trade long before France did), the French were seemingly always interested in expansion. In 1892 they sent a force of four thousand men, including eight hundred Foreign Legionnaires, to conquer Dahomey (now Benin). Dahomey was neither the richest nor the most powerful of the West African kingdoms, but its population of 300,000 or more was large enough for its king to be able to call up thousands of men for military service. Its army was reasonably well disciplined and well armed, but its greatest notoriety came not from its men but its corps of women soldiers, referred to by Europeans as "Amazons" after the Greek myth. The women soldiers fought in the front ranks of the Dahomean army and were its shock troops, its bravest and most ferocious soldiers. In 1851, when the Dahomeans attacked the principal city of their traditional enemies, the Yoruba, the Amazons led the assault. The battle was a terrible defeat for Dahomey, and the corps of six thousand women warriors was destroyed.

A decade later, Sir Richard Burton was the British Consul in Dahomey. He was rarely impressed by anything African, and he quickly concluded that the Dahomean army was second-rate at best, but he was impressed by the "Amazons" (Dahomeans called them "our mothers" or "the king's wives''). Burton counted 2,038 of them in one parade, ''grumpily trudging along.'' They were hefty, powerful women who looked the part of ferocious warriors. Among many other restrictions on their lives, Amazons were permitted to have sexual relations only with the king. Given the number of Amazons in Dahomey, the king (*any* king) must have been sorely tried to accommodate all of his women warriors. Various European observers concluded that the Amazons' ferocity must be a result of their enforced chastity. There were five corps of Amazons, each wearing a different uniform and each carrying a different type of weapon: guns, swords, bayonets, and bows and arrows. They marched and danced as they passed Burton. He thought that these women would fight more bravely than Dahomean men, but most of all he was impressed by their ''stupendous'' buttocks.[11]

When the French forces began their march toward the Dahomean capitol, the eight hundred Foreign Legionnaires led the advance. The Dahomean army met them in a series of small battles in which the Amazons led what the French called ''suicidal attacks.'' The Dahomean women pressed their charges so fiercely that Foreign Legionnaires had to bayonet them, and more than one Legionnaire had his nose bitten off in savage hand-to-hand fighting.[12] It comes as no great surprise that some Legionnaires found this kind of fighting against women demoralizing. The French and Dahomeans fought dozens of small battles. In a typical fight, like the one at a place called Pognessa, two hundred Dahomeans were killed (twenty of them Amazons) against only eight French. Still, battle casualties and disease took a heavy toll of the French. When the war ended in August 1893, barely half of the eight hundred Foreign Legionnaires were still alive.

Although the Foreign Legionnaires might have doubted it, the Dahomean army was by no stretch of the imagination the best one in West Africa. Since about 1700, the Asante state (usually written as ''Ashanti'') had been the dominant force in West Africa.[13] The Asante kingdom was large, wealthy, and sophisticated. Its dominance, as well as its central role in the slave trade, was due to the power of its large standing army and the skill of its government in using its military power to control trade with neighboring states. European traders were obliged to accept Asante rule—including their control over prices—until early in the nineteenth century, when the British decided to take control for themselves. In 1824, the British sent a mixed force of British and African soldiers against the Asantes. There was a bizarre prelude to battle in which the two sides engaged in an exchange of music—the British played, ''God Save the King'' and the Asantes responded with a martial number of their own. The two armies repeated the serenade several times before the Asantes, apparently tired of it all, attacked and won a resounding victory.

Fifty years passed before the British challenged the Asantes again. This time they gave the job to none other than General Sir Garnet Wolseley, at that time Britain's youngest general and, many—including Wolseley himself—would say, its best. Wolseley hand-picked a staff of enterprising officers, most of whom would fight against the Zulus five years later, and sailed for the Gold Coast (now Ghana) where he soon discovered that the Fante, who were Britain's allies, wanted no part of another war with the Asantes. Wolseley had to send for British troops. He received an army of four thousand men, including the famed kilt-wearing Highland regiment, the Black Watch. In deference to the climate, the Scotsmen left their kilts on board ship, however, and like the other regiments dressed in lightweight gray uniforms. They also donned pith helmets, spine pads (to prevent sunstroke), and flannel waistbands (known as cholera belts, thought to prevent cholera by keeping the abdomen warm at night) before marching off into the dense, dark, and steaming forests of Ghana.

Wolseley wrote a remarkable pamphlet for his officers. Among other things, it assured them: "It must never be forgotten by our soldiers that Providence has implanted in the heart of every native of Africa a superstitious awe and dread of the white man that prevents the negro from daring to meet us face to face in combat."[14] Wolseley had apparently not heard of the Asante War of 1824. The Asantes of 1874 were obviously unaware of their "awe and dread" of Wolseley's white men, because their troops quite cheerfully engaged them in battle. In fact, they amazed British officers with the discipline they displayed in carrying out complex maneuvers and with their battlefield skill and courage. One British officer wrote, "The Ashantis stood admirably and kept up one of the heaviest fires I was ever under."[15] The British finally won the battle, thanks mainly to the great superiority of their rifles and the exceptional bravery of the men of the Black Watch, who charged with their bagpipes playing "The Campbells Are Coming," and the Royal Welch regiment, led by the son of a lord with the unforgettable name of Colonel the Honorable Savage Mostyn.

When the British reached the Asante capital, Kumasi, they were again astonished by their enemies. Although the British were disgusted by the ample evidence they found that human sacrifice was common in Kumasi, they found the huge Asante capital immaculately clean, with beautifully laid-out streets and finely made, elegantly decorated houses built around lovely courtyards. Although the Asantes had removed many of the treasures from the immense royal palace of their king, Kofi Karikari ("King Coffee" to the British), the British were awed by silks, fine furniture, silver, and beautifully carved solid gold necklaces, bracelets, belts, masks, and a 42-ounce gold carving of a ram's head. Needless to say, the British took everything they could as the "spoils of war." They found fine Hollands gin and champagne, which they drank, as well as Persian rugs, delicate Bohemian vases, engravings of the Duke of Wellington, rows of books in many languages, and some British newspapers dating from 1843.

Although the British had occupied Kumasi, the Asante army was still a large and formidable force. Wolseley's men were too tired and sick to pursue the Asantes farther into the rain forest, so Wolseley burned Kumasi and marched back to the coast with no hopes of a treaty with "King Coffee," much less a resounding victory. To Wolseley's surprise and relief, the Asantes (under the mistaken impression that a small force they had spotted was another large British army bearing down on them) chased after Sir Garnet and agreed to a treaty, handing over some gold to seal the bargain.

Wolseley later wrote that his six-month campaign against the Asantes had been the "most horrible" war he had ever taken part in (he had been in several previous wars and was badly wounded in both Burma and the Crimea). Although Wolseley had escaped personally unscathed, seven members of his staff were dead, and thirty-one others were wounded or sick. All told, Wolseley's "triumph" had cost sixty-eight British dead, 394 wounded, and more than one thousand invalided home. Wolseley and his surviving officers wanted nothing more than to forget the campaign as quickly as possible and to leave the miserable Gold Coast.[16] For them, the war had been anything but a success, but to their surprise Britain proclaimed the war a great victory and Wolseley a national hero. The reasons were rooted in factionalism within the army and in some creative newspaper reports (Henry Stanley, who "found" Dr. Livingston, was one of several reporters who had gone on the campaign), but Wolseley and his men were not inclined to reject adulation. Wolseley was made a permanent major general (all his officers were promoted, too); Queen Victoria granted him an audience; both houses of Parliament thanked him; the universities of Oxford and Cambridge both granted him honorary degrees; the Grand Cross of the Order of St. Michael and St. George was awarded to him; and he was made Knight Commander of the Bath. Not least, in a time when a gentleman could manage nicely on £5,000 a year, Sir Garnet was given an award of £25,000!

Pleased that the British had sailed away, the Asantes rebuilt Kumasi, ignored the provisions of Wolseley's treaty, and continued their dominant role in the Gold Coast for twenty-five more years, until another British army, this time equipped with machine guns, finally conquered them.

The partition of Africa among the European powers was settled upon at the Berlin Conference of 1885. Belgians, Germans, Italians, French, British, and Portuguese scrambled to stake their claims to "bits" of territory that were usually much larger than their home countries. They did so with the same weapons that later slaughtered millions in World War I. Single-shot rifles were replaced by rifles that fired five to ten rounds from a magazine before having to be reloaded; Gatling guns, large, heavy, and temperamental, were replaced by lightweight "Maxim" machine guns, which fired bullets more rapidly than veteran soldiers could comprehend. In memorable doggerel, Hilaire Belloc wrote the last word about colonial armies: "Whatever happens, we have got, the Maxim gun, and they have not!" True, and European forces also had artillery. Older muzzle-loading cannon were supplanted by mobile, breech-loading, rapid-firing artillery pieces that could place shrapnel or high-explosive shells on distant targets with great precision. Against those weapons, African soldiers added a motley of muskets and single-shot rifles to their traditional weapons. Their firearms were almost always castoffs, the kinds of weapons European troops had discarded years earlier. Sometimes they were antiques. Usually ammunition was in short supply. The battles that Africans fought against Europeans had always been uneven, but after 1885 or so they were monstrously so. Africans fought, nonetheless, and won more than a few battles. At the battle of Adwa in 1896, an Ethiopian army shattered an invading Italian force of more than 10,000 men, killing or wounding 75 percent of them and capturing all their artillery and most of their rifles.[17] Not until Mussolini's armies returned in 1935 with their airplanes, tanks, and poison gas did the Italians win.

One of the bloodiest of the colonial wars was fought in the Sudan in 1885 between British troops, armed with modern magazine rifles, machine guns, and artillery, and Muslim African tribesmen known variously to the British as "Arabs," "Dervishes," or "Fuzzy-wuzzies." The Dervish army was on a holy war—a *jihad*—to cleanse the Sudan of corrupt Egyptian rule. The Dervishes' divine mission, in fact, their state itself, was created by a man who claimed descent from Muhammed. He did not mind being considered the reincarnation of the Prophet. He called himself *Mahdi,* "the expected one." He was a spellbinding, magnetic orator cut from the traditional cloth of the warrior-priest of Islam. He was also a strict Muslim whose austerity would make the religious leaders of Iran today seem frivolous by comparison. Yet Europeans who saw him reported that he always smiled benevolently, even when he was ordering torture and death for wrongdoers.

For many reasons, including the brutality and corruption of the Egyptian officials sent south from Cairo to govern the Sudan, men flocked to the Mahdi's cause. The Egyptians were outrageously corrupt. For one thing, they were involved in the slave trade, which took more than 50,000 captives out of the Sudan every year. The men who joined the Mahdi's army, known as *ansars*—helpers—were almost as diverse as the Sudan itself. The Mahdi's cavalry and most of his officers came from the Baggara tribe of horse nomads, who were similar to the Bedouins. Some were as Caucasian-looking as any North African Bedouin, but others were darker-skinned, reflecting centuries of mixture with black Africans, including slaves, from the south of the Sudan. Some of these men actually wore medieval armor to battle—helmets, breastplates, and chain mail—and carried huge broadswords. It was bizarre enough that those relics of the Crusades should have found their way to one of the hottest places on earth (it was often 120 degrees Fahrenheit in the shade, and there was no shade in battle); it was even more remarkable that men actually attacked British machine guns wearing fourteenth-century armor. Other Dervishes were Beja and Hadendoa tribesmen, who like the Baggara were partly Caucasian, but mixed with more Negroid peoples. It was their hair style—poking up in every direction like a fright wig—that led to the condescending fuzzy-wuzzy epithet. Many of the men in the Dervish army were black Africans from the non-Muslim south—Dinka, Shilluk, and Nuba. The Dervishes despised those "pagans" and sent their devout Muslim troops to attack them, but they respected them as warriors. One way or another, sometimes by capture, thousands of the dark-skinned men found their way into the Dervish ranks, where they were led by lighter-skinned officers.

To the call of war trumpets made from elephant tusks, the Mahdi's army defeated garrison after garrison of Egyptian soldiers, captured modern weapons, and attracted more men to the cause. When the Egyptian government mounted an expedition of eight thousand men led by a British colonel, William Hicks, and other British officers, 50,000 Dervishes attacked them, killing all the British officers, including Hicks. Only about two hundred Egyptians survived. The Dervish army also besieged the city of Khartoum, where British General Charles Gordon had been set up as the Governor-General of the Sudan.

After much delay, the British sent a relief column to "save" Gordon.

The column was led by General Sir Garnet Wolseley, once again. The army moved slowly, and several times the Dervishes attacked it with astonishing bravery. Twice they broke through the ranks of soldiers in the British "square," something that had never been done before. The idea of African horsemen in suits of armor swinging their broadswords at bayonet-wielding, kilted Scottish infantry in temperatures that reached 165 degrees in the sun is almost too much for a modern imagination, but it happened.[18] To compound their feat of arms, the Dervishes captured some British machine guns before they were driven off. Their heroism inspired these famous lines by Kipling:

> So 'ere's to you, Fuzzy-Wuzzy, at your
> 'ome in the Sowdan;
> You're a pore benighted 'eathen but
> a first-class fighting man;
> An 'ere's to you Fuzzy-Wuzzy, with
> your 'ayrick 'ead of 'air—
> You big black bounding beggar—for
> you bruk a British square.[19]

When word came that Khartoum had fallen, Wolseley's army marched away, leaving the Sudan to the Dervishes. A few months later the Mahdi died mysteriously, but his successor held the Mahdist state together and strengthened its army. Thirteen years later, when the British belatedly decided to avenge Gordon's death, the Dervish army numbered more than 100,000 men, 80,000 of whom had rifles, more than half of them modern military weapons. They also had some machine guns and seventy-five modern artillery pieces. Actually, the British decision to march on Khartoum had much less to do with avenging Gordon (although vows of revenge were marvelous for Victorian morale) than with the fear that the French were about to extend their domination of the eastern Sudan to the west by seizing the upper Nile.

The British army of 25,000 men included many distinguished regiments, such as the 21st Lancers, the Grenadier Guards, and more Highland Scots (the Camerons and the Seaforths), but only one-third of the Army was British. The rest were Egyptian peasant soldiers and black Sudanese troops, some of whom had previously fought with the Dervishes before they deserted or were captured. This time the British army was led by General Horatio Herbert Kitchener, he of the walrus mustache and steely eyes, pointing his finger and saying "Your country needs *YOU*" in the famous World War I recruiting poster. As a major of intelligence, Kitchener had served in Wolseley's unhappy expedition. He knew Arabic and, despite his appearance (he was a bulky 6′2″ with strikingly blue eyes), he often dressed as a Bedouin and rode off into the desert in search of information, carrying a bottle of poison in case of capture. Now he was the ultimate man of war, cold, ambitious, efficient, and thoroughly ruthless.[20] Along for the ride was a young officer named Winston Churchill. Although Churchill was a serving officer with the 4th Hussars in India, he managed to take leave and used the considerable influence of his wealthy and beautiful mother, the mistress of several powerful men, including the man who would succeed Queen Victoria as King Edward VII, to wangle his way into serving as a lieutenant with the 21st Lancers.

As with the Zulus in 1879, most of the British officers feared that the Dervishes would not fight, but in case they did, the soldiers were encouraged to take the precaution of cutting an X into the nose of their bullets. It seemed that standard issue bullets tended to go through the Dervishes without stopping them. Dum-dums, which blew a fist-size hole in a man, were more effective. Cursing the heat, dust, sand, flies, scorpions, and large tarantulas, the British army marched on toward Omdurman, the Mahdist capital. They expected something like the splendors of Damascus or the opulence of Samarkand, but Omdurman was as unimpressive a conglomerate of mud hovels as ever became a large city. Stretching for 6 miles along the Nile across from Khartoum, Omdurman was 3 miles wide in some places, and more than 100,000 people lived in its single-story mud-brick houses. Except for the Mahdi's tomb and a few other buildings in the center of the city, Omdurman was no more than a vast, sprawling village. Ahead of Kitchener's army, many scouts rode forward searching for the Dervishes. Churchill, predictably, was one of the first to sight them. He was ordered to ride back to Kitchener with the information. Kitchener didn't recognize him, which was just as well, since Kitchener heartily disliked Churchill for publishing criticisms of his senior officers (many of the other officers disliked him simply as a brash and arrogant twit). However, another officer, Sir Reginald Wingate, did recognize Winston, and in a scene at least as strange as that of nineteenth-century black men wearing medieval armor in a blistering African sun, Churchill was invited to join Kitchener and Wingate for lunch. As the Dervish army "jog-trotted" toward them at a rate Churchill had estimated at 4 miles per hour, the gentlemen officers chatted politely while they were served lunch on a white linen table cloth. They drank from crystal and ate with proper silverware, seemingly indifferent to the heat, the flies, or the Mahdist army of 60,000 men or more that was bearing down on them. When the meal was finished, they went back to the work of war.[21]

The Baggara cavalry charged the British lines and died to the last man. Not one came closer than 30 yards. Next, the infantry attacked, time and again, dying by the thousands before the British fire. A war correspondent for the *Daily Mail*, G. W. Steevens, wrote: "No white troops would have faced that torrent of death for 5 minutes, but the Baggara and the blacks came on."[22] What is more, those who survived did not run away from the British guns, they walked, slowly and disdainfully.[23] On one flank of the battle, the 21st Lancers rode out in the last great cavalry charge in British history. At the head of a troop of twenty-five men was Churchill, who shot several Dervishes at point-blank range, just missing one man who wore medieval armor. The Lancers fought bravely, as did the British infantry, but their part in the battle was a sideshow. The brunt of the Dervish attack was taken and broken by the black Sudanese soldiers of the ill-fated Colonel Hector Macdonald's brigade. It was the steadiness and fire of those African troops that won the battle, not the heroics of the Lancers or the battle honors of the famous British regiments, whose position in the British defense line was not seriously attacked.

The British counted more than 10,000 dead Dervishes on the battle-ground; 15,000 or so others lay wounded. Many of these were finished off by British, Egyptian, and Sudanese troops. In a subsequent battle, British artillery fired high-explosive shells against a Dervish defensive position. The Dervish soldiers could have retreated, but they chose to stay in their trenches, where more than three thousand of them died. The Dervishes gave no quarter in war, and they expected none. No quarter is what they got, and Kitchener outdid even his most brutal soldier. He ordered the Mahdi's tomb dug up, had the corpse's head severed, and took it away with him, presumably as an act of primitive revenge for Gordon, who had been decapitated against the Mahdi's order (the Mahdi had ordered Gordon taken alive so that he could be converted to the "true faith"). Word that Kitchener had taken this grisly trophy and intended to use the skull as an inkstand or drinking cup, depending on whose version one believed, reached Queen Victoria, who was not amused. She ordered the head properly reinterred, and Kitchener was obliged to write the Queen a letter of apology. (In 1879, unknown British officers dug up the grave of the former Zulu king, Mpande. King Mpande's remains were never returned to Zululand.)

It was a strange war, pitting Islamic religious zeal against terrible Christian revenge. Most ironic is the fact that many of the best soldiers on both sides were "pagan" African tribesman from the southern Sudan. Whether on the side of the Mahdi or the British, those tall, thin-legged black men (they averaged over 6 feet in height) fought with skill, discipline, and reckless bravery. It is unlikely that very many of those men cared greatly for either Islam or Christianity or that they fought confident that death in war would lead them to Paradise or Heaven. They were simply warriors. The British, who usually called all Africans "niggers," called these Sudanese soldiers "sambos." It was not meant as a term of respect, but in this war, those black warriors on both sides won everyone's admiration.

"The River War," as Churchill called it in a book he lost no time in writing,[24] was well publicized in Europe, but other savage wars in Africa went almost unnoticed. Every colonial power in Europe turned its machine guns on Africans at one time or another. For example, thousands of British-led African soldiers (including some Sudanese) equipped with Maxim guns required almost a decade to defeat and capture Kabarega, the Nyoro King, in Uganda. Casualty figures were not reported.[25] When the Ndebele and the Shona peoples of Southern Rhodesia rebelled against white rule in the 1890s, the result was another major conflict. It took the British (with help from the Portuguese in neighboring Mozambique) years of fighting to put down the resistance.[26] It is not clear how many Africans died from British gunshot wounds, although nearly five thousand dead were acknowledged.[27] Others died in prison, from disease and starvation. Even minor conflicts that hardly earned a place as historical footnotes involved deadly fighting. When the British in Kenya used force to put down the resistance of the Gusii people in 1904 and 1905, British machine guns and rifles killed hundreds. At the same time, the Nandi tribesmen a little farther north in Kenya challenged the British. The British took such challenges seriously. Against the Nandi, armed only with bows and arrows, the British assembled a force of eighty British officers, more than 1,300 African soldiers of the King's African Rifles, one thousand Maasai, one hundred Somali volunteers, five hundred armed porters, 260 armed police, and 3,500 unarmed porters. In addition to their more than two thousand Lee-Enfield magazine rifles, this army had an armored train and ten machine guns. This largely African army was well disciplined for killing (some were flogged for indiscipline, even though flogging had been illegal in the British army for more than twenty years), and it did its work with enthusiasm. One of their British officers, who killed several Nandi himself, estimated that the Nandi lost 70,000 sheep and goats, 10,000 head of cattle, and five hundred or so warriors.[28] The British had less than one hundred casualties, almost all of them wounded.

Much worse fighting took place in Germany's new territories. For reasons that are still obscure, but certainly involved competition with

France, newly unified Germany felt compelled to acquire African territories. Aided by agreements struck by the European powers at the Berlin Conference of 1885, Germany's Imperial Chancellor, Otto von Bismarck, claimed dominion over Togo, the Cameroons, South West Africa, and Tanganyika—in all, lands many times larger than Germany.

Although German entitlement to those vast territories had been agreed to by the other colonial powers, the Africans who lived there still had to be convinced. The Germans set about the task of conquest with what one might call vigor. As early as 1575, a Portuguese priest in Angola wrote to his Jesuit superiors that the Africans would have to be conquered by force of arms, because "the conversion of these barbarians will not be attained by love."[29] The Germans wasted no time loving Africans. Carl Peters, an adventurer who led the German colonial cause in Tanganyika, wrote that the African was "a born slave, who needs his despot like an opium addict needs his pipe."[30] Peters was so willing to serve as a despot that even his fellow German colonialists protested the sadistic punishments he inflicted on Africans. To be judged a sadist in Tanganyika at that time was really quite special, as ordinary Germans savagely flogged Africans whenever the whim struck them. The German Colonial Government was no less severe; between 1901 and 1913, 64,652 Africans were sentenced to corporal punishment.[31]

When flogging was not enough, guns were used. The German conquest of Tanganyika began along the coast, where German Imperial Marines from ships could easily come ashore to provide armed force. They did this often, "killing everyone they saw," as one contemporary observer put it.[32] Conquering the interior was more difficult. Some tribes in the interior chose to negotiate or even cooperate with the Germans, but others resisted. Where the land was suitable for guerrilla war, the Germans had no easy time of it. For example, in 1891 the Germans sent a large column equipped with machine guns and artillery to subdue the Hehe people in the southern highlands of Tanganyika. Under their chief, Mkwawa, the Hehe dominated a large area, and they had no intention of accepting German rule. Armed only with spears, they routed the German column, killing most of the troops, including the German commander. The war did not end until 1898, when Mkwawa finally killed himself to avoid capture. By that time, German forces had established German rule over all of Tanganyika.

In 1905 African hatred of German rule in Tanganyika exploded in what came to be known as the *Maji-Maji* rebellion. Inspired by a religious prophecy that a particular medicine—maji; literally, water—would protect men against German bullets, much of southern Tanganyika rose against its "masters." German machine guns killed the insurgents by the thousands. Guerrilla tactics replaced massed assaults, and the war continued. When the Germans intentionally destroyed crops and prevented harvests, famine followed. By the time the fighting ended in 1908, somewhere between 250,000 and 300,000 Africans were dead. On the German side, only fifteen Europeans and about 400 of their African soldiers had been killed.

It is likely that quite a few educated Americans have heard of the Maji-Maji rebellion—it has a catchy ring to it—although it is doubtful that very many know what the rebellion was about or even where it took place. At the same time that the Maji-Maji bloodshed was taking place between Africans and Germans, an almost completely unknown but equally terrible war was taking place on the opposite side of the continent in German South West Africa. South West Africa (now commonly known as Namibia) was then, and still is, a dismal-looking place, huge, barren, and desolate. Except for the very north, the country is so arid that agriculture is impossible. Almost the entire country is hotter and more arid than any part of Tanganyika. Cattle herding is possible in some areas, and several tribes, principally the Hereros, herded cattle and goats over vast grazing lands in the interior. Much of the country was simply desert, occupied only by wild animals, the San (the so-called Bushmen), and, in 1905, refugees from German rule.

Effective German colonization of South West Africa began about 1870, and by 1904 most of the Hereros had been reduced to living as wage laborers on German ranches. Like other African cattle pastoralists, the Hereros were proud, and like their distant Bantu-speaking relatives, the Zulus, they had a military tradition. German rule deprived all but the richest Herero chiefs of their cattle, and it demeaned the Hereros, whom the Germans called baboons and treated like baboons. African women were raped more or less with impunity, and both men and women were flogged brutally for trivial offenses or for none at all (Carl Peters was not the only sadist among German colonists). In German South West Africa, Hereros who offended German settlers for whatever reason—nonpayment of a small debt, for example—were flogged, not on the back or buttocks, a brutal enough punishment for anyone, but on the stomach and between the legs. Men and women alike were stretched out on their backs and flogged, their intestines exposed, their testicles destroyed, their unborn children torn to bits in what was less a form of punishment than a sadistic execution.

Confronted by growing Herero resistance, which included a few small battles, the Germans quietly surrounded a Herero dissidents' camp in

1905 with orders to "annihilate" them. The attack killed 150 people, including seventy-eight women and children, but many men escaped, including the Herero leader, known to the Germans as Hendrik Witbooi. After that attack the war spread, and it did not go well for the Germans. Despite their superior weapons, the Germans lost battle after battle to the "baboons." More and more Imperial German troops arrived in the country, but there were still equipment shortages (their machine guns and artillery used ammunition at an alarming rate), so for a while the Germans were obliged to fight with great caution. The Hereros, armed with spears and obsolete rifles, taunted the Germans, daring them to come out from behind the walls of their forts and fight like men. When the Germans refused, the Hereros charged the German forts, urged on by wildly chanting women. Against stone walls and machine guns, the Hereros lost; when the Germans were caught in the open, the Hereros defeated them.

The German commander and governor-general, Major Theodor Leutwein, was shocked. "Public opinion in Germany," he wrote, "including many men with experience in Africa, has dramatically underestimated the Hereros. Even we in the colony had not expected such resistance. The Hereros apparently believe that they can expect no quarter and are therefore fanatically determined."[33] Kaiser Wilhelm was shocked too. Despite his insistence that he wanted no colonies, his pride in German arms had been offended. He dispatched more and more troops and armaments to distant South West Africa. The Kaiser also replaced Leutwein with General von Trotha, who had acquired a well-deserved reputation for ferocity by his service in Tanganyika. "I know the tribes of Africa," von Trotha announced. "They are all alike. They respond only to force. It was and is my policy to use force with terrorism and even brutality."[34]

Von Trotha was true to his word. With nearly 20,000 Imperial German troops, the pick of the strongest army in the world at that time, armed with machine guns and heavy artillery, he destroyed the Hereros and their Hottentot allies. When the war turned into a rout, the German troops indulged themselves in an orgy of killing. Women and children by the thousands were shot, bayoneted, and burned alive. The Hereros had fought savagely, too, killing in ways that were cruel by any standard, but the Germans easily outdid them.

When the war finally ended in 1907, German losses amounted to more than 1,300 dead, seventy-six missing and presumed dead, and a thousand or so wounded. Those were considerable losses against poorly armed Africans, but they were nothing compared to the losses of the Hereros and Hottentots. Before the war, there were about 80,000 Hereros;

at the end there were only 15,130. Some Hereros escaped into the desert or to neighboring countries, but it is probable that 50,000 men, women, and children died. About 10,000 Hottentots died as well.

Despite the horrors of German rule in Tanganyika and South West Africa, and British punitive campaigns in East Africa, nothing matched the death toll in the Belgian Congo (now Zaîre). The Berlin Conference of 1885 gave the Congo to King Leopold of Belgium as his personal property. The Congo was enormously rich in rubber, ivory, and minerals, but King Leopold's armed men committed such wholesale slaughter in exploiting the Congo's wealth that by 1908, when world opinion forced the Belgian government to take over administration of the Congo, probably 5 million Africans had died—25 percent of the population. Some writers think that estimate is low, contending that Leopold's men killed more Africans in the Congo than Hitler killed Jews in World War II. World opinion generally, however, has given this episode of genocide scant attention.[35]

War in Africa did not end with the destruction of the Hereros. There were bloody rebellions in other parts of Africa about the same time.[36] During World War I, African soldiers fought one another under the flags of France, Italy, Belgium, Great Britain, and Germany. World War II began for Africa with the Italian attack on Ethiopia. Later, African soldiers wearing British uniforms defeated Italian soldiers from Somalia to North Africa. Others fought the Japanese in Southeast Asia.[37] After World War II, African wars of rebellion continued. The Mau Mau rebellion in Kenya during the 1950s was the first, and it was particularly bloody. Among the British troops who fought the Mau Mau rebels were men of the Black Watch, the same regiment that three-quarters of a century before had fought the Asante. When the Belgians suddenly declared Zaîre (then the Belgian Congo) independent in 1960, Zairan soldiers fought with and against soldiers from scores of nations in Africa, Europe, and elsewhere. How many Zairans died will never be known. In the 1960s Nigerians fought a terrible civil war when the Eastern Region, Biafra, declared its independence from the Federal Government. Biafra received military aid from France, Portugal, Israel, South Africa, and the People's Republic of China; the Federal Government was aided by the Soviet Union and Britain. A unified Nigeria emerged from the war in 1977 with the largest standing army in Africa, 250,000 men,[38] but before the war ended after thirty months of fighting, 500,000 people had died. There is fighting today in Mozambique, Zimbabwe, Uganda, Angola, Chad, Botswana, Sudan, and other countries of Africa, including, of course, South Africa.

Africa may never match Europe or the Middle East for continual wars of conquest and revenge, but Africa *was* a continent of warriors. Among those warriors, the Zulus are the most celebrated, and their battles against the British in 1879 still stand as epics of men at war. Men of war in Africa, or anywhere else in the world for that matter, have seldom displayed greater courage, and the Zulus richly deserve the respect they have received for their valor in defending their homeland. But the Zulus were not the only people in Africa who fought valiantly against European invaders.

# Epilogue

There are some striking parallels between the British conquest of the Zulus and the U.S. Army's defeat of the Indian tribes of the Great Plains. The way of life of those Indians was doomed by the westward expansion of the American population, but the end was hastened, and made bloodier, by the discovery of gold in the Black Hills, an area that had been ceded to the Sioux by the United States. Miners flocked to the Black Hills, the Sioux fought back, and in 1876, 210 men of the 7th Cavalry died with General Custer as the U.S. Army attempted to control the Sioux and their allies by force. The Zulu Kingdom was also destroyed after the discovery of mineral wealth, and the Zulus too defeated the first troops sent against them. As if to symbolize their shared fate, when the Sioux were finally defeated, the U.S. troops were led by a colonel named McKenzie, and when the Zulus rebelled in 1906, the troops who defeated them were also led by a colonel named McKenzie.

Americans glamorized the cavalrymen who fought against the Plains Indians. Custer, for example, was almost deified. The Plains Indians became "noble savages" whose warriors epitomized martial splendor for generations of Americans. For generations of Britons the heroes were officers like Bromhead and Chard, and their ideas about the glamor of "savage" warfare were formed by images of Zulu warriors. The Anglo-Zulu War immediately generated an outpouring of popular and scholarly writing. It still does. With the exception of the most recent scholarly writing, the war has been painted in broad strokes as either glamorous or tragic, sometimes as both. The British were gallant, needless to say, and the Zulus were either fearless opponents or inhuman, death-dealing monsters. For example, H. Rider Haggard's adventure novels about the Zulus became enormously popular. His novels of African war and adventure, such as *Dawn, King Solomon's Mines,* and *People of the Mist,* made him one of Britain's most popular writers and earned him a knighthood. "Their bloodstained grandeur" and "their superstitious madness" were among his favorite phrases. Within a few months after the British troops were "massacred," and before all Zulu resistance had ended, enterprising showmen brought Zulu "warriors" (actually noncombatant Zulu refugees from neighboring Natal) to Prague and other European cities, as well as to London music halls, and even today "Zulu musicals" play in Britain. Zulu costumes soon became a part of "traditional" Welsh ceremonies (many of the soldiers who fought against the Zulus were Welsh). The Zulus' warrior image quickly spread to America, too, where, for example, Zulu martial themes and costumes still play a prominent part in New Orleans's Mardi Gras.

The Anglo-Zulu War also inspired film-makers, who began to realize that Americans, like the British, could become fascinated by the Zulus. First there was *King Solomon's Mines,* then *Untamed,* a lavish, almost $4 million 1952 production starring Tyrone Power and Susan Hayward, which depicted battles between the Boers and Zulus. *Variety* (March 2, 1955) dismissed the movie as a "western with fiery Zulus supplanting the Redmen, and Boers taking the place of the western pioneers." In 1964, *Zulu* presented a romantic portrayal of the battle at Rorke's Drift mission station. It starred Michael Caine as Lieutenant Gonville Bromhead. In 1979, an even more "spectacular" production of the war was released: *Zulu Dawn.* It attempted to deal with events leading up to the war, and it provided a graphic, if confused, version of the war's first great battle at Isandlwana. It featured Peter O'Toole as Lord Chelmsford, John Mills as Sir Bartle Frere, and Burt Lancaster as Colonel Durnford. Both films did well at the box office, and they still appear on television. In 1986, the life of King Shaka was recreated in a lavish $24 million, ten-hour television "miniseries" that screened in the United States, Britain, and Europe.

Like the Plains Indians, Zulu warriors have fascinated our popular imagination. Although there are some similarities between the colonial experiences of the two peoples, in the century since they were defeated they have taken different paths. The Plains Indians were never numerous. Since being segregated on reservations they have existed as tiny enclaves in the vastness of an ever growing American population. It has been different for the Zulus. They were a large population at the start of the Anglo-Zulu War, and despite their defeat, followed by a period of civil war and years of economic hardship, their numbers have grown. Today, Africans of Zulu ancestry are the largest ethnic group in South Africa, outnumbering the white population of that embattled country.

# Notes

CHAPTER 1 (pp. 1–22)

1. Emery (1977:92).
2. This estimate is based on Zulu recollections of deaths in each regiment. It is only an estimate, because after the battle the regiments dispersed to their homes, where many died of their wounds. See, for example, Clarke (1984:157).
3. *The Times*, February 12, 1879, p. 10.
4. Harrison (1908:136).
5. White (1933:79).
6. Furneaux (1963:196).
7. Morris (1965:39)
8. Cope and Guy (1979). It is possible that Dingiswayo was influenced by an English doctor named Cowan, but Cowan's influence was unlikely to have affected military developments. *C.f.* Morris (1965).
9. Otterbein (1967).
10. Omer-Cooper (1966).
11. Welsh (1971:178).
12. Brookes and Webb (1965:87). The one observer to mention Indian laborers was a naval surgeon who spend some time on the coast where the sugar plantations were located. Norbury (1880).
13. Etherington (1981:22).
14. *Ibid.*, p. 36.
15. Fuze (1979).
16. Guy (1979)
17. Etherington (1981).
18. Guest (1981:61).
19. Etherington (1981:43) and Kennedy (1976).
20. Morris (1965) estimates 57 pounds.
21. Clarke (1984).
22. *Ibid.*, p. 68.
23. Parr (1880:101).
24. Furneaux (1963:27).
25. Beach (1932:10).
26. Chadwick and Hobson (1979).

27. Guest (1981:65).
28. Morris (1965) states that the Zulu army was already mobilized at Ulundi to celebrate the annual first fruits ceremony. That is an error. The army was not mobilized until after the British began their invasion. See Webb and Wright (1982).

CHAPTER 2 (pp. 23–47)

1. *Punch,* April 5, 1879, p. 154.
2. Guy (1979).
3. Gon (1978:195).
4. Barnett (1970:319).
5. See, for example, Spencer (1965).
6. Webb and Wright (1976:312).
7. Krige (1950:74; 105).
8. *C.f.* Blood (1933:201) and Isaacs (1970).
9. After the war, when one of the executioners, Sihayo's son Mehlokazulu, was captured and handed over to British authorities in Natal, the court could find no legal basis for charging him with a crime.
10. Colenbrander (1981:90).
11. Kennedy (1981:35).
12. Lugg (1975).
13. Farwell (1973).
14. Webb and Wright (1976:53).
15. DuToit (1975).
16. Krige (1950) and Samuelson (1929).
17. Webb and Wright (1979:56); Cannibalism was said to have arisen after the famine caused by Shaka's raids. *C.f.* Webb and Wright (1976:53, 201, 302) and Webb and Wright (1979:14).
18. Durnford (1882:15); for a discussion of Zulu dancing and singing, see Krige (1950) and Samuelson (1929).
19. Kunene (1979) and Cope (1968).
20. Webb and Wright (1976:253).
21. Gardiner (1836:144).
22. *Ibid.*, p. 58.
23. Krige (1950:iii).
24. Lugg (1949:35).
25. Webb and Wright (1982).
26. Laband (1979).
27. Webb and Wright (1982:319).
28. Webb and Wright (1982:306–7).
29. *Ibid.*, p. 307.
30. Samuelson (1922:53)
31. Furneaux (1963) describes them as the world's finest athletes and best light infantry.
32. Isaacs (1870:147; 204).
33. Moodie (1879:344); see Smail (1969) for a discussion of Zulu tactics and weapons.
34. Guy (1970).
35. Guy (1979).
36. Binns (1963:176).
37. Samuelson (1929:37). Lord Baden-Powell, founder of The Boy Scout Movement, modeled his ''wood badge'' after these beads.

38. Wood (1906, II: 12) and Child (1978:80).
39. Lugg (1975:13).
40. Gardiner (1836:130).
41. See Gluckman (1960) and Ritter (1935). Morris (1965) repeats this interpretation.
42. For Shaka's sexual preferences see Fynn (1950), Isaacs (1870), and Webb and Wright (1976, 1979, 1982)
43. Webb and Wright (1976:83).
44. Webb and Wright (1979:179, 247) and Kunene (1979).
45. Ngubane (1977).
46. Lugg (1975:33).
47. Binns (1975:118).
48. Clarke (1979).
49. Bryant (1929). *C.f.* Vilikazi (1962), Ngubane (1977), and Berglund (1976).
50. Ngubane (1977).
51. Fuze (1979:39).
52. Blood (1933:191).
53. Krige (1950:225).
54. Stuart (1913).
55. Webb and Wright (1982).
56. Krige (1950:270). I have been unable to determine who Neal was or how he was killed.
57. Binns (1963:67); also see Kennedy (1976).
58. Webb and Wright (1982:322).
59. Guy (1979).
60. *Ibid.*, p. 130.

CHAPTER 3 (pp. 48–70)

1. Featherstone (1966).
2. Farwell (1981:76).
3. Frey (1981:23).
4. Skelley (1977).
5. *Ibid.*, and Emery (1977).
6. Skelley (1977).
7. Farwell (1973:362).
8. DeWatteville (1954:114).
9. Laffin (1966:110).
10. Blood (1933).
11. Grenfell (1925).
12. Skelley (1977:151).
13. Lucas (1878).
14. Holmes (1986); Hamilton-Browne (1911).
15. Skelley (1977:136).
16. *Ibid.*, p. 82.
17. Frey (1981).
18. Trustam (1984:119).
19. Adams (1968).
20. Gon (1979).
21. *Ibid.*

22. Grenfell (1925).
23. Emery (1977:64).
24. Smith-Dorrien (1925)
25. Child (1978:24).
26. Hamilton-Browne (1911:49).
27. Norris-Newman (1880).
28. Emery (1977:63).
29. *Ibid.*, p. 66.
30. Barnett (1970:343).
31. Dixon (1976).
32. Farwell (1981:135).
33. Baynes (1967:123).
34. Honey (1975:22).
35. Meadows and Brock (1975:113).
36. *Ibid.*, p. 101.
37. Laslett (1965).
38. Blood (1933:202–3).
39. For various examples, see Emery (1977), Clarke (1984), Child (1978), and virtually anything else written by British officers at that time.
40. Baynes (1967:210).
41. Holmes (1986:98–99).
42. Montague (1880:3).
43. Farwell (1973).
44. Clarke (1984:217,224).
45. Emery (1977:50).
46. Blood (1933).
47. Meinertzhagen (1960).
48. Hamilton (1944).
49. Farwell (1981:116).
50. Farwell (1985:197).
51. Barthorp (1980:49).
52. Farwell (1981:43).
53. Tylden (1959).

CHAPTER 4 (pp. 71–91)

1. Sergeant Morley of H Company, 2d Battalion, 24th Regiment, who survived Isandlwana, wrote to one of his comrades about the Zulus that "they were like lions and not afraid of death." Emery (1977:101). The Zulus said the same thing about the British. Webb and Wright (1982:304).
2. Mitford (1883:147).
3. Hamilton-Browne (1911:108).
4. Child (1978:20); Morris (1965) reports this episode, but he has many of the details wrong.
5. Jackson (1965).
6. Lloyd (1975:16).
7. *Ibid.*
8. Burnett (1879).
9. Emery (1977:185).

10. Courtenay (1879).
11. Norris-Newman (1880:86).
12. French (1939:134).
13. British Parliamentary Papers, LIV, 1878–79 (C.2454), sub-enc. in enc. 1 in no. 34: "Statement of Sihlahla taken by J. W. Shepstone, 3 June 1879."
14. *The Natal Mercury*, Supplement, January 22, 1929.
15. Clarke (1984:126).
16. *Ibid.*, and Durnford (1882).
17. Clarke (1979:65).
18. Hamilton-Browne (1911:116).
19. Furneaux (1963:51).
20. Laband (1985:11).
21. A survivor, Captain Cochrane, was present when Durnford spoke to Pulleine. Moodie (1879:236).
22. Clarke (1979:68).
23. Smith-Dorrien (1925).
24. *Ibid.*
25. Hattersley (1938).
26. Webb and Wright (1982:307).
27. It had been generally accepted that the British infantry withdrew toward the camp because they were out of ammunition (Morris [1965]), but better analysis of survivor's reports and the battle itself suggest that the only troops who were short of ammunition at this point in the battle were Durnford's men. Jackson (1965).
28. Mitford (1883:92).
29. Morris (1965) mistakenly reported that Anstey died on the firing line.
30. Moodie (1879:202).
31. Cochrane, *The Times*, February 8, 1879.
32. Hattersley (1938:156).
33. Moodie (1879).
34. Norris-Newman (1880:80).
35. *The Natal Mercury*, Supplement, January 22, 1929.
36. Norris-Newman (1880:83).
37. Parr (1880:220).
38. Mitford (1883:220).
39. Zulus were able to convey information rapidly by a combination of hilltop shouting, smoke signals, and long-distance runners.

CHAPTER 5 (pp. 92–107)

1. Maxwell (1979:5).
2. *Ibid.*, p. 6.
3. Hamilton-Browne (1911:140–41).
4. Montague (1880).
5. Child (1978) and Mitford (1883).
6. Jackson (1965:35).
7. Glover (1975).
8. Barthorp (1980:72).
9. Mitford (1883).
10. Some writers believe that a narcotic was mixed into the snuff, but the evidence is equivocal. For a fuller discussion, see Chapter 8.

11. Morris (1965) reports that James Rorke died "about 1875," but a man by that name was trading in Zululand when the war began. Clarke (1984:158). Perhaps this was Rorke's son.
12. Morris (1965).
13. One of these men, Lieutenant James Adendorff, may have stayed to assist in the defense. Morris (1986).
14. Child (1978:40).
15. Montague (1880).
16. Clarke (1984:131).
17. Glover (1975).
18. Preston (1973:112).
19. *Ibid.*, p. 320.
20. Emery (1977:241).
21. There is controversy about the part that a shortage of ammunition played in the British defeat at Isandlwana. Morris (1965, 1986) believes that the British ammunition boxes were so difficult to open that the troops could not be fully supplied. Jackson (1965) downplays the ammunition shortage in his account of the battle. Whatever the truth of the matter, no one who was at Rorke's Drift mentioned having difficulty opening the ammunition boxes.
22. Hook (1905).
23. Preston (1973:92).
24. Hook (1905).
25. Parr (1880:212).
26. Maxwell (1979:6–7).
27. Emery (1977:140).
28. Maxwell (1979).
29. Hamilton-Browne (1911:150).
30. *Ibid.*, p. 151.
31. Webb (1978:12).

CHAPTER 6 (pp. 108–37)

1. Laband (1985).
2. Webb and Wright (1978:36).
3. *Ibid.*, p. 37.
4. Moodie (1888:487).
5. Vijn (1880:28).
6. Webb and Wright (1982:304).
7. Webb (1979:13).
8. Vijn (1880:41).
9. Webb and Wright (1978).
10. See Furneaux (1963) and Durnford (1882).
11. Durnford (1882:346). Frere's correspondence with Durnford's surviving brother, also a colonel, is both arrogant and deceitful. Chelmsford's was little better.
12. Clarke (1984:135).
13. Many of those letters are printed in *ibid.*
14. *Ibid.*, pp. 131–32.
15. *Ibid.*, p. 132.
16. Child (1978).
17. Hamilton-Browne (1911:164).

18. Maxwell (1979:14).
19. Emery (1977:160).
20. Tucker (1943:185).
21. Mitford (1883:277–78).
22. Wood (1906, vol. II).
23. *Ibid.*, II:50.
24. Vijn (1880). It was rare for Zulu women to take part in battle. As far as I know, they never did so with a royal regiment.
25. Mossop (1937:50).
26. *Ibid.*, p. 51.
27. *Ibid.*, p. 63.
28. Wood (1906, vol. II).
29. Moodie (1879:284).
30. Gon (1979:148).
31. Moodie (1879:289–90).
32. Montague (1880:263).
33. Vijn (1880:113). Laband (1979:32) has pointed out that a printer's error caused Morris to locate the Ngobamakosi on the Zulu left, rather than the right.
34. Vijn (1880:114).
35. Wood (1906, vol. II).
36. British Parliamentary Papers, LIV of 1878–179, C. 2454.
37. Emery (1977:169).
38. Snook (1879).
39. *Ibid.*
40. Emery (1977:169).
41. Jervis (1879).
42. Moodie (1879:281).
43. *Ibid.*, p. 288.
44. Jervis (1879).
45. Wood (1906, vol. II).
46. Vijn (1880:114).
47. Mitford (1883:279).
48. *Ibid.*
49. Vijn (1880:115).
50. Mitford (1883).
51. It is now spelled Gungundhlovu.
52. Barthorp (1980:80). See also Norbury (1880).
53. See Morris (1965).
54. Hutton (1928:71).
55. Anonymous (1879).
56. Emery (1977:204).
57. Norris-Newman (1880:141).
58. Hamilton-Browne (1911:206–7).
59. Clammer (1973:163).
60. Hamilton-Browne (1911:211–13).
61. Powis (1879).
62. Norbury (1880:234).
63. Moodie (1879).

CHAPTER 7 (pp. 138–65)

1. Stuart (1913:275)
2. Ashe and Wyatt-Edgell (1880) and Morris (1965)
3. Colenso (1880:361)
4. Hamilton-Browne (1911). He has been criticized by Morris (1965) for his racist attitudes and his brutality to Zulus, among other things. The charges are true, and he was also an anti-Semite. It should be noted, however, that many British officers shared his attitudes and behaved brutally. Hamilton-Browne was also a brave and competent officer.
5. Hutton (1928:68).
6. Hamilton-Browne (1911:171–72).
7. Ashe and Wyatt-Edgell (1880:314–15).
8. Preston (1973:47).
9. Blood (1933:190).
10. Clarke (1984:267).
11. See *Ibid.*
12. Preston (1973).
13. Clarke (1984:229).
14. Montague (1880:184).
15. Webb and Wright (1978a:27) and Laband (1985:43). The action taken by the umCityo was more than defiant bravado. They knew that Cetshwayo could not meet all of Chelmsford's peace conditions, so they concluded that the cattle would simply be wasted. Colenso (1880) and Durnford (1882).
16. Clarke (1984:241).
17. Clarke (1979:149).
18. Jervis (1879).
19. Clarke (1984:237).
20. British Parliamentary Papers, L of 1880 (c.2482), enc. in No. 32: Statement of Ungungunga, taken by T. Shepstone, Junior, July 4, 1879.
21. Clarke (1984:238).
22. *Ibid.*, p. 244.
23. Moodie (1879:356).
24. Grenfell (1925:66).
25. Unnamed sergeant of the 17th Lancers, *North Devon Herald*, September 18, 1879.
26. Emery (1977:235).
27. Blood (1933:176).
28. Mossop (1937:94–95).
29. Anonymous sergeant of the 17th Lancers, *North Devon Herald*, September 18, 1879.
30. Colenso (1880:438).
31. Wilmot (1880).
32. Clarke (1984:239).
33. Preston (1973)
34. Child (1978:73). Sir Herbert Stewart was killed in 1884 during Wolseley's abortive campaign to relieve General Gordon in Khartoum.
35. Guy (1979:62).
36. Vijn (1880:72).
37. *Ibid.*, p. 87.

38. *Ibid.*, p. 100.
39. *Ibid.*, pp. 102–3.
40. Preston (1937)
41. Hamilton-Browne (1911).
42. Vijn (1880:172).
43. *Ibid.*, p. 175.
44. Barthorp (1980:166).
45. Norris-Newman (1880:396).
46. Laband and Thompson (1983).
47. Norris-Newman (1880:141).
48. Chadwick and Hobson (1979:177). See also Laband and Thompson 1983:35.
49. Mitford (1883) and Parr (1880).
50. Preston (1973:210).
51. Colenso and Durnford (1882).
52. Child (1978:83).
53. Samuelson (1929:228–31).
54. *Ibid.*, p. 230.
55. Guy (1979:130).
56. Binns (1963:189).
57. Guy (1979:202).
58. Binns (1963:260).
59. Kanya-Forstner (1969:47–48).
60. Samuelson (1929:53).
61. Brookes and Webb (1965).
62. Marks (1970).
63. Stuart (1913:393).
64. Ritter (1935:xii).
65. Binns (1963:221).
66. Brookes and Webb (1965:229).
67. Fischer (1950:55–56).

CHAPTER 8 (pp. 166–94)

1. For a review of this complex material the reader should begin with Holmes (1986) and Keegan (1978).
2. Webb and Wright (1982:316).
3. Persico (1977).
4. Mitford (1883:160).
5. *Natal Mercury*, Supplement, January 22, 1929.
6. Marshall (1947).
7. Keegan (1978).
8. Emery (1977:21).
9. Hook (1879).
10. Emery (1977:198); also Clarke (1984).
11. Emery (1977:162).
12. *Ibid.*, p. 122.
13. Banks (1879).
14. Holmes (1986:286).
15. Durnford (1882:167).

16. Manchester (1983:254).
17. Walters (1970:142).
18. Hamilton-Browne (1911); Child (1978); Clarke (1984).
19. Blood (1933:196).
20. Preston (1973:70). The regimental colors were not at Isandlwana. For some reason, they had been left with a reserve company of the 2d Battalion at Helpmekaar.
21. Laband (1979, 1985).
22. Webb and Wright (1982:11).
23. Clarke (1979:73).
24. Elliott (1978:90).
25. Walker (1961:167).
26. Fuze (1979:101–2).
27. *Ibid.*, p. 106.
28. DuToit (1975:97).
29. Keegan (1976). During the Anglo-Zulu War, most British officers and soldiers drank alcohol after battle, not before it. White NCOs with the N.N.C. were an exception. They were drunk much of the time, including during battles.
30. DuToit (1975).
31. Codere (1975).
32. DuToit (1975).
33. Tedder (1968:59).
34. Binns (1963:217).
35. Samuelson (n.d.:40).
36. Samuelson (1929:319–21).
37. Mitford (1883:287–88). For a broader perspective on the role of dance in the African warrior tradition, see Hanna (1977).
38. Gluckman (1959:9).
39. Bryant (1929:647).
40. Moran (1950) and Holmes (1986:213–14).
41. Holmes (1986).
42. Vijn (1880:38). Norbury (1880:40,157) reported that the Naval Brigade also kept monkeys as pets.
43. Montague (1880:310–11).
44. Hattersley (1938:16).
45. Fynn (1950) and Isaacs (1970). For a discussion of the bravery of men of high rank, see Webb and Wright (1982:260).
46. For another analysis of this possibility, see Guy (1979).
47. Durnford (1882:311).
48. Heathcote (1980).
49. Fynn (1950:227).
50. Mitford (1883:145).
51. Webb and Wright (1982:320).
52. Child (1978:72–73).
53. Mitford (1883:266).
54. *Ibid.*, p. 144.
55. Montague (1880:274).
56. Mitford (1883:174).
57. Montague (1880:280–81).

58. Webb (1978:21).
59. *Ibid.*, p. 16.
60. Clarke (1984:266).
61. Fuze (1979).

CHAPTER 9 (pp. 195–213)

1. Meinertzhazen (1960:105).
2. Trevor-Roper (1963).
3. In general, bows and arrows were more common in West Africa than elsewhere, but some East African societies, such as the Nandi, also relied on bows and arrows in their battles against European troops.
4. Mazrui (1977).
5. Curtin (1969).
6. Davidson (1966).
7. Ajayi and Smith (1964).
8. Muffett (1978:280).
9. Kanya-Forstner (1969).
10. *Ibid.*, p. 37.
11. See Burton (1966:262) and Ross (1978:149).
12. Hubert (1938). See also Wellard (1974).
13. Goody (1971).
14. Lloyd (1964:88).
15. *Ibid.*, p. 109.
16. *Ibid.*
17. Rotberg and Mazrui (1970), Del Boca (1969).
18. Ziegler (1973).
19. Kipling (1899:9).
20. Farwell (1985).
21. For a lively account of this campaign see Churchill (1899).
22. Steevens (1898:264).
23. Grenfell (1925:122).
24. Churchill (1899).
25. Beattie (1960).
26. See Ranger (1967) and Palmer (1972).
27. Gann and Duignan (1978).
28. Meinertzhagen (1957:249).
29. Bender (1978:137).
30. Iliffe (1979:150).
31. *Ibid.*
32. *Ibid.*, p. 93.
33. Bridgeman (1981:103).
34. *Ibid.*, p. 112.
35. Okumu (1963).
36. For example, see Ogot (1972) and Isaacman (1976).
37. Lunt (1981).
38. Ocaya-Lakidi (1977).

# References

Adams, J.
1968 *The South Wales Borderers.* London: Hamish Hamilton.
Ajayi, J. F. A., and R. Smith
1964. *Yoruba Warfare in the Nineteenth Century.* Cambridge: Cambridge University Press.
Anonymous
1879 *The Watchman,* April 23.
Ashe, M., and E. V. Wyatt-Edgell
1880. *The Story of the Zulu Campaign.* London: Sampson, Low, Marston, Searle & Rivington.
Axelson, Eric
1967. *Portugal and the Scramble for Africa, 1875–1891.* Johannesburg: Witwatersrand University Press.
Banks, J.
1879 *The Dover Express,* June 6.
Barnett, C.
1970. *Britain and Her Army 1509–1970: A Military, Political and Social Survey.* London: Allen Lane.
Barthorp, M.
1980. *The Zulu War.* Poole: Blandford Press.
Baynes, J.
1967. *Morale: A Study of Men and Courage.* London: Cassell.
Beach, V. H.
1932 *Life of Sir Michael Hicks Beach.* London: Edward Arnold.
Beattie, J.
1960. *Bunyoro: An African Kingdom.* New York: Holt, Rinehart & Winston.
Bender, G. J.
1978. *Angola Under the Portuguese: The Myth and the Reality.* Berkeley: University of California Press.
Berglund, A.-I.
1976. *Zulu Thought-Patterns and Symbolism.* Cape Town: David Philip.

Binns, C. T.
1963. *The Last Zulu King: The Life and Death of Cetshwayo*. London: Longmans.
1975. *The Warrior People*. London: Hale.
Blood, Sir Bindon
1933. *Four Score Years and Ten: Sir Bindon Blood's Reminiscences*. London: G. Bell & Sons.
Bridgeman, J. M.
1981. *The Revolt of the Hereros*. Berkeley: University of California Press.
Brookes, E. H., and C. de B. Webb
1965. *A History of Natal*. Pietermaritzburg: University of Natal Press.
Bryant, A. T.
1929. *Olden Times in Zululand and Natal*. London: Longmans, Green.
Burnett, J. W.
1879 *The Dover Express*, March 14.
Burton, Sir Richard
1966. *A Mission to Gelele, King of Dahome*. London: Routledge & Kegan Paul.
Chadwick, G. A., and E. G. Hobson.
1979. *The Zulu War and the Colony of Natal*. Mandini, Natal: Qualitas Publishers.
Child, D. (ed.)
1978. *The Zulu War Journal of Colonel Henry Harford, C.B.* Pietermaritzburg: Shuter & Shooter.
Churchill, W. S.
1899. *The River War: An Account of the Reconquest of the Sudan*. London: Eyre & Spottiswood.
Clammer, D.
1973. *The Zulu War*. London: Pan.
Clarke, S. (ed.)
1979. *Invasion of Zululand, 1879*. Johannesburg: The Brenthurst Press.
1984. *Zululand at War 1879: The Conduct of the Anglo-Zulu War*. Houghton, South Africa: The Brenthurst Press.
Clements, W. H.
1936. *The Glamour and Tragedy of the Zulu War*. London: John Lane, The Bodley Head.
Codere, H.
1975 "The Social and Cultural Context of *Cannabis* Use in Rwanda." In V. Rubin (ed.), *Cannabis and Culture*. The Hague: Mouton, pp. 220–27.
Colenbrander, P. J.
1981. "Confronting Imperialism: The People of Nquthu and the Invasion of Zululand." In A. Duming and C. Ballard (eds.), *The Anglo-Zulu War: New Perspectives*. Pietermaritzburg: University of Natal Press.
Coleuso, F. E., and E. C. L. Durnford
1880 *History of the Zulu War and Its Origin*. London: Chapman & Hall.
Cope, R. L., and J. J. Guy
1979. *The Anglo-Zulu War: Two Centenary Lectures*. Johannesburg: University of Witwatersrand.
Cope, T.
1968. *Izibongo: Zulu Praise-Poems*. Oxford: At the Clarendon Press.
Coupland, R.
1948. *Zulu Battle Piece: Isandhlwana*. London: Collins.

Crowder, M. (ed.)
1978. *West African Resistance: The Military Response to Colonial Occupation*. London: Hutchinson University Library for Africa.
Curtin, P. D.
1969. *The Atlantic Slave Trade*. Madison: University of Wisconsin Press.
Davidson, B.
1966. *A History of West Africa: To the Nineteenth Century*. New York: Doubleday.
Del Boca, A.
1969. *The Ethiopian War 1935–1941*. Trans. from Italian by P. D. Cummins. Chicago: University of Chicago Press.
DeWatteville, H.
1954 *The British Soldier: His Daily Life from Tudor to Modern Times*. London: J. M. Dent.
Dixon, N.
1976. *On the Psychology of Military Incompetence*. London: Jonathan Cape.
Duminy, A., and C. Ballard (eds.)
1981. *The Anglo-Zulu War: New Perspectives*. Pietermaritzburg: University of Natal Press.
Durnford, E. C. L. (ed.)
1882. *A Soldier's Life and Work in South Africa, 1872 to 1879: A Memoir of the Late Colonel A. W. Durnford*. London: Sampson, Low, Marston, Searle & Riverington.
DuToit, B.
1975. "Dagga: The History and Ethnographic Setting of *Cannabis Sativa* in Southern Africa." In V. Rubin (ed.), *Cannabis and Culture*. The Hague: Mouton, pp. 81–116.
Elliott, A.
1978. *Sons of Zulu*. London: Collins.
Emery, F.
1977. *The Red Soldier: Letters from the Zulu War, 1879*. London: Hodder & Stoughton.
Etherington, N. A.
1981. "Anglo-Zulu Relations, 1856–78." In A. H. Duminy and C. C. Ballard (eds.), *The Anglo-Zulu War: New Perspectives*. Pietermaritzburg: University of Natal Press, pp. 13–52.
Farwell, B.
1973 *Colonial Small Wars, 1837–1901*. Newton Abbot: David & Charles.
1981. *For Queen and Country*. London: Allen Lane.
1985. *Eminent Victorian Soldiers: Seekers of Glory*. New York: W. W. Norton.
Featherstone, D. F.
1966. *All for a Shilling a Day*. London: Jarrolds.
Featherstone, D.
1973. *Captain Carey's Blunder: The Death of the Prince Imperial*. London: Lee Cooper.
Fischer, L.
1950. *The Life of Mahatma Gandhi*. New York: Harper & Brothers.
Forbes, A.
1880. "Lord Chelmsford and the Zulu War." *The Nineteenth Century*, February 1880.
French, G.
1939. *Lord Chelmsford and the Zulu War*. London: John Lane, The Bodley Head.

Frey, S. R.
1981. *The British Soldier in America: A Social History of Military Life in the Revolutionary Period.* Austin: University of Texas Press.
Furneaux, R.
1963. *The Zulu War: Isandhlwana and Rorke's Drift.* London: Weidenfeld & Nicolson.
Fuze, M. M.
1979. *The Black People: And Whence They Came.* Ed. A. T. Cope. Pietermaritzburg: University of Natal Press, 1979.
Fynn, H. F.
1950. *The Diary of Henry Francis Fynn.* Comp. and ed. by J. Stuart and D. McK. Malcolm. Pietermaritzburg: Shuter & Shooter.
Fynney, F. B.
1967. *Zululand and the Zulus.* Pietermaritzburg: Horne, n.d.; repr., Pretoria: The State Library.
Gann, L. H., and P. Duignan
1978 *The Rulers of British Africa, 1870–1914.* London: Croom, Helm.
Gardiner, Captain A. F.
1836. *Narrative of a Journey to the Zoolu Country in South Africa.* London: Wm. Crofts.
Gillings, K.
1979. "Inyezane, Gingindlovu and the Relief of Eshawe." *Military History Journal,* vol. 4, no. 4.
Glover, M.
1975. *Rorke's Drift: A Victorian Epic.* Cape Town: Purnell.
Gluckman, M.
1959 *Custom and Conflict in Africa.* Glencoe: The Free Press.
1960. "The Rise of the Zulu Empire." *Scientific American,* 202:157–68.
Gon, P.
1979. *The Road to Isandlwana.* Johannesburg: Donker.
Goody, J.
1971. *Technology, Tradition, and the State in Africa.* London: Oxford University Press.
Grenfell, F. W.
1925. *Memoirs of Field Marshal Lord Grenfell.* London: Hodder & Stoughton.
Guest, W. R.
1981. "The War, Natal and Confederation." In A. H. Duminy and C. C. Ballard (eds.), *The Anglo-Zulu War: New Perspectives.* Pietermaritzburg: University of Natal Press, pp. 53–77.
Guy, J.
1971. "A Note on Firearms in the Anglo-Zulu War." *Journal of African History,* 11:561–63.
1979. *The Destruction of the Zulu Kingdom.* London: Longmans.
Hamilton, I.
1944 *Listening for the Drums.* London: Faber & Faber.
Hamilton-Browne, G.
1911. *A Lost Legionary in South Africa.* London: T. Werner Laurie.
Hanna, J. L.
1977 "African Dance and the Warrior Tradition." In A. A. Mazrui (ed.), *The Warrior Tradition in Modern Africa.* Leiden: E. J. Brill, pp. 111–33.

Harrison, R.

1908 *Recollections of a Life in the British Army During the Latter Half of the 19th Century*. London: John Murray.

Hattersley, A. F. (ed.)

1938. *Later Annals of Natal*. London: Longmans, Green.

Heathcote, T. A.

1980. *The Afghan Wars, 1839*. London: Osprey.

Holmes, R.

1986. *Acts of War: The Behavior of Men in Battle*. New York: The Free Press.

Honey, J. R. de S.

1975. "Tom Brown's Universe: The Nature and Limits of the Victorian Public Schools Community." In B. Simon and I. Bradley (eds.), *The Victorian Public School: Studies in the Development of an Educational Development*. Dublin: Gin & Macmillan, pp. 19–33.

Hook, H.

1879 *The North Wales Express*, April 18.

1905 "How They Held Rorke's Drift." *The Royal Magazine*, February.

Hubert, Charles

1938. *Le Colonel Domine*. Paris: Berger-Levrault.

Hutton, General Sir Edward

1928. "Some Recollections of the Zulu War, Extracted from the Unpublished Reminiscences of the Late Lieut.-General Sir Edward Hutton." *The Army Quarterly*, 16:65–80.

Iliffe, J.

1979. *A Modern History of Tanganyika*. Cambridge: Cambridge University Press.

Isaacs, Nathaniel

1970. *Travels and Adventures in Eastern Africa Descriptive of the Zoolus, Their Manners, Customs*. Rev. and ed. by L. Herman and P. R. Kirby. Cape Town: C. Struik.

Issacman, Allen F.

1976. *The Tradition of Resistance in Mozambique: The Zambesi Valley 1850–1921*. Berkeley: University of California Press.

Jackson, F. W. D.

1965. "Isandhlwana, 1879—The Sources Re-Examined." *Journal of the Society for Army Historical Research*, 43: 30–43, 113–32, 169–83.

Jervis, E.

1879 *The Dover Express*, September 5.

Kanya-Forstner, A. S.

1969. *The Conquest of the Western Sudan: A Study in French Military Imperialism*. Cambridge: Cambridge University Press.

Keegan, J.

1978. *The Face of Battle: A Study of Agincourt, Waterloo and the Somme*. New York: Penguin.

Kennedy, P. A.

1976. "The Fatal Diplomacy: Sir Theophilus Shepstone and the Zulu Kings, 1839–1879." Unpublished Ph.D. dissertation, University of California, Los Angeles.

1981. "Mpande and the Zulu Kingship." *Journal of Natal and Zulu History*, 4:21–38.

Kipling, R.
1899. *Barrack Room Ballads and Other Poems*. New York: T. Y. Crowell.
Krige, E. J.
1950. *The Social System of the Zulus*. Pietermaritzburg: Shuter & Shooter.
Kunene, M.
1970. *Zulu Poems*. New York: Africana Publishing Co.
1979. *Emperor Shaka the Great: A Zulu Epic*. London: Heinemann.
Laband, J.
1985. *Fight Us in the Open: The Anglo-Zulu War Through Zulu Eyes*. Pietermaritzburg: Shuter & Shooter.
Laband, J. P. C.
1979. "The Zulu Army in the War of 1879: Some Cautionary Notes." *Journal of Natal and Zulu History*, 2: 27–35.
Laband, J. P. C., and P. S. Thompson
1983. *A Field Guide to the War in Zululand, 1879*. Pietermaritzburg: University of Natal Press.
Laffin, J.
1966. *Tommy Atkins: The Story of the English Soldier*. London: Cassell.
Laslett, P.
1965 *The World We Have Lost: England Before The Industrial Age*. New York: Scribners.
Lloyd, A.
1964. *The Drums of Kumasi: The Story of the Ashanti Wars*. London: Longmans.
Lloyd, W. N.
1975. "The Defence of Ekowe." *Natalia*, 5:15–28.
Lucas, T. J.
1878 *Camp Life and Sport In South Africa*. Johannesburg: Africana.
Lugg, H. C.
1975 *Life Under a Zulu Shield*. Pietermaritzburg: Shuter and Shooter.
Lunt, J.
1981. *Imperial Sunset: Frontier Soldiering in the 20th Century*. London: MacDonald.
Manchester, W.
1983. *The Last Lion: Winston Spencer Churchill—Visions of Glory, 1874–1932*. New York: Dell.
Manington, George
1907. *A Soldier of the Legion*. London: Murray.
Marks, S.
1970. "The Zulu Disturbances in Natal." In R. I. Rotberg and A. A. Mazrui (eds.), *Protest and Power in Black Africa*. New York: Oxford University Press, pp. 213–57.
Marshall, S. L. A.
1947 *Men Under Fire*. New York: Morrow.
Maxwell, J.
1979. *Reminiscences of the Zulu War*. Ed. Leonie Twentyman Jones. Cape Town: University of Cape Town Libraries.
Mazrui, A. A. (ed.)
1977 *The Warrior Tradition in Modern Africa*. Leiden: A. A. Brill

McBride, A.
1976 The Zulu War. London: Osprey.
Meadows, A. J., and W. H. Brock
1975. "Topics Fit for Gentlemen: The Problem of Science in the Public School Curriculum." In B. Simon and I. Bradley (eds.), *The Victorian Public School: Studies in the Development of an Educational Development*. Dublin: Gin & Macmillan, pp. 95–114.
Meinertzhagen, R.
1957 *Kenya Diary, 1902–1906*. Edinburgh: Oliver and Boyd.
1960 *Army Diary, 1899–1926*. London: Oliver and Boyd.
Melville, C. H.
1923. *Life of General the Right Hon. Sir Redvers Buller* . . . 2 vols. London: Edward Arnold.
Miller, C.
1974. *Battle for the Bundu: The First World War in East Africa*. New York: Macmillan.
Mitford, B.
1883. *Through the Zulu Country*. London: Kegan Paul, Trench.
Molyneaux, W. C. F.
1896. *Campaigning in South Africa and Egypt*. London: Macmillan.
Montague, W. E.
1880. *Campaigning in South Africa: Reminiscences of an Officer in 1879*. Edinburgh: William Blackwood & Sons.
Moodie, D. C. F.
1879. *The History of the Battles and Adventures of the British, Boers, and the Zulus in Southern Africa,* Vol. I. Adelaide: George Robertson.
1888 *The History of the Battles and Adventures of the British, the Boers, and the Zulus in Southern Africa,* Vol. II. Cape Town: Murray & St. Leger.
Moodie, D. C. F. (ed.)
1886 *John Dunn, Cetywayo and the Three Generals*. Pietermaritzburg: Natal Printing & Publishing.
Moran, Lord
1966. *The Anatomy of Courage*. 2d ed. London: Constable.
Morris, D. R.
1965. *The Washing of the Spears*. London: Jonathan Cape. Revised edition, 1986.
Mossop, G.
1937. *Running the Gauntlet*. London: Thomas Nelson.
Muffett, D. J. M.
1978. "Nigeria-Sokoto Caliphate." In M. Crowder (ed.), *West African Resistance: The Military Response to Colonial Occupation*. London: Hutchinson Library for Africa, pp. 268–99.
Ngubane, H.
1977. *Body and Mind in Zulu Medicine: An Ethnography of Health and Disease in Nyuswa-Zulu Thought and Practice*. New York: Academic Press.
Norbury, H. F.
1880. *The Naval Brigade in South Africa During the Years 1877–78–79*. London: Sampson Low, Marston, Searle & Rivington.

Norris-Newman, C. L.
1880. *In Zululand with the British Throughout the War of 1879*. London: W. H. Allen.
Ocaya-Lakidi, D.
1977. "Manhood, Warriorhood and Sex in Eastern Africa." In A. Mazrui (ed.), *The Warrior Tradition in Modern Africa*. Leyden: E. J. Brill, pp. 134–65.
Ogot, B. A. (ed.)
1972. *War and Society in Africa: Ten Studies*. London: Frank Cass.
Okumu, W.
1963. *Lumumba's Congo: Roots of Conflict*. New York: Obolensky.
Omer-Cooper, J. D.
1966. *The Zulu Aftermath: A Nineteenth-Century Revolution in Bantu Africa*. Evanston, Ill.: Northwestern University Press.
Otterbein, K. F.
1967. "The Evolution of Zulu Warfare." In P. Bohannan (ed.), *Law and Warfare: Studies in the Anthropology of Conflict*. Austin: University of Texas Press, pp. 351–58.
Palmer, P. H.
1972. "War and Land in Rhodesia." In B. A. Ogot (ed.), *War and Society in Africa*. London: Frank Cass.
Parr, H. H.
1880. *A Sketch of the Kafir and Zulu Wars*. London: Kegan Paul.
Persico, J. E.
1977. *My Enemy, My Brother: Men and Days of Gettysburg*. New York: Pocket Books.
Powis, E.
1879 *The Cambrian*, July 11.
Preston, A. (ed.)
1973 *The South African Journal of Sir Garnet Wolseley, 1879–80*. Cape Town: A. A. Balkema.
Ranger, T. O.
1967. *Revolt in Southern Rhodesia 1896–97*. Evanston, Ill.: Northwestern University Press.
Ritter, E. A.
1935. *Shaka Zulu: The Rise of the Zulu Empire*. London: Allen Lane.
Ross, D.
1978. "Dahomey." In M. Crowder (ed.), *West African Resistance: The Military Response to Colonial Occupation*. London: Hutchinson, pp. 144–69.
Rotberg, R. I., and A. A. Mazrui
1970. *Protest and Power in Black Africa*. New York: Oxford University Press.
Samuelson, L. H.
n.d. *Some Zulu Customs and Folk-Lore*. London: The Church Printing Co.
Samuelson, R. C. A.
1929. *Long, Long Ago*. Durban: Knox Printing & Publishing Co.
Skelley, A. R.
1977 *The Victorian Army at Home*. London: Croom Helm.
Smail, J. L.
1969. *With Shield and Assegai*. Cape Town: Howard Timmins.

Smith-Dorrien, H.
1925 *Memories of Forty-Eight Years' Service*. London: John Murray.
Snook, J.
1879 *The North Devon Herald*, May 29.
Spencer, P.
1965. *The Samburu: A Study of Gerontocracy in a Nomadic Tribe*. Berkeley: University of California Press.
Steevens, G. W.
1898. *With Kitchener to Khartum*. New York: Dodd, Mead.
Stuart, J.
1913. *A History of the Zulu Rebellion 1906 and of Dinuzulu's Arrest, Trial and Expatriation*. London: Macmillan.
Tedder, V.
1968. *The People of a Thousand Hills*. Cape Town: C. Struik.
Trevor-Roper, H.
1963. "The Rise of Christian Europe." *The Listener*, November 28, pp. 871–75.
Trustram, M.
1984. *Women of the Regiment: Marriage and the Victorian Army*. Cambridge: Cambridge University Press.
Tucker, C.
1943 "The Battle at Intombe River." *Journal of the Society for Army Research*, 22:180–86.
Turney-High, H. H.
1971. *Primitive War: Its Practice and Concepts*. Columbia: University of South Carolina Press.
Tylden, Major G.
1959. "Commandant George Hamilton-Browne of the Colonial Forces." *Journal of the Society for Army Historical Research*, 37:153–60.
Vijn, C.
1880. *Cetshwayo's Dutchman, Being the Private Journal of a White Trader in Zululand During the British Invasion*. Trans. J. W. Colenso. London: Longmans, Green.
Vilakazi, A.
1962. *Zulu Transformations: A Study of the Dynamics of Social Change*. Pietermaritzburg: University of Natal Press.
Walker, O.
1961. *Zulu Royal Feather*. London: Hutchinson.
Walters, J.
1970. *Aldershot Review*. London: Jarrolds.
Webb, C. de B. (ed.)
1978. "A Zulu Boy's Recollections of the Zulu War and of Cetshwayo's Return (orig. compiled by G. H. Swinny)." *Natalia*, 8:6–21.
Webb, C. de B., and J. B. Wright (eds).
1976. *The James Stuart Archive of Recorded Oral Evidence Relating to the History of the Zulu and Neighboring Peoples*. Trans. Webb and Wright. Pietermaritzburg and Durban: University of Natal Press and Killie Campbell Africana Library. Volume One.
1978 *A Zulu King Speaks: Statements Made by Cetshwayo KaMpande on the History*

*and Customs of His People*. Pietermaritzburg and Durban: University of Natal Press and Killie Campbell Africana Library.

1979. *The James Stuart Archive,* Volume Two.

1982 *The James Stuart Archive,* Volume Three.

Wellard, J.

1974. *The French Foreign Legion.* London: Andre Deutsch.

Welsh, D.

1971. *The Roots of Segregation: Native Policy in Colonial Natal, 1845–1910.* London: Oxford University Press.

White, T. H.

1933. *Farewell Victoria.* London: Jonathan Cape.

Wilkinson-Latham, C.

1978. *Uniforms and Weapons of the Zulu War.* New York: Hippocrene Books.

Wilmot, A.

1880. *History of the Zulu War.* London: Richardson & Best.

Wood, Field-Marshal Sir Evelyn

1906. *From Midshipman to Field Marshal.* 2 Vols. London: Methuen.

Ziegler, P.

1973. *Omdurman.* London: Collins.

# Index

# Index